THE GREAT RIGHT NORTH

CARLETON LIBRARY SERIES

The Carleton Library Series publishes books about Canadian economics, geography, history, politics, public policy, society and culture, and related topics, in the form of leading new scholarship and reprints of classics in these fields. The series is funded by Carleton University, published by McGill-Queen's University Press, and is under the guidance of the Carleton Library Series Editorial Board, which consists of faculty members of Carleton University. Suggestions and proposals for manuscripts and new editions of classic works are welcome and may be directed to the editorial board chair, Jody Mason, at jody.mason@carleton.ca or to any member of the editorial board.

254 *Mrs Dalgairns's Kitchen*
Rediscovering "The Practice of Cookery"
Edited by Mary F. Williamson

255 *Blacks in Canada*
A History, Fiftieth Anniversary Edition
Robin W. Winks

256 *Hall-Dennis and the Road to Utopia*
Education and Modernity in Ontario
Josh Cole

257 *University Women*
A History of Women and Higher Education in Canada
Sara Z. MacDonald

258 *Canada to Ireland*
Poetry, Politics, and the Shaping of Canadian Nationalism, 1788–1900
Michele Holmgren

259 *Harriet's Legacies*
Race, Historical Memory, and Futures in Canada
Edited by Ronald Cummings and Natalee Caple

260 *Regulatory Failure and Renewal*
The Evolution of the Natural Monopoly Contract, Second Edition
John R. Baldwin

261 *Trade and Commerce*
Canada's Economic Constitution
Malcolm Lavoie

262 *Eye of the Master*
Figures of the Québécois Colonial Imaginary
Dalie Giroux
Translated by Jennifer Henderson

263 *Canadian Literary Fare*
Nathalie Cooke and Shelley Boyd, with Alexia Moyer

264 *Small Stories of War*
Children, Youth, and Conflict in Canada and Beyond
Edited by Barbara Lorenzkowski, Kristine Alexander, and Andrew Burtch

265 *Confessions of an Immigrant's Daughter*
Laura Goodman Salverson

266 *Statesman of the Piano*
Jazz, Race, and History in the Life of Lou Hooper
Edited by Sean Mills, Eric Fillion, and Désirée Rochat

267 *The Great Right North*
Inside Far-Right Activism in Canada
Stéphane Leman-Langlois, Aurélie Campana, and Samuel Tanner

THE GREAT RIGHT NORTH

INSIDE FAR-RIGHT ACTIVISM IN CANADA

Stéphane Leman-Langlois
Aurélie Campana
Samuel Tanner

Carleton Library Series 267

McGill-Queen's University Press
Montreal & Kingston • London • Chicago

ISBN 978-0-2280-2283-1 (cloth)
ISBN 978-0-2280-2284-8 (paper)
ISBN 978-0-2280-2324-1 (ePDF)
ISBN 978-0-2280-2325-8 (ePUB)

Legal deposit fourth quarter 2024
Bibliothèque nationale du Québec

Printed in Canada on acid-free paper that is 100% ancient forest free (100% post-consumer recycled), processed chlorine free

This book has been published with the help of a grant from the Federation for the Humanities and Social Sciences, through the Awards to Scholarly Publications Program, using funds provided by the Social Sciences and Humanities Research Council of Canada.

Funded by the Government of Canada | Financé par le gouvernement du Canada | Canada

Canada Council for the Arts | Conseil des arts du Canada

We acknowledge the support of the Canada Council for the Arts.

Nous remercions le Conseil des arts du Canada de son soutien.

McGill-Queen's University Press in Montreal is on land which long served as a site of meeting and exchange amongst Indigenous Peoples, including the Haudenosaunee and Anishinabeg nations. In Kingston it is situated on the territory of the Haudenosaunee and Anishinaabek. We acknowledge and thank the diverse Indigenous Peoples whose footsteps have marked these territories on which peoples of the world now gather.

Library and Archives Canada Cataloguing in Publication

Title: The great right north : inside far-right activism in Canada / Stéphane Leman-Langlois, Aurélie Campana, Samuel Tanner.
Names: Leman-Langlois, Stéphane, 1965- author. | Campana, Aurélie, author. | Tanner, Samuel, 1975- author.
Series: Carleton library series ; 267.
Description: Series statement: Carleton library series ; 267 | Includes bibliographical references and index.
Identifiers: Canadiana (print) 20240378296 | Canadiana (ebook) 20240378318 | ISBN 9780228022831 (cloth) | ISBN 9780228022848 (paper) | ISBN 9780228023241 (ePDF) | ISBN 9780228023258 (ePUB)
Subjects: LCSH: Right-wing extremists—Canada. | LCSH: Radicalism—Canada.
Classification: LCC HN110.Z9 R3 2024 | DDC 303.48/40971—dc23

Set in 10/14 Radiata with Oswald and Neue Haas Unica Pro

Book design & typesetting by Garet Markvoort, zijn digital

CONTENTS

TABLES

THE GREAT RIGHT NORTH

INTRODUCTION

The Canadian Far Right: A Newly Visible Object

On 3 February 2021, the Canadian government published an expanded list of groups considered to be terrorist entities. While far-right groups, like Blood and Honour, were already on the list, the addition of four like-minded new groups – Atomwaffen Division, the Base, the Proud Boys, and the Russian Imperial Movement – came as a surprise to many observers. A few weeks after the assault on the US Capitol in Washington, the activities of several groups that were born in Canada, have links with Canadian groups, or are suspected of trying to export their branding to Canada were perceived as a potential threat to Canadian security. This decision contrasts with previous assessments by law enforcement and intelligence agencies of the threats posed by the groups and individuals operating within this movement. The extreme or far right was, generally speaking, considered to be a negligible phenomenon not worthy of interest.

It must be said that until the mid-2010s, far-right groups were rather discreet in Canada. Few, made up of a small number of members and marked by considerable instability, sought to occupy the public arena. Preferring to keep to themselves, most were not visible. People were generally surprised when the authors of this book announced in late 2013 that they were starting a research project on Canadian far-right groups, as if such groups did not exist in Canada. By and large, most policing and intelligence organizations also assumed that the violent far right was a small collection of crackpots that did not present much of a threat to the public (see chapter 6) or, at worst, were a local police matter.

The context has evolved dramatically since then, in large part due to increased media attention. A number of very public controversies helped resurrect the classic themes of the right and far right: morality, economic hardship, identity, immigration and integration, social order and security, etc. Among others: in 2013, the province of Quebec attempted (and failed) to enact a *charte des valeurs* (cultural values charter); in 2014, Zunera Ishaq challenged the ban on niqabs during her Canadian citizenship ceremony, triggering a scandal for parts of the population; in 2016, Canada accepted some 50,000 refugees from Syria; since 2017, protests against colonialist monuments have accelerated and spread countrywide; at the same time Haitian and other refugees started entering Canada from the US via uncontrolled and illegal crossings; between 2020 and 2022, COVID-19 restrictions served as a flashpoint for far-right groups eager to capitalize on widespread resentment and fear. Each of these not only exposed deep political cleavages in Canadian society but also turned the media spotlight towards groups who expressed more extreme views than those typically heard in Canada.

At the same time, the far-right scene was in a deep process of metamorphosis, in large part driven by the massive cultural impact of information technologies. New movements like Pegida Canada, the Soldiers of Odin, Storm Alliance, and La Meute emerged – some exclusively on social media. This effervescence was especially beneficial to groups that were in the throes of organizational and financial difficulties, for instance helping them survive the arrest of their leaders and internal discord by increasing their social acceptability. Once almost invisible, since 2015 the movements that compose the Canadian far-right nebula have been gaining more and more political traction. This has also been true in the United States and in Europe. While most of the groups active in 2015 or earlier have now disappeared, rebranded, or otherwise transformed, many other groups have emerged. In particular, the government response to the COVID-19 pandemic has led to major reconfigurations: new leaders and influencers have emerged (and disappeared since), multiple forms of rule breaking have led to clashes with various authorities, and some aspects of the public health response have led to massive, albeit temporary, federation of otherwise incompatible entities.

What has changed far less, if at all, is the official attitude towards the far right in Canada. Most politicians have had little to say about the phenomenon, other than insisting that it is happening elsewhere – where they have neither responsibility nor jurisdiction. Police organizations have also been disturbingly slow to react. Ottawa's inept, paralytic response to its (predicted) invasion by the "Freedom Convoy" in 2022 is paradigmatic. Canada's high-policing national security agency continued to argue, until 2019 at least, that the rise of the far right is a negligible quantity, mostly made of individual, and often psychologically unbalanced, actors. The January 2021 assault on the Capitol in Washington, DC, has led to the addition of right-wing extremist groups such as the Proud Boys, the Base, and Division Atomwaffen to the list of terrorist organizations in Canada (the USA only maintains a list of *foreign* terrorist entities). But the general awareness of the danger, even the threat, posed by some of these groups and individuals remains low, especially when compared with the anxiety generated by "jihadi" groups. Of course, merely adding a group name to the already highly dubious list of enemies is not likely to cause much of a stir in the hornet's nest, as we shall see later.

In North America the 2016 election of Donald Trump to the presidency of the United States – as well as his loss in 2020, in fact – has contributed to boosting the far-right discourse, its proposed solutions, and, especially, the form of language deemed adequate to describe the world. This new public discourse, with its far lowered bar for the social acceptability of vulgar, contemptuous, vengeful, and xenophobic language, has pulled many far-right groups into mainstream politics in the USA and in Canada (Gest, Reny, and Mayer 2018; Galbraith 2017; Newman et al. 2021). Only the most radical still choose to remain underground. Paradoxically, extreme explosions of violence, such as the terrorist attack against a Quebec City mosque in late January 2017, far from bringing about a moment of pause and re-evaluation, in fact seem to open up new political opportunities. Local groups were able to exploit the aftermath of the massacre to advance their "de-demonization" strategy, mostly by demonstrating that they are not *that* extreme.

Given these developments, we cannot but conclude that the Canadian far right is getting bolder and bolder everywhere in Canada. They eagerly use social media to disseminate their propaganda and to organize demonstrations and meetings, they unfold banners asking for the "deportation of immigrants" (La Presse Canadienne 2017), put up posters in the streets or in public venues such as universities in Ontario and Quebec (e.g., Krishman 2015; Ouellet-Vézina 2017), and have intensified their recruitment efforts.

Yet this social and political phenomenon remains largely understudied. Indeed, there is a paradox between the high level of attention these groups have received in the media and the paucity of research on them. Research published in the 1990s and the early 2000s offered important insights into the past of the Canadian far right (Barrett 2015 [1987]; Ross 1992, 1995; Young 1997; Kinsela 2001) but is now clearly outdated. A few recent studies have admittedly explored the Canadian contemporary far right. Parent and Ellis (2014, 2016), Perry and Scrivens (2015, 2017, 2019), as well as Perry, Gruenenwald, and Scrivens (2022) do provide a general picture of right-wing movements across the country, analyzing their main characteristics, ideology, and repertoires of actions. Scrivens and Perry (2016) also look at ways of countering the potential resonance of the hate discourse these groups have been propagating in the virtual and real worlds. Based on a social network analysis, Momani and Deschamps (2021) analyze the discourses that circulated online in 2020 within what they call the Canadian Right-wing Extremism network. They show how diverse they are and who play the strongest role in their elaboration and circulation.

Some research focuses more specifically on individual Canadian provinces. In this respect, the province of Quebec is certainly the one that has drawn the most attention from researchers as far-right groups multiplied between 2015 and 2019. Indeed, Tanner and Campana (2014) examined the process of radicalization within right-wing skinhead groups in the province of Quebec. Nadeau and Helly (2016) examined the rise of right-wing discourses on Facebook following the debates around the Quebec Charter of Values. Nadeau, Geoffroy, and Qchiqach (2021) drew a chronology of violent events in the province of Quebec between 2010 and 2020, while Nadeau (2020) analyzed the pathways into the Quebec right-wing sphere through an ethnographic approach.

In a significant departure from the dominant literature, the main objective of this book is not to discover ways to prevent so-called radicalization, to defuse the far-right expansion, or to block, censor, and de-platform extremists. Though some of us are directly involved in street-level CVE (countering violent extremism) efforts, the present book is motivated by our desire to better understand the group dynamics, the discourse, the logic, the contradictions, and the workings of far-right groups and individuals to provide a big-picture, comprehensive analysis of the Canadian far-right scene and its myriad participants, repertoire of actions, contexts, and technologies. Beyond the multiplication of banners and acronyms, is there a tangible resurgence of the far right in several Canadian provinces and, if so, how can it be explained? Is this process uniform across Canada? How has the Canadian far right evolved since the early 2010s and how have the groups that compose this nebula become visible political actors? Who are the individuals who are active within these groups? Why do far-right discourses seem more attractive than they were in the recent past and how do these organizations garner support? What are the main social and political implications of their rise for Canadian politics? How do various forms of government attention (extremism prevention, censorship, criminalization, surveillance, etc.) interact with the internal organization and the external actions of the groups and their members?

Far-right oppositional groups: what are they?

No consensus exists on the definition of "right-wing" or "far-right" extremism within the literature. The term *extremism* itself is at the centre of many debates, which too often conflate it with terrorism (Schmid 2014) – not to mention that it is purely relative, with no objective boundaries. What is more, in the public sphere the slightest disagreement routinely gives rise to outbursts of accusations and counteraccusations of "radicalism," "extremism," "communism," "fascism," etc. In this era of (real and hyped) acute political divides, the field is heavily mined. Finally, since extremism is generally viewed as pejorative and undesirable, any observation of its multiple aspects is always coloured by the imperative of finding ways to neutralize it. Nevertheless, we have elected to proceed with the classic naiveté of the researcher, disregarding the potential political, strategic, or ideological pitfalls.

Before we begin, one final caveat is necessary: our theoretical and definitional frameworks are only meant to apply to Western liberal democracies and to the Canadian situation. The likelihood that our categories are directly relevant elsewhere across the globe is rather low.

Extremism and radicalism

First, we believe that it is helpful to distinguish between *extremism* and *radicalism*. Mudde (2010, 1169) has convincingly shown the usefulness of distinguishing between "radical" and "extremist" when comparing far-right parties and groups. Following him, we will use *radicalism* as the idea that valid social and political change must reach to the *roots*. This usually involves challenging the founding principles of the polity or countering them with "purer" or "truer" versions thereof. Alternatively, it may also involve a completely new set of principles and an altogether different, if not opposed, ideology. In that, radicalism could be progressive or conservative and may call for moderate or revolutionary action, incremental or rapid change, overt or covert action, etc. In liberal democracies, however, most "radical" parties accept the rules of the political game and democracy as an organizing principle (even when, for instance, denouncing some of the core values of liberal democracy [Mudde 2017]).

Extremist groups and individuals, for their part, may not reject the political system as a whole – though it is likely that they object to a substantial part of it. But they think that the current political system is not a proper vehicle for change, that their voices cannot be heard or do not count. Consequently, they do not want to discuss or negotiate and do not believe that opponents have the basic legitimacy that qualifies them as political counterparts.

What distinguishes radicalism and extremism, then, is their relation to Western-style democracy as a principle – radicalism usually respects most of the basic tenets of democracy, while extremism rejects them – and to the state – most radicals want to transform it from within, while extremists tend to put its intrinsic legitimacy into question.

Of course, the contours of both concepts are highly subjective. Both are also relative and depend on what is considered moderate or tolerable in a given cultural context: they refer to ideologies, discourses, actions, and strategies that are located "outside the mainstream political thinking of a given society" (Schmid 2014, 14). Finally, both have, in most democratic countries, a pejorative connotation and few groups or individuals self-identify as "extremists."

Left–right

Second, there is also the matter of the "right" end of the political spectrum. The concept is dated and is largely difficult to apply to persons or groups. To make matters worse, both being on the right and on the left are used as *ad hominem* arguments in ideological contests. There are, however, some types of framing and some types of issues that can be categorized as "right-wing." The preservation of social order, of traditions, and of a particular set of cultural norms deemed to be fundamental to the "character" of a polity are a few examples. Oftentimes the social order idealized by the right rests on a set of inequalities or hierarchies of individuals and populations deemed to be "natural" (Mudde 2007). Following that, the term "far right" will be used in this book to represent the subset of those who adhere to right-wing ideas with more intensity, pushing concepts, arguments, and definitions to their extremes – for instance, when cultural preservation becomes racism.

Much confusion comes from the idiosyncratic use of "right-wing," "radical right," "conservative right," or "far right" in the literature. In 1995 Mudde could already identify twenty-six different definitions of these concepts and the matter has not been settled since. One reason for the confusion is the recurrent self-reinvention of the far-right militants themselves. This produces a constantly renewed vocabulary and rapid changes in self-designations. Usually, this results from a quest for social respectability, from a need to deflect police attention, or simply when a schismatic group wishes to distance itself from its former peers. The re-invention also often involves increasing confusion around political objectives. For instance, the short-lived term "alt-right," an abbreviation derived from "alternative right" (where the "alt" prefix also refers to the movement's heavy, or even exclusive, presence in Internet forums), quickly became a buzzword after being coined by one time superstar white supremacist Richard Spencer in the USA. It then disappeared equally suddenly, as did its creator.

Observers usually agree on at least three main ideological signposts present in the far-right culture at large (Carter 2005, 14): i) ultranationalism; ii) fundamental criticism of democracy and its institutions, and in particular its pillars of egalitarianism and pluralism, and iii) a rejection of "Others," a designated enemy population whose identity often varies according to context. Sometimes groups will try to escape the far-right label by pointing out that they *also* support environmental causes, labour unions, or the rights of women, for instance (see chapter 2). While we accept that group labels may not apply to every member or to every collective or individual act, we recognize a group to be on the far right if its discourse and action *mostly* align with far-right culture. While groups tend to adopt different modes of action (Caiani et al. 2012) and different goals, most of them position themselves as challengers to the established political and social order and adopt both symbolic and physical violence as legitimate means of action. We will explore these aspects further in chapters 1 and 2.

Group structure

Third, some precision is needed on the notion of "group." How closely, how often, and about what do individuals have to interact in order to be considered a group? In what follows we adopt the widest possible definition of the notion, one that encompasses both small, closely knit, highly active formations as well as broad, low-investment, open groups, and everything in between. We will point out these differences when pertinent. While this allows us to be inclusive and to account for connections and interactions between like-minded groups and individuals, it should be clear from the outset that a large proportion of these formations are quite removed from the mythical clandestine, violent, fanatic gangs that dominate the popular imagination.

In their 2005 article "White Supremacists and the Internet," Adams and Roscigno use the concept of "oppositional culture" to explain the inner cohesion of social movements. The authors argue that there are "three functions or processes of social movements or oppositional culture … (1) identity building and solidarity maintenance, (2) providing followers and/or potential recruits with an alternative frame for interpreting grievances, and (3) promoting a sense of efficacy relative to group grievances outlined in the frame" (2005, 761). These functions converge on the one fundamental characteristic of these groups: their oppositional nature. They consciously and strategically adopt marginalized positions within society, promoting, following, and defending alternative rules and norms. While most attempt to gain general political visibility, they do so by mobilizing populations that are unambiguously dissatisfied with their democratic institutions. Others simply choose to remain or to go completely underground, becoming "clandestine groups" (Della Porta 2013, 7). Becoming clandestine is of course a process contingent on the nature, intensity, and social acceptability of government responses.

In a nutshell, we believe that far-right groups can be better understood as instances of "oppositional social movements" (Tanner and Campana 2014). This concept has heuristic value in that it reveals a common thread that runs through myriads of ideological nuances: it considers *wilful marginality* as their core characteristic. Relations to other actors and to the state can be seen as its visible manifestation. This also conveys the idea that the group survives because it provides a supportive milieu for its members, as well as ready-to-use representations, discourses, and worldviews that build their identity. This means that although the group primarily defines itself through its outgroup, what and whom it *opposes*, it also engages in intensive processes of identity construction, of structuring the ingroup, as a central component of its emergence and survival (Melucci 1995). Furthermore, since it is a negative concept, its power is not diminished by the absence, or underdevelopment, of alternative objectives for society. It can survive simply by condemning, deriding, or denigrating the current status quo.

Our approach takes into consideration the structuring role of identity formation and transformation, the influence of the sociocultural context and the political landscape (in particular, whether the state apparatus appears to tolerate, in part or in whole, the discourse and the actions of the group), as well as the quality and density of interpersonal relationships between members of the group. We contend that the group's symbolic identity is created through a dynamic process that entails continuous transactions between its members, with other groups (friendly or not), and with the immediate and distant environment (Tilly 2003, 5). Identity formation requires that members of the group reach at least a minimal consensus on the meanings generated during their interactions. Some of these meanings will revolve around the negotiated construction of common goals (Melucci 1995). Diani (2013) notes that "identity plays a crucial role here as it connects actors to longer-term collective projects, thus making their relation different from that between actors engaged in purely instrumental coalitions." In practice that never works very long and, consequently, groups split or dissolve quickly.

The connection between militants does not take place only through shared collective experiences; pre-existing affective ties also play a crucial role in the dynamics of mobilization and in sustaining social movements over time (Lefranc and Sommier 2009). More specifically, emotional factors contribute to creating and maintaining a sense of solidarity. This is especially true of groups that seek to distance themselves from the dominant social order, where solidarity is based mainly on trust, as trust both expresses mutual understanding and defines the nature and scope of interactions between the group's members and between the group and the "outside world." Oppositional groups in general can be seen as "networks of trust," in Tilly's sense: "we can think of trust as an attitude or as a relationship with practices attached" (2007, 6). According to him, trust "consists of placing valued outcomes at risk to others' malfeasance, mistakes, or failures" (4). Networks of trust are thus "ramified interpersonal connections, consisting mainly of strong ties, within which people set valued, consequential, long-term resources" (6). These networks can be based on family or close peers or develop around common interests or shared representations. A network of trust exists when the following conditions are created:

> the relation has a name mutually known to its participants ... involvement in that relation gives all participants some minimum

> of shared rights and obligations ... participants have means of communicating and representing their shared membership [and] participants mark and maintain boundaries separating all members from outsiders. (Tilly 2005, 44)

Fieldwork under defiance

From the outset, we elaborated the project as one based on multiple qualitative methods and triangulation. First, we conducted interviews and non-participant observations in four Canadian provinces: Quebec, Ontario, British Columbia, and Alberta. Such a strategy was innovative when we started to do fieldwork in 2014. Few researchers had succeeded in contacting volatile groups that didn't seek visibility in the public space. As discussed above, over the following years of "de-demonization" and "mainstreaming," this general shyness slowly evaporated. A second strategy involved documentary research, the collection and analysis of the materials (pamphlets, magazines, posters, published testimonies, etc.) produced by the groups and individuals. Also included in our sample are multiple court proceedings. Finally, we also analyzed online publications and discussions through discourse analysis and online ethnography.

When we started our project, the groups and individuals we were working with were mainly using traditional websites, forums, and Facebook. Online practices evolved over time, as new platforms emerged and became popular in the far-right nebula (as elsewhere). Twitter (now X), YouTube, TikTok, Reddit, 4Chan, and Gab ... have become the new sites for exchange, discussion, convergence, or competition. We therefore had to adapt our data collection and analysis tools to the new platforms. Three platforms were subjected to systematic data collection: Facebook, YouTube, and Twitter (now X). On Facebook, we used screen captures of posts from the La Meute public group page on two occasions. The first involved logging onto the group's page daily and taking screenshots of all publications from October 2015 (when the page was created) to September 2016. A second data collection was carried out during the five days following the Quebec City mosque attack in January 2017. In total, this represents 232 screenshots including text, images, memes, and GIFs.

Some of the data also comes from YouTube. We looked at the YouTube channel of a radical right-wing influencer known in Canada and, more generally, in North America: Lauren Southern. Based on a theoretical approach documented in chapter 4, we carried out a careful analysis of a video of the influencer, filmed live as part of an operation in the French Alps in April 2018. In reportage format, this video "documents" an operation by a European anti-immigration group (Génération Identitaire) that is live-commented by Southern. We show later (chapter 4) how this video is illustrative of the manufacture of radical right-wing discourse, resulting from a hybrid process between humans and machines that, little by little, participates in the manufacture of memes affecting public representations. Finally, Twitter (now X) also provided a platform from which our data was collected. Using in-house software developed by our research centre's programmer, we automatically collated tweets produced by what we have elsewhere described as the "anti-sanitary measures tweetosphere" (Tanner and Campana 2022). As we have seen, this vast, amorphous movement was partly – but not exclusively – assembled by people already involved in the far-right networks we had been following since 2014.

In the next few paragraphs, we present the strategies we adopted and adjusted in the course of this long journey and discuss the two interrelated phases of our research.

Phase 1: Mapping

Our first objective, after getting our ethics clearance – which proved an adventure on its own – was to draw a broad portrait of the Canadian far right in order to distinguish clues and indicators that would allow us to identify groups, places, and, eventually, individuals of interest. We wanted to gather as much data as possible from open sources and for this we turned to the Internet and social media, which we scraped with the help of various automated tools. Also very useful were articles in the press related to events implicating far-right groups or individuals. Finally, we consulted articles posted on antifascist websites, like FachoWatch. Though rich in terms of information, and well documented and valuable for our objectives, we used these sources with great caution since their content providers are far from objective observers of the scene.

Once we had a partial mapping, our second step was to look for the names of those affiliated with these movements on social media, particularly on Facebook. This led to a snowball effect, whereby more and more data, including pictures, comments, and discussions, became accessible. A vast network map was drawn from this data, showing multiple persons and groups in interaction. In addition to the procedures described above, we used three applications to retrieve data on the Internet: Aspira for Facebook, an in-house PHP script for Twitter (now X), and a combination of web crawlers and WordStat for more traditional websites and blogs. Exploration of the web and social media also provided us with valuable information that was useful in preparing for interviews with members of oppositional movements. We of course also greatly benefited from testimonies written by former far-right militants who disengaged for various reasons from the movement to which they were affiliated.

We collected documents and used information in cases involving former or current members of far-right oppositional groups who had been convicted of criminal offences. These documents are available on the QuickLaw database. The keywords used to retrieve the data were *right-wing extremism, *racism, *anti-Semitism, *hate propaganda, and *Skinhead, which directed us to 967 files. Criteria of inclusion and exclusion were defined based on the objectives of our research. We eliminated all court sentences that did not concern specifically far-right militants, whatever the criminal offences for which they had been convicted. This research strategy has a number of limitations. First, cases settled out of court are not included in the database. While there were no figures available for this group, our impression is that it represents a number significantly higher than our collected court cases. Second, we realized in the course of fieldwork that the database we consulted does not include all sentences involving far-right militants. For instance, some of our interviewees spoke of their past convictions, but we could not find them in our database. Obtaining information then involved going to the different provincial and municipal courts, names in hand, and consulting court documents one by one, a time-consuming process.

Our effort at mapping also included ideological discourses. Using frame analysis and more precisely micro-discourse analysis (Johnston 1996, 241), we looked at how different individuals and groups shape the meaning of an object (for instance, immigration), as well as the solutions foreseen to solve the perceived problems. As frames are not static, we looked at the ways in which messages, references, stereotypes, images, etc. were used and sometimes transformed. Although framing is based on texts, it is strongly related to organizational practices and shaped by inter-organizational and eventually intra-organizational competition. This competition develops mainly into a struggle over signification, based on different "interpretative repertories" (Potter and Wetherell 1988, 172). Frames and discourses are then inextricably related; the former "organize and interpret discourse or talk within concrete interactional contexts" (Snow 2004). Following Johnston's methodological proposal, we used micro-discourse analysis to better map the frame's structure and content.

Finally, mapping also involves a focus on the practice of Internet and social media usage. In addition to our analysis of websites and social media texts as a collection of static empirical material, we also followed the evolution of groups and individuals over the years.

We stopped short of a now traditional statistical social network analysis (SNA), though it might certainly have been interesting. However, social network analysis would have produced a picture of the relations between specific groups and persons, most of whom would no longer occupy the far-right scene by the time of publication. We instead elected to proceed with a digital ethnography in order to analyze how discourses are constructed online and how social media are used daily. To build our sample of websites, we mapped the far right infosphere using mainly the snowball effect. We started with an initial list of websites and then followed the connections between groups and individuals. We updated our map of far-right movements at least three times a year, to take into account their extreme fluidity.

Phase 2: Interviews

Our second step consisted in conducting interviews with current and former members of far-right oppositional groups. This step was crucial for our research since, given the dearth of research on the Canadian far right, we needed direct information from those in oppositional groups in order to obtain the finest-grained material available on individual trajectories, values, identity building, and ingroup dynamics. This approach proved very valuable since we encountered difficulties in exploiting the data available on the web, due to very efficient social control exercised by the groups. For example, despite numerous attempts, we were never able to locate a skinhead concert or a meeting organized by one of the groups we identified before it happened. We would see flyers on different Facebook pages but those never revealed the actual location of the concert. Since *in situ* observations were part of our methodology, we needed to meet at least one person who could provide us with such information.

Once we identified individuals or places, we established a list of persons to contact. In order to diversify our approach and maximize our data collection, we used multiple strategies, including visits in bars and other such places that appeared in social media as regularly frequented by members of far-right groups. Although we expected to have some difficulty in establishing contact with members of these oppositional groups, we did not imagine it would be as difficult as it turned out to be.

Seasoned experts in "fieldwork under difficult conditions" (Boumaza and Campana 2007), we were confident that we would be able to overcome these complications when we first realized the degree of complexity of this project and the many obstacles that lay ahead. We succeeded for the most part, but to our surprise we were confronted by an extremely high level of distrust and defiance. Perhaps things would have gone more smoothly if we had started our field research in 2016 or 2017, when many far-right groups chose to become more publicly visible, some even adopting high-profile marketing strategies. Beginning in early 2017 we found that our prospective research participants seemed less reluctant to speak candidly about their adherence to far-right ideas, tactics, and networks. Now, both leaders and members of these groups more readily agree to meet journalists and researchers. Just a few years before, the conditions were completely different and we faced contempt, suspicion, and sometimes outright abhorrence. These circumstances made our project more challenging and may have had an impact on its results – not to mention its duration (data collection for what follows spanned almost eight years).

We faced many reactions after first contacting prospective participants. One person we contacted replied at length, explaining why they didn't want to take part in the study. Since they explicitly told us that they did not wish their motivations to be exposed in the research, we can say no more. Yet this attitude contrasts with the one we most frequently encountered: most did not return repeated calls, emails, or text messages. Some explained that they were frightened of discussing themselves or their group; a few even attempted to intimidate and threaten us. Most of the responses we obtained consisted of various kinds of personal justifications for their refusal to meet. One answered that their interest in a far-right group was too personal to be discussed with researchers.

On many occasions, we had to explain the role of the researcher. The amalgam between researchers and journalists and the anti-science posture of several far-right movements clearly made our task more complex. Our work as researchers has been repeatedly called into question and the scientific nature of our (or any) research mocked. For one of our contacts, the mention that we have an ethics certificate from our institutions prompted a sign of total mistrust, because "the University–Industrial Complex has NO ETHICS!" (May 2015). Another refused the conditions of anonymity we offered. On the contrary, he wanted to use the recorded interview to publicize his group's actions and philosophy. Not only did they ridicule our research processes, but they intended to instrumentalize us at every stage of the research, a position that proved deeply uncomfortable for us.

Likewise, we have on several occasions been associated with the "far-left lobby." It appeared that most of the persons we contacted adhere to conspiracy theories that characterize universities as institutions infiltrated by Zionists, Freemasons, or "cultural Marxists," and academics as corrupted, manipulated, incompetent, or too far left to deserve consideration. On other occasions, the people we contacted declined our request for an interview on the grounds that we benefited from a grant from a federal agency. One stated that they didn't want to be associated with the Canadian federal government, "a criminally convicted body" (March 2015). Others responded to our initial email in condescending ways, asking what was in it for them. We didn't offer any financial compensation, but we were open to compensating respondents who agreed to meet us with a non-alcoholic drink or food. Of course, a group with close ties to the skinhead movement did not take kindly to such a response and answered very aggressively, asking for beers and other alcoholic drinks.

At times, the way we introduced our research project caused some unexpected reactions. For example, one potential participant responded in a very aggressive way, categorically refusing to be assimilated to the far right and threatening to file a complaint with our university for slander. After an hour-and-a-half-long telephone conversation, the person finally decided to participate in this research.

Finally, some did agree to meet us but didn't show up for the interview. One group spontaneously contacted us, after months of silence, to agree to meet one member of the research team but, at the last minute, disappeared completely from our radar and was never heard from again. Their website was shut down a few weeks later. Did the group disband? Was one of its leaders arrested? We never got a definitive answer to our questions.

These difficulties led us to rethink our strategy for approaching potential respondents. What proved to be the most prejudicial was our respective past research projects on terrorism, criminal gangs, and civil wars (of course the first reaction of persons who received a request for an interview was to google our names). Our previous programs of research and our publications turned out to be a poor business card to approach far-right groups and individuals! Some of those we convinced to be interviewed told us, once the recorder had been turned off, that they were afraid we'd think of them as terrorists in the making. We can hypothesize that such fears may have been the reason for several refusals. Since we couldn't, for ethical reasons, hide our identities and disappear from the Internet (or even from our universities' respective websites), our options were limited. We created a generic contact address for people of interest, so as not to put ourselves in the front line too directly. That strategy was not as successful as we had hoped, since the body of the email still mentioned our names and functions.

Our publication agenda was at the centre of another decision. In 2014 two of us published a report on skinhead groups in Quebec (Tanner and Campana 2014). In it, we offer a definition of right-wing skinheads and discuss, although briefly, the relationships their members have developed with other kinds of far-right movements. While many of our respondents reject the label *far right*, the publication of this report unfortunately helped to entrench certain beliefs about our alleged bias or so-called political "leftist" agenda. We therefore decided to stop disseminating our research results before ending our fieldwork. Such an adjustment has come at a cost for us, since we had to rethink our publication strategy. It nevertheless appeared to be the best approach.

In 2017, after we decided to stop contacting potential respondents, two of us presented some of our empirical results at a scientific conference. Two days later, our paper was ridiculed in a video posted on YouTube by an individual who could be considered at that time as one of the main influencers of the alt-right movement in the province of Quebec. One of us was also intimidated and our research mocked. This rather stressful experience shows, if needed, that doing this type of fieldwork requires resilience and a high degree of adaptability on the part of researchers. As widely discussed in the literature, doing fieldwork is an emotional experience (Stodulka et al. 2019; Weiss et al. 2023). When there is no compatibility between the researcher's political beliefs and the ones of their respondents, challenges are high. "Emotional management" and distance are two key ingredients to maintain objectivity (Hedlund and Sampson 2023). Our experience as researchers has prepared us for this type of field research, even if we naively thought we wouldn't have to face such major challenges. Those challenges are, however, also a result in themselves. Besides the high level of distrust and suspicion expressed by many prospective respondents, our difficulties reveal that, between 2014 and 2017, agreeing to speak with outsiders about one's engagement and commitment to a far-right group was a momentous decision.

The stigmatizing effect of the term "far right" was especially high for women. All of those we contacted refused to grant us interviews. They seemed especially wary of the research process: while they were open to talking about their political engagement, they seemed to fear stigmatization if the interview were to reveal their personal details. They also tended to be more concerned with the way law enforcement agencies might use information that would eventually be published in scientific papers. We tried to reassure them about the integrity of the research procedure and our personal ethics; we underlined that we were fully committed to safeguarding their privacy and repeated that we would not, under any circumstances, disclose their personal information. Ultimately these arguments did not persuade them.

Despite these enormous difficulties, we did manage a respectable, and in fact unprecedented, fifty semi-structured interviews with respondents from four different provinces: we conducted twenty-five interviews in Quebec, fourteen in Ontario, four in Alberta, and seven in British Columbia. All interviewees were male, aged between twenty and seventy. Most were middle-aged, in their thirties or forties. They came from various socio-economic backgrounds, but at the time of the interviews most were lower middle-class, had a family, and were working in a variety of sectors, except for education. In addition to these interviews, we met with various observers of the far-right galaxy: social actors who monitor mainly street groups and skinhead gangs; journalists who have been on the far-right "beat," and former antifascist militants who gave us a glimpse of what the movement had been like in the 1990s and 2000s. We also conducted a dozen non-participant observations, mostly in Quebec and Ontario, where we followed demonstrations, meetings, and concerts, which were often announced at the very last minute. (This is why we were not able to attend such events farther west, for instance to fly to Alberta or to British Columbia at the drop of a hat.)

We decided to stop fieldwork and particularly interviews in early 2017. However, we continued to follow the groups and individuals we had included in our sample through their online activities and included the new groups that appeared from 2017 to 2022. Of course, the data generated by the analysis of their online activities did not allow us to address some of the questions we had handled through the interviews, such as the motivation of individuals or the sinuousness of their trajectory. Such a strategy did, however, provide us with a window on major organizational changes, networking, competitions, and collaborations and evolutions in ideological positioning.

Outline of the book

This book focuses on far-right extra-parliamentary oppositional groups that have been active across Canada between 2012 and 2022. Based on original empirical data, it provides a comprehensive analysis of the Canadian far right, exploring "macro" issues such as the evolution of the movement, its structure, and its membership, as well as "micro" aspects like the identity-processes and propaganda strategies adopted by groups and individuals. It intends to contribute both theoretically and empirically to the growing literature on far-right movements and politics, in the Canadian context.

We first articulate a theoretical framework that accounts for the development of a plethora of fringe groups in Western countries following the turn of the twenty-first century, feeding off mounting cynicism towards governing elites and defiance towards the state. At the same time, we shed new light on the understudied Canadian context, where the far-right galaxy has been rebuilding since the mid-2010s. In that respect we will map the main trends in the Canadian far-right movement over the last decade, accounting for the volatility of our subject: since 2010 groups have been created and disbanded, only to be born again. We will then offer explanations for the manner in which these groups are structured and their strategies for occupying the public sphere and creating and managing conflicts. We will also explore their attempts at "autonomization," breaking away from a "system" they view as corrupted. We will also investigate their recruitment strategies and the progressive engagement of would-be militants within groups. Finally, we will examine the way information and communication technologies are mobilized and how cyberspace contributes to the evolution of these groups.

Chapter 1 clears up some of the definitional issues and identifies remaining theoretical challenges. After discussing the literature on far-right movements in their multiple national and transnational expressions, it develops an original theoretical framework that cross-references literature on far-right extremism, social movements, and especially contentious politics, subcultures, and political engagement at both the collective and individual levels. We also call on ethnomethodology in order to account for the construction of a system of representations and a corresponding language within the social group. In this way our explanatory model crosses over the usual macro–micro divide. This framework aims at theorizing the different strategies from contention to autonomization. Based on a relational approach, it examines concomitant processes like identity building and propaganda building, visibilization and enlargement of their membership and their social base. It also further analyzes the relationships these groups maintain with the state as a principle and an organization, as well as with democracy as a value.

Chapter 2 offers further insights into the developments of the Canadian far right and presents a broad picture of the main categories of groups and influential individuals that constitute it. The Canadian far right is marked by a high degree of fragmentation and never-ending competition between groups that sometimes have a very short lifespan. As in other Western contexts, Canadian far-right groups form a "complex galaxy composed of different ideological tendencies, mobilising around different issues, and using distinct repertoires of action" (della Porta 2012). They are Christian identity, neo-Nazi, fascist, white supremacist, anti-government, anti-establishment, antisemitic, homophobic, anti-immigration, anti-Muslim, ultra-conservative, ultranationalist, etc. movements. Some of them combine different ideological features and, in an attempt to seize political opportunities, adapt them to immediate social and political issues as well as current events when opportunities arise.

One reason that explains this persistent fragmentation lies in the ideological diversity that characterizes these groups. Ideological discourses are group-specific, which generates the current patchwork of various neo-Nazi, white supremacist, racialist, religious, anti-immigration conspiracy theories and, in rare cases, left-wing references. In this context, typologies based on ideology and targets are difficult to operationalize. We therefore propose a new typology based on the way entities position themselves in relation to violence, institutions, and minorities.

Given this high degree of fluidity and the force of interpersonal relations in forging and dismantling these groups, chapter 3 focuses on discursive strategies used by groups to maintain cohesion, build up membership, and popularize their worldview. Acting as classic moral entrepreneurs, groups identify and relentlessly build up an issue they think will serve as a rallying point. While these issues are usually specific and immediate, they are often inserted in anti-Muslim/Arab and/or antisemitic worldviews, and Nazi symbolism continue to provide strong references. In classic form, these discourses are systematically framed around the notion that the white majority is being victimized or threatened. In many cases governments are also accused of willingly or naively promoting public policies that end up favouring dangerous minorities. This in turn raises the question of the legitimacy of the government, if not of the entire political and social system.

The repertories of action of the far right are diverse, and groups tend to construct their unique combination in order to voice demands or gain visibility and, as of late, social legitimacy. Respectability and acceptability have become sought after by a number of groups and individuals who strive to participate in mainstream politics. They adopt various "de-demonization" strategies meant to smooth out, tone down, and reframe the language – often by cherry-picking the more conventional parts of their platform. Obviously, their approach will differ (including the use of violence) according to the role they intend to play: to reorient the political debates from within, to replace a state viewed as corrupt and inefficient, or to alter the rules of the game.

Chapter 4 looks at the all-important presence of Canadian far-right entities on the Internet and various social media, which have become the central tools for propagandist strategies. The chapter discusses the circulation of ideas and symbols and presents the diverse ways in which the Internet can give life to virtual communities that extend well beyond the boundaries of nation states. The Internet has become a space where groups can easily fulfil their "mission" to raise political awareness and to enlighten a "misinformed" public. The objective is to create new political fractures in order to induce a process of reconfiguration of the political scene where they would play a direct or indirect role. While not all groups intend to intervene directly in political and public debates, they do work to garner more support for the ideas they defend and use the Internet to do that. It has become commonplace to say that the Internet has opened incredible opportunities for all sorts of oppositional groups, but our take on the situation is somewhat different. We analyze the situation as a perpetual, ongoing co-construction of multiple actors with highly variable agendas, relationships, discourses, strategies, and technological know-how *as well as* the platforms and devices they use, with their highly specific limitations and requirements, that transform the discourse and the users, *and* the audiences that both influence and seek influence.

Chapter 5 explores the engagement and disengagement processes that are at the basis of individual and group mobility. In particular, we tackle issues related to recruitment and active participation in group activities (legal, culturally appropriate, or otherwise). We will use the twin concepts of "engagement" and "commitment" to account for group formation and maintenance, instead of the contested and overused term "radicalization," because it allows us to introduce a distinction between convictions and actions and to underline the differential in personal investment and risk. This distinction is also valid for so-called "lone wolves," who can be said to "engage" with a radical ideology or "commit" to it with actual action. This is important if we are to account for the diversity of individual trajectories and analyze the role of the main variables behind engagement and commitment (ideology, peer influence, sense of community, fascination with violence ...). The chapter also explains the mirror process of disengagement, often forgotten but a major factor in personal and group biographies.

The closing chapter analyzes the official and non-official responses that have been mounted against far-right extremists and groups over the last decade. It looks at both security intelligence and national security policing as well as criminal policing and criminal justice.

The following will call on multiple theories and hypotheses in order to account for various specific aspects of the state of the far right in Canada. However, a few of these run through every chapter:

- Our selected definition of course shapes what we are looking at and attempting to account for. Despite our use, for simplicity's sake, of the term "far right," we suggest that in fact what defines the entities is not a common, recognizable, uniform ideology (some even claim to be on the left) but a vague number of concepts, imagery, and modes of relation to populations and institutions.
- The old concept of radicalization doesn't begin to account for what we have uncovered. In fact, it obfuscates what is a vastly complex interaction of factors and actors, including the often-neglected actions and reactions of institutions and the public at large. Hence "radicalization" will not be found in this book, at least not as an explanatory concept.
- Everywhere, at absolutely every level, the physical and the virtual, or informatic, intertwine and produce the various phenomena at hand. This was already true when we began our scientific journey in 2013, but it is vastly more so today (2022).
- Finally, societal responses, especially in the form of political discourse, laws, private regulation, policing, and popular

reaction, have several significant effects on far-right groups and individuals, be they intended or unintended (the latter, positive or counter-productive). In other words, societal responses are part of the context that has shaped the far right into what it is today.

1 DEFINITIONS AND CONCEPTS

Introduction

Carter holds that academics have reached a high degree of consensus on the main characteristics of right-wing parties. She suggests that "the parties' authoritarianism, their anti-democracy, and their exclusionary and/or holistic nationalism should all be considered defining properties of right-wing extremism/radicalism" (Carter 2018, 175), with xenophobia, racism, and populism seen as accompanying features. If Carter uses the generic term "right wing," her review of the literature includes articles and books that resort to other terms. The most used include "extreme-right," "radical right," "new right," "radical right populism," etc. Indeed, while a consensus may be emerging about the predominant ideological characteristics of these parties, many concepts continue to be used interchangeably or, at times, as competing (Backes 2001, 14). Often, they are not defined at all, as if they spoke for themselves. Perhaps this is the consequence of the contemporary cultural context, where the rise of far-right parties and movements has become a global phenomenon, making them major players in national and international forums. Yet, as Mudde put it, "differences in definitions vary as much between terms as within terms" (2002, 13). The creation of new concepts, such as the alternative right or alt-right, only adds to the conceptual cacophony.

Three main problems arise with concepts describing the far right. The first one is that they are relational and context-sensitive. They do not refer exactly to the same political phenomenon in France and in

Canada – or even within Canada. Indeed, a far-right party in Denmark is unlikely to have the same ideological contours or political agenda as its counterpart in the United States, though both may share some common characteristics. As case studies multiply, so do definitions.

The second problem is that these concepts are used indiscriminately to characterize political parties, extra-parliamentary groups, think tanks, "alternative" media, and grassroots activists as well as self-proclaimed experts, pundits, intellectuals, or agitators who are not affiliated with any organization but promote far-right ideas. All these actors tend to rely on similar ideological references and thus are related in some way – although the level of proximity varies. However, they do not share the same objectives; they do not always frame their discourse in the same way nor do they adopt the same organizational structures, repertories of actions, or agendas.

The third problem concerns the fact that these terms are not only used for scientific purposes but also for political ones (Mudde 2002, 10). The meaning of these politically charged terms varies from one era to another, but since World War II, the terms "extreme right" and "far right" have served a larger strategy aimed at drawing a "cordon sanitaire" around undesirable political parties (Downs 2002; Heinze 2018). It is also important to note that many of the new phrases were coined by far-right ideologues for "marketing" and propaganda purposes – like "alt-right" or "alt-lite" – before being adopted, sometimes without any critical distance, by academics and the media. Journalists have played an instrumental role in popularizing some of these terms during the 2016 US presidential election campaign. This circulation of terms and concepts and the multiple significations attached to them also contribute to the conceptual inflation and confusion.

Should the definition of "far right" be based only on ideological features or should it encompass other aspects, such as the structure and the nature of the groups or their (changing) political objectives? In a context where the "extraordinary diversity of key themes in the far-right arsenal" (Feldman and Pollard 2016) results in a high degree of ideological fragmentation, the definitional problem seems more intractable than ever. Not to mention a slew of other developments, such as the tensions generated by the influence of transnationalization on the trajectory of far-right groupings and movements, combined with the persistence of local issues; the constantly moving goalposts of conservative and far-right values regarding contentious social and political issues like immigration, abortion, globalization, and now pandemics and vaccines; the recent rise of an anti-immigration left, as illustrated by the emergence of the political party Aufstehen in Germany in 2018 (Olsen 2018); the convergence of right-wing and left-wing anti-elitism and anti-globalization discourses; and the prevalence of semi-serious, semi-mocking trolls that proliferate online and contribute to the diffusion of far-right symbolism and fake news.

To date, most of the research has focused on official political parties. Little has changed since Pedahzur and Weinberg noted, in 2001, the lack of interest scholars have in extra-parliamentary politics (55). The same observation still applies at the time this book was written, though some progress has been made (Rydgren 2018, 9; Caiani 2017; Mudde 2007). But to the extent that scholarly focus remains on far-right political parties, the main definitions of the far right discussed in the literature do not take fully into account the specificities of extra-parliamentary groups, their fluidity, and their diversity at both the ideological and organizational levels. By fluidity, we refer to the high degree of flexibility in ideological discourses and organizational structures, as well as the dynamism of movements, structures, and processes. "The perspective of fluidity emphasizes the cultural sides of movements – the transformations of meaning – and the interactive sides of consequences – the less public aspects of life" (Gusfield 2000, 156). Of course, some students of the far right have researched – sometimes extensively – non-institutionalized groups and movements. However, most of these studies gloss over definitional challenges, with the noticeable exception of some seminal specialists of social movements (e.g. Caiani, della Porta, and Wagemann 2012; Fielitz and Thurston 2016).

We contend that a useful definition of far-right politics should comprise as many non-party organizations as possible, including Internet-based organizations, as well as self-proclaimed experts and agitators. We claim that a definition that accounts for the variations at both the ideological and organizational levels is indispensable to the proper study of the different forms far-right movements take and the intersection of different groups, movements, and individuals with local, national, and transnational networks. Also, as will be discussed elsewhere in this book, the far-right phenomenon should be viewed through a lens that accounts for how the Internet, as well as automation propelled by algorithms and artificial intelligence, impacts it and may transform it in the near future (Daniels 2018). Far-right content, its circulation and diffusion vectors within the public sphere, and the way it affects diverse audiences must now all be analyzed with attention to the role of machines.

Ideological variations on the right of the right

Ideology is the best entry point to assess variations on the right of the right. Despite the lack of consensus on a definition of right-wing extremism, most authors agree on the fact that it is a particular form of ideology (Mudde 1995, 203–5) with a unique combination of features. We define ideology, following Van Dijk, as "social representations that define the social identity of a group; that is, its shared beliefs about its fundamental conditions and ways of existence and reproduction" (2006, 116). Although ideology provides a "sense of certainty, safety and identity" (Jost 2017, 168), it is not fixed. Influential personalities, group leaders, and activists can draw on it, refine it, or repackage it depending on their objectives, resources, and context (Payerhin and Zirakzadeh 2006; Koelher 2015, 27).

Our intent is not to discuss extensively the features that characterize far-right ideology, but rather to better understand its high degree of fragmentation, variability, and fluidity. True, some ideological features remain strongly constitutive of the far-right ideology. As Mudde shows, nationalism, internal homogenization, xenophobia, welfare chauvinism, and law and order were already at the core of European far-right political parties active in the 1980s and the 1990s (2002, 176). For his part, Jamin (2009) shows that the far-right ideological universe revolves around three main domains: the inequality between races and "civilizations"; nationalism as a project to counter the perceived inequalities, as well as a finality; radicalism and extremism as means of action. Mainly based on empirical studies of European political parties, neither definition discusses other ideological features that also tend to be found in American and European parties and groups as well: nativism, Christian identity, libertarianism, white supremacism, vigilantism, conspiracy theorists, survivalism, etc. (e.g. Sprinzak 1995; Durham 2007; Mudde 2009). The proliferation of parties and activists has two *a priori* contradictory consequences: the increase in ideological fragmentation and the multiplication of the connections between these overlapping ideological strands.

The waves in the far right

Indeed, far-right ideology constantly evolves, and this movement has accelerated with the evolution of the technological environment. But students of right-wing extremism usually distinguish between different waves of post-war, right-wing extremism (Von Beyme 1988). Ignazi for instance makes a distinction between "old" and "new" types of parties (Ignazi 1992): the former has a strong "fascist imprint"; the latter develops an anti-system attitude (1992, 3). Von Beyme identifies three waves: the post-war neo-fascism; the Poujadist type of right-wing extremism; and the rise of right-wing extremist parties, which "free[s] right-wing extremism from its ghetto" (1988, 12). This third wave started in the 1980s and has seen a profound transformation of right-wing political parties from outsiders to "institutionalised and integrated members of the political system" (Mudde 2016, 16).

Bernauer claimed, in a 2017 conference paper, that it was "too early to tell whether we are moving towards a fourth wave of [right-wing] populism" (2017). It may be time to reassess that claim. As the authors cited above show, changes in the social and political environment have had an impact on the actors' strategies and on the ideological references being mobilized within the movement. The shift to the right in most Western countries and the accompanying technological advances have altered both the frontiers of the far-right national and transnational scenes and the way ideological discourses are shaped. Thus, we may in fact be entering a fourth wave, one characterized by the electoral successes of many far-right parties from Hungary to France; by the blurring of the traditional boundaries between conservatism and far-right extremism; by the higher visibility of far-right, extra-parliamentarian movements in most Western countries; by the greater diversity of actors involved in ideology- and identity-building;

and by the larger range of issues being tackled. The role played by far-right groups in the 2016 presidential campaign in the USA perfectly illustrates how fringe ideas are brought into the mainstream (Barkun 2017).

Needless to say, in the last decade the Internet has played an instrumental role in creating transnational far-right communities in which ideological references can circulate. A sense of collective identity has emerged in online forums and on social media (Scrivens 2017). However, the mobilization of ideological references depends on the availability of tangible local issues or imported transnational ones. Consequently, discourses tend to remain group-specific, as most groups and individuals thrive on various but unique combinations of native and imported references more than on a shared, but abstract, ideology. In other words, the influence of transnational networks extends dramatically, but far-right groups remain shaped by the local historical, political, and social context in which they emerge.

The influence of local history cannot be overstated. Beyond the complex organization and constant evolution of national far-right movements, they are the products of past movements and ideological traditions. In the United States, the KKK, which emerged from the Civil War, has left a long-lasting imprint on the different waves that have marked US far-right history (Hamm 2009). The contemporary US white supremacist movement is deeply rooted in the 1970s and 1980s, when far-right organizations started to instrumentalize resentments expressed at the end of the Vietnam War. It grew by recruiting veterans who wanted to avenge what they perceived as a betrayal of the state in the conduct of the war (Belew 2018). In Europe, for obvious reasons, right-wing parties and organizations usually try to keep their distance from any Fascist or Nazi lineage, but "some lines of continuity" remain inescapably obvious (Mammone, Godin, and Jenkins 2013, 5). The persistence of strong national – and sometimes local – specificities, as well as the existence of cultural differences, partly explains the huge diversity in movements and political parties that draw on the far-right ideological arsenal. It remains to be seen if the emergence of a leading movement or personality might reconcile and restructure disparate far-right ideological traditions (7).

Blurred boundaries

For the last decade or so, the opportunities opened up by the Internet have significantly increased the malleability of ideology. The sheer number of actors involved in the remodelling and diffusion of ideology today exacerbates the ideological fragmentation and blurs the traditional ideological boundaries of right-of-centre politics. Two examples are worthy of mention and discussion.

The first example refers to the terms coined by far-right ideologues in the United States – "alt-right" and "alt-lite" – to gain more visibility and legitimacy on the political scene in the 2010s. These terms capture a key trend for the far right in the United States, one that appeared well before the Trump presidency and rapidly reached far beyond American borders. According to Marwick and Lewis, the alt-right consisted of "an amalgam of conspiracy theorists, techno-libertarians, white nationalists, Men's Rights advocates, trolls, anti-feminists, anti-immigration activists, and bored young people" (2017, 3). While popular figures such as Richard Spencer or Milo Yiannopoulos briefly appeared as central, many scholars note that the alt-right never had a "real organisational structure" (Wendling 2017, 5) and thus could "scarcely be called an organised movement" (Hawley 2017, 11). That was, perhaps counterintuitively, its main strength. It was influential in the mainstream conversation in large part because of its appropriation and intensive use of digital media (Hankes 2016) but especially for its use of a new repertoire of action involving "trolling" and other aggressive attention-getting activities (Nagle 2017; Philips 2015; Lewis 2018). Contrary to previous online activity by right-wing groups, which was generally confined to members-only websites (e.g., stormfront.org), the alt-right online discourse spread beyond these platforms, moving from specialized channels such as 4chan or 8chan/8kun to mainstream social media platforms such as Twitter/X or YouTube and finally to traditional media (Wendling 2017; Scrivens et al. 2021). As protests mounted and platforms removed hateful content, it simply migrated to new providers that were constantly emerging. In other words, the alt-right tide acted as a powerful federating force for a movement that had been atomizing.

A "lighter" form of the alt-right, the so-called "alt-lite," adopted a similar repertoire of action, while avoiding calls for violence and other extremist views. Perhaps consequently, the alt-lite was considered to have gained a "much larger audience" (Hawley 2019, 185). It made inroads in broader conservative media and opinion platforms, where its adherents adopted "a strong populist and confrontational style, frequently deriding so-called political correctness" (187). Examples of such platforms included Breitbart in the United States and Rebel Media in Canada. Both promoted anti-immigration and pro–white nationalist discourses, always taking great care not to devolve into hate speech.

Both the alt-right and the alt-lite contributed to the elaboration of new strategies to facilitate far-right participation in political debates. Their adherents made it more politically palatable to openly belong to far-right groups or to echo their ideology. These strategies include 1) constantly redefining the ideological boundaries of far-right politics; 2) popularizing far-right online forums and, to some extent, making them common and banal; and 3) increasing individual, group, and ideological presence within mainstream media. Each brought about a new "normality" for the far right, allowing it to progressively invade the traditional political grounds of mainstream conservative parties and movements. They also contributed to the ongoing redefinition of extraparliamentary politics by generating a massive impact on the attention economy and by rattling the public trust in institutions as well as in the traditional media (Donovan and Boyd 2019, 4).

The second example illustrates how far-right organizations, activists, or supporters can hijack marginalized social issues and give new visibility to ideological strands that used to be confined to the Internet abyss or obscure forums. One is the hateful masculinism of "Incels," once a small group meeting on an unknown subreddit. Incels are self-described "involuntary celibates," men willing but forbidden to partake in what they conceive as a highly sexualized but exclusive culture that has rejected them as undesirable. They in turn respond to this perceived injustice with hatred for feminists and women in general, resentment towards the men who they imagine to be getting disproportionate sexual attention, and general animosity towards a society that has allowed those to exist.

While Incels do not entirely fit within the far right, their outlandish theory about male and female sexual behaviour does share in the same widespread misogynistic and antifeminist/masculinist rhetoric. Kimmel (2013) has shown the central importance of masculinity in many far-right groups in the USA, some of whom the alt-right has helped to rehabilitate (Kelly 2017). He also argues that masculinity (or perceived threats to it) has been one of the most powerful motivations for young men to engage with far-right violent extremism and indeed violent extremism in general (2018). In fact, far-right groups who have adopted a masculinist rhetoric have contributed to shaping discourse in the *manosphere* as a whole (Koulouris 2018). The term refers to a loose assemblage of various online forums that claim to defend men's rights by adopting a masculinist, antifeminist perspective (Ging 2017, 3). They all adhere to the so-called "red pill philosophy" which works to "awaken men to feminism's misandry and brainwashing" (4). The red pill trope is quite common in the far-right online discourse. The term comes from *The Matrix* film series in which a red pill awakens one from the dream-like, manipulative, and exploitative matrix, itself an embodiment of the classic (Marxist) concept of false consciousness. The loose coalition of far-right groups and activists who took on this thesis went one step further, accusing not only feminism but also liberalism and leftism of no less than destroying Western civilization (Ganesh 2018).

The Proud Boys in the US and in Canada have made masculinity a core ideological component of their identity. Although they pretend to be "Western chauvinists" first and foremost and display the corresponding racist, and especially anti-Muslim, feelings, they also describe themselves as a club for white men only and have multiple rules concerning women and (hetero)sex. As stated on the USA chapter website (proudboysusa.com), "Our group is and will always be MEN ONLY (born with a penis if that wasn't clear enough for you leftists)! If you are (and were born) a woman and you would like to be involved, there is a girls' group. They call themselves Proud Boys' Girls and they're our second-biggest demographic."

The Internet, and social media in particular, has exacerbated several trends that began years ago. First, it has created spaces for the emergence of online communities whose discourse may circulate and resonate with far-right organizations. Consequently, it increases opportunities for far-right groups or activists to instrumentalize and reframe existing – and often marginalized – social issues and to attempt to hijack, or hack, them in order to strengthen their political agenda and to gain more social and political visibility and ultimately legitimacy. Finally, the two examples on which we based our discussion illustrate the fluidity of the ideological strands that constitute the far-right ideological universe. We now turn to discussing a revised definition that takes into consideration that fluidity and diversity, at both the ideological and organizational levels, which characterizes far-right non-party politics.

Towards a definition of far-right non-party movements

Crafting a definition that is at the same time consistent, discriminant, and simple is a challenging endeavour and, beyond simple semantics, it directly affects the contours of the objects we are to observe. It doesn't help, of course, that we all have our own political views and that "right" or "far right" are relative concepts. That is why we have attempted to identify key connections at the heart of the identity of social movements and discrete organized groups that position them at the edge of the political spectrum.

A social movement like any other?

Kincaid (2017) maintains that right-wing social movements are unique in several ways and deserve special treatment from social movement scholars. According to him, organizationally speaking, the main difference between left-wing and right-wing movements is that the latter act on behalf of an advantaged, empowered majority, which has access to diverse political and social resources. However, this distinction overlooks the change-oriented activities of most far-right groups and activists, who vow to transform values, styles of government, and, consequently, society and the state that governs it. It also underestimates the variety of *target audiences* of these movements and the repertoires of actions and practices they use to mobilize people (on social movements' audiences, see Blee and McDowell 2012). Audiences can include, according to Earl (2019), current activists, potential recruits, "uninformed or uncommitted bystanders" (756); movement's opponents; movement's main target (governments and political, economic, and cultural elites); and external institutions, like education and the media. We would add to this list other like-minded movements, with whom they seek to connect domestically or internationally. Clearly, not all these audiences are advantaged or empowered. Instead, following Hirsch-Hoeffler and Mudde (2013), we adopt a more "neutral" conception of far-right social movements, one that focuses on their distinctive features.

It is also helpful to underline that most of these movements and organizations are proactive in raising awareness among the public, more specifically within the so-called "victimized white communities," in lobbying potentially sympathetic political parties and in shaping an "alternative" social and political order. In that, far-right movements are classic social movements. This is why Gattinara reckons that to better understand far-right non-party politics we need to focus especially on the complex "intersections of social movement dynamics and far-right politics" (Gattinara and Pirro 2018, 8).

Party and non-party politics

According to many authors (e.g., Koopmans et al. 2005, 185–7; Giugni et al. 2005; Kriesi 2012), the existence of a strong, official far-right party with representatives in the national parliament leaves far-right movements a very narrow political space. That is because almost every political or cultural event, controversy, or other opportunity to intervene directly or indirectly in the public debate is immediately fully colonized by the official party.

This trade-off hypothesis suffers, however, from two shortcomings. First, it overlooks the interconnectedness between party, movement, and activists and, more largely, the interpenetration of society, movement, and party. Institutionalized and non-institutionalized politics are two faces of the same coin and interplay with each other. For instance, political parties may develop "out of movements, in response to movements or in close association with movements" (Goldstones 2003, 2). Pedahzur and Weinberg established that far-right political parties and social movements often view themselves as partners and may actively cooperate (2001, 66–7). During a crisis of representation, social movements can transform into a political party, support the creation of a new party, and create opportunities for the emergence of a new political party (Hutter, Kriesi, and Lorenzini 2019, 330). More generally, interactions between actors in far-right politics can take the form of cooperation, agenda appropriation, co-optation/penetration, rejection, competition, exclusion, agenda-setting, attack, to no interaction at all (Caiani and Císař 2019c, 236–41). Interactions also operate at different levels: ideological, strategic, organizational, etc. (236). In the same vein, the trade-off hypothesis does not consider hybrid actors that "are located at the intersection between the party and the social movement" (Gattinara 2019, 92).

The second shortcoming relates to the interconnection and interconnectedness of conservative (i.e., right of centre but still mainstream) and far-right values, an overlooked issue that deserves attention, despite the difficulties in unpacking the "cultural messiness" of contentious politics (Busher and Morrison 2018, 227). Far-right and conservative political views play with many of the same themes: national identity, traditional values, religion, citizenship, immigration control, social control and order, and various anti-abortion positions. Oftentimes, far-right groups will claim to be merely "more honest" about the issues, the worldview, the projects, and the goals that are commonly found in mainstream conservative parties. That said, Blee and Creasap (2010) did identify a central distinction between the merely conservative right and the far right based on their relationship to violence, where the latter are suffused with the symbolic and tangible forms of violence. This is not, however, always obvious, as more and more far-right movements adopt, at least in public, a sanitized, non-violent version of their ideas in order to bring them into the mainstream.

Mainstream conservatism comes in a variety of incarnations and expressions and both conservative movements and parties are extremely heterogeneous and context-dependent. Movements like the Tea Party in the United States (which would later morph into Trumpism); political parties like the Conservative Party in Canada, the Wild Rose and Alliance (now defunct) parties in Alberta, or the People's

Party of Canada; and media like the Daily Wire or Fox News in the United States and Rebel News in Canada are fragments of a wide nebula that includes people and organizations from different backgrounds but who tend to share key ideological components (Blee and Creasap 2010). Mudde argues that what he coins the "populist radical right" "is well connected to mainstream ideas and much in tune with broadly shared mass attitudes and policy positions" (2010, 1178). These interconnections operate at the elite and mass levels as well. Starting in the 1960s, most conservative parties started shifting further and further to the right, as right-wingers were slowly capturing power from within (sometimes with the assistance of activists and intellectuals outside the party, as in the case of the US Conservative Party; Brennan 1995). The growth of official extremist right-wing parties, like the Front National in France, accelerated or precipitated this process, depending on context. Economic crises and terrorist attacks such as that on 9/11, as well as other contextual fluctuations, provided opportunities for some of these parties to increase their share of votes. Finally, most conservative and far-right movements took a grassroots orientation, following the strategies elaborated by the so-called New Right in the US in the 1970s (Blee and Creasap 2010). The New Right was successful in mobilizing diverse populations, from low-social-status groups to the economically successful upper-middle class. This gave parties an enlarged social base and contributed to the resonance of their ideas.

The changes in the conservative political landscape – the so-called "right turn" – and the rise of far-right movements and parties are independent but interconnected processes that resulted in part in blurring the boundaries between the right and the far right. The literature usually examines two issues: 1) Do the electoral successes of far-right and radical right-wing parties push them into the mainstream (e.g., Akkerman, de Lange and Rooduijn 2016)? 2) How and to what extent do fringe ideas impact the agenda of mainstream parties (e.g., Han 2015)? Most studies show that the attitudes of mainstream parties vary from one context to another and depend on many factors (Heinze 2018); however, it is generally agreed that mainstream parties of the right and far right converge on at least three central issues, which are often conflated: immigration, integration, and multiculturalism (e.g.,

Bale 2008; Bale et al. 2010; Akkerman, 2012; Alonso and Claro da Fonseca 2012; Han 2015). But convergence is not influence. Though there are instances of far-right parties influencing less radical formations at specific moments in national histories, that influence is far from uniform and is probably less significant than it has sometimes been predicted (e.g., Mudde 2013; Akkerman 2015; Meyer and Rosenberger 2015). Akkerman considers that it has been overestimated (2015, 63), while Rooduijn et al. show that mainstream parties "have not become more populist in the past two decades" (2014, 569). Indeed, Mudde convincingly demonstrates that if far-right parties have had an indirect influence on people and parties, "their success was enabled by the pre-existence of a fertile breeding ground of popular resentment around immigration, crime and party politics" (2013, 11).

These very important results give a much-needed perspective on the rise of far-right parties and movements. Yet they only look at the interactions of the conservative/right wing and the far right at the level of their generic public discourse on values and concerns. On many specific political and societal issues, the two groups essentially overlap. For instance, far-right raging Islamophobia directly connects with conservative concerns about immigration, the preservation of a so-called threatened culture, and so on. Indeed, anti-Islam and anti-Muslim positions have become one of the main features of the contemporary far right (Hafez 2014). Islamophobia itself is on the rise in most Western countries (e.g., Gottschalk and Greenberg 2007; Satzewich 2011; Lean 2012; Bail 2014), in a context where the "national identity axis" is again prevalent (Ellinas 2010). Particularly since 11 September 2001, Islam has been presented as both an international threat and a national, domestic fifth column ready to pounce. According to Hafez (2014), in many countries Islamophobia has become a form of "accepted racism." Traverso shares this conclusion and considers that "Islamophobia is fully acceptable, in a European culture whose colonial inheritance remains alive and well" (2016, 95). Canada is no exception, and hostility towards Muslims and Islam has been growing since at least 9/11 (e.g., Poynting and Perry 2007; Helly 2012; Perry 2014).

The political shift to the right in Europe and in the United States coincides with a rapid acceleration in the dissemination – especially on the Internet – of stereotypes about Muslims. This special context has helped make some far-right themes more widely acceptable. One reason is the "porosity in the discourse between the more extreme articulations [of Islamophobia] widely condemned in the mainstream, and the more normalised and insidious ones, which the former tend to render more acceptable in comparison" (Mondon and Winter 2017, 2152–3). Most far-right official parties maintain an intentional ambiguity towards Muslims, although some of their members occasionally express anti-Muslim sentiments and positions. The French Rassemblement national (RN, formerly Front national) has developed an ethno-nationalist agenda and pursues a strategy elaborated in the early 2000s, which consists of focusing its discourses on immigration, integration, and the "authentic" French cultural heritage rather than targeting a community in particular (Frigoli and Ivaldi 2017, 31). However, RN discourses on identity, often peppered with ethnocentric and racist tropes and references, invariably indirectly target Islam, both fostering and exploiting widespread anti-Muslim sentiments within the French far right. As Schmuck and Matthes (2019) convincingly show, explicit anti-Islamic and anti-Muslim statements, as well as implicit ("dog whistle") political rhetoric in political campaigns, are commonly used to leverage hostile attitudes towards Muslims in order to affect voting preferences in many Western countries.

Far-right non-party organizations take an active part in this process. The strategies vary according to their political agenda and objectives. Some groups define themselves as specifically anti-Islam (i.e., Pegida and its national and local chapters), while others promote anti-Islam and anti-Muslim positions among other themes (i.e., the Soldiers of Odin, an anti-immigration group with a particular focus on Muslim immigrants). Most, in an attempt to portray themselves as less radical or extreme than they are, deliberately follow a "de-demonization" strategy that inserts ambiguity at the discursive level in order to promote far-right ideas, values, and ideals to a wider public (Campana and Tanner 2020). In so doing, they also contribute to the crystallization of far-right and conservative values into a uniform ideological package that epitomizes the convergence of far-right and conservative party and non-party politics.

This smooth ideological packaging, however, conceals the complexity and conflicts that characterize far-right social movements across the globe and, most importantly, the gap that remains between far-right oppositional movements and mainstream conservative political parties. This is especially true in Canada, where there exists no far-right official political party at this time. Canadian conservative parties continue to participate in, and approve of, the basic tenets of liberal democracy and the rule of law. They also mostly stay away from using the rhetorical function of violence, contrary to far-right movements.

To offer a definition that accounts for the specifics of the far right, its central themes, its internal conflicts, and constant change, as well as to properly distinguish it from its neighbouring groups and concepts, we adopted a "3D" definitional matrix.

A 3D definitional matrix

Any far-right social movement family is a composite actor or, as Gattinara and Pirro put it, a "variegated milieu" (2018, 3), fluid in nature and structure. As discussed earlier, there are significant differences between the types of non-institutionalized groupings that compose these movements. Although ideology certainly represents a transversal characteristic and allows for the coexistence and co-constitution of different "subcultures" or "schools of thought," the heterogeneity and fluidity of far-right politics calls for a definition that addresses this diversity and accounts for non-institutionalized politics and its interaction with party politics.

Following Futrell et al. (2019), we consider that extremism is not a "fundamentally different unit of analysis that requires fundamentally new or distinct theories and concepts." The same applies to radicalism. Yet we argue that a classic, rigid definition would confine the study of the far right to an overly narrow framework. We need a certain degree of flexibility in order to account for the variety, the constant shifting, and the "de-demonization" tactics described above. Moreover, this definition should encompass contextual and relational dimensions and especially the interpenetration between society, party, and far-right movements. Therefore, we propose, following the method suggested by Brodeur, to define contested social phenomena that are characterized by a high degree of variation and evolution, a "matrix of features" ("matrice de traits" [Brodeur 2009, 35]).

Composed of three main facets, our definitional matrix attempts to take into account the different natures, structures, and ideologies that far-right groupings adopt and their evolution across time and contexts. It analyzes these movements, resorting to a relational and processual approach (Delpéteau 2018).

Relationship with political and social institutions

The first facet is the manner in which far-right groups envision their relationship with political and social institutions. The term "institutions," here, refers to the institutions that are constitutive of the state, that symbolize the norms, principles, and rules that govern social and political relations within a given context, as well as to routine political processes. As Freilich et al. (1999) remind us, fringe movements usually engage in the explicit promotion of an ideology that moves away from accepted social and political norms. They also aim at challenging the "existing systems of authority" (Snow and Soule 2010). The "law and order" theme, usually developed around issues relating to immigration control and immigrant integration (or lack thereof), represents a core feature of most far-right groups. It comes with the call for a stronger state and the adoption of authoritarian stances and attitudes (Carter 2018, 169). It involves an ambivalent position towards the state, at the same time denouncing it for its current permissiveness and demanding that it capture more power to control or stop the flow of immigrants.

Anti-elitism, while not unique to this aspect of the matrix, is part and parcel of the populist style adopted by many far-right groups and parties. It is usually expressed through a limited set of familiar variations: some groups adopt anti-establishment views; others target explicitly political, social, economic, and cultural elites and reject the system partially or as a whole; others attack democracy and the system of values attached to it more explicitly. It is worth noting that mainstream conservative parties, which share similar outlooks on some of the issues far-right groups pretend to address, are nevertheless considered part of the problem. They are viewed as traditional parties, no better than their more progressive counterparts, because their leaders and representatives are members of the establishment and because they represent a vehicle for individual political ambitions.

Indeed, far-right groupings go from a posture of contesting the legitimacy of elites, to denouncing, to outright rejecting political, social, cultural, and media organizations as well as all international, national, and regional forms of order. Therefore, relationships with political and social institutions can take different forms and degrees: from a denunciation of the liberal order to the more radical rejection of the democratic order. This distinction closely matches the distinction we made in the introduction between radical and extremist groups and movements.

Relationship to violence

The second facet refers to the relationship to violence. It depends on many factors but primarily ideological orientation, cultural context, and, especially, the role of violence in ordinary social interactions (i.e., whether violence is considered potentially legitimate by a statistically significant proportion of citizens), and the role of violence in the repertoires of action of other social movements. Borjno and Ravndal (2019) make a distinction between far-right *violence*, which includes both symbolic and physical acts of violence, and far-right *terrorism*. They also discuss a third type of violence, which may or may not cause physical harm: hate crimes (5). They acknowledge that definitions of hate crimes vary from one country to another and that this type of crime is not the exclusive domain of the far right (6). Furthermore, the use of three categories to analyze far-right violence can create ambiguities, as databases that compile acts of far-right violence do not rely on the same definitions and, very often, will classify a given act in different categories (7), not to mention the well-documented, gross underreporting of hate crimes and other minor violent acts committed against persons or property. Consequently, in what follows we adopt a simpler approach, shrinking the number of categories to two: physical and symbolic violence.

Radical groups, movements, and parties have a different relation to violence than extremist ones. As already stated in the introduction, the latter may value and even promote the use of physical violence as a legitimate means of action to intimidate "others" or "the state"; to "wake up" the so-called "silent white majority"; to redress a perceived downgrading in symbolic, political, or economic status; to provoke a reaction from the state or declared enemies; or to avenge a perceived outrage or prejudice. Some extremist groups even vow to replace the state institutions that they deem incompetent or corrupt by the creation of vigilante or militia groups, who will patrol the streets and forcefully impose their conception of social and political order. Violence is here far from being only defensive; it can meet an offensive and disruptive objective. It can also be spontaneous and explosive (Bornjo and Ravndal 2019, 5), especially when used by members of skinhead groups and cliques. Lastly, it can take a variety of forms: from vandalism and damage to symbolic venues (e.g., a synagogue, a mosque, a gay bar) to physical assaults and terrorism as defined in the Criminal Code.

Violent behaviours and attitudes are most common in extremist groups and the individuals they inspire. Symbolic violence, however, is present in both extremist and radical groups, as they are based on a logic of suspicion, rejection, and, for some, dehumanization. According to Bourdieu (1999), symbolic violence is a type of violence produced by discourses that depict and legitimate an alternate, ideal structure of power relations. It irremediably includes latent threats of violence, at least through the desired collapse and replacement of existing structures and the security they provided. Of course, the proposed structure is usually aimed at directly (further) fragilizing the political position of targeted groups, which directly impacts their sense of security – when it's not explicitly used to intimidate them. Brodeur considers symbolic violence to belong to the psychological, communicational, and political register (2009, 29). Propaganda, symbols, tropes, and narratives appearing on digital platforms, on banners and placards waved during demonstrations, or on walls (graffiti, etc.) serve two goals. First, they aim at recruitment, mobilization, and cohesion within the group. Second, they also participate in the process of altering perceptions, creating and fostering social tensions, and, ultimately, social and political polarization. In doing so, they contribute to a climate of open defiance and increasing vulnerability.

Construction of otherness

The rejection of pluralism and egalitarianism is the main characteristic of both radical and extremist groups composing the far-right social movements family. The third facet of our definitional matrix concerns the construction and relationship to otherness. All types of far-right discourse are systematically filled with positive self-presentation and negative depictions of "others" (Van Dijk 2006, 126). This negative depiction can turn into dehumanization. As most radical far-right groups attempt to gain additional visibility and present themselves as a viable alternative to dominant political thinking and traditional political parties, many adopt subtler language and moderate the tone of their messages at public appearances. Alternatively, some adopt and adapt a strategy devised by Grand Wizard David Duke in the 1980s when he stressed that the KKK was "pro-white" rather than "anti-black."

Extremist groups, however, display their anti-pluralist and anti-egalitarian views and attitudes far more explicitly. Their targets are multiple and the identification of outgroups varies from one to another, but since 2001 two overarching forms of racism have been dominant: Islamophobia, still on the rise (e.g., Gottschalk and Greenberg 2007; Satzewich 2001; Lean 2012; Bail 2014), and classic antisemitism, which still persists as a beacon for far-right social movements, where centuries-old expressions of antisemitism coexist with new ones (Wodak 2018, 62–4, 81).

The conception of otherness is central to the definition of the nation that far-right movements aspire to construct. Bar-On states that nationalism provides far-right movements and parties "a stable anchor" and "daily oxygen" (2018, 18). Indeed, as shown by Mudde (2007, 2017b), Betz (2017), Rydgren (2007, 2018), and Art (2020), among others, traditional nativism remains a defining feature of the far right. Lubbers defines nativism as a claim "to protect the interests of an ingroup against those of out-groups, protecting the homogeneity of the nation state against threats by non-native elements" (2019, 449). Nativism is therefore a form of exclusivist nationalism for many authors. According to Bergmann (2020), nativism comes in waves; the third, contemporary wave is clearly linked to the rise of anti-immigration sentiments.

Far-right social movements, much like far-right political parties, base their ideology and propaganda on ethnic nationalism and are explicitly opposed to a more modern, civic, legally and territorially defined, and thus more inclusive, nationalism (on the civic–ethnic distinction, see Kohn 1944; on the persistent debates it gives rise to, Jaskulowski 2010 and Özkirimli 2010). Although authors use different concepts (from nativism and radical nationalism to "ethno-cultural exclusionary nationalism," Caiani and Kröll 2017), there is a quasi-consensus within the literature on the ethnicity-driven nature of far-right nationalism. As always, the contours of this ethnonationalism do vary from one group to another. The main differences concern the figure of the others: some groups defend limited inclusiveness, accepting those whom they recognize as having approximately similar objective traits, a common cultural background, and shared interests with themselves. Other groups promote exclusionary ethnonationalist ideas and reject any form of inclusion.

The typology drawn by Bjørgo and Ravndal (2020, 3), based on Berntzen (2018), captures these differences well. The authors distinguish between "cultural nationalism," "ethnic nationalism," and "racial nationalism." Cultural nationalists generally focus on cultural differences and mostly (but not exclusively) point to Islam and the so-called Islamization of Western societies as the main threat facing Western societies. Generally speaking, far-right movements adapt who they are targeting to current events and to the evolving political and social context. During the COVID-19 pandemic, anti-Asian racism was on a dramatic rise and some anti-Muslim groups temporarily "converted" to anti-Asian discourses and attitudes. Cultural nationalists claim that the social, political, cultural, demographic, and economic threats posed by outsiders can be defused by their assimilation or, if they are unwilling to submit, their expulsion.

Ethnic nationalists can be found among both the radical and the extremist movements, depending on the means they consider legitimate to bring on the separation of ethnic groups. They are often referred to as "Identitarians" and promote the near-mainstream idea that "whites" are an ethnic group that should be preserved, sometimes promoting the unpalatable solution of "returning" peoples of other ethnic groups to their country of origin. Finally, racial nationalist movements state that the "white race" is simply superior, that violence is legitimate and necessary to preserve the purity of the race by deporting or exterminating peoples from other races. They obviously reject democratic order and call for the creation of totalitarian states (Berntzen 2018, 4–5).

In many ways, this last facet is the most important of the three: the relationship to otherness plays the key role in delimiting far-right nationalism. Though pride, nationalism, and patriotism are often played up and used to sanitize the discourse and make it more broadly acceptable, as Lubbers (2019) shows, the "threat framework" is far more mobilizing than any feeling of pride or belonging to the so-called nation. Nevertheless, we suggest that we should also take into account the definition of cultural features (what does it mean to be "white") and the role of history. The "glocal" nature of most far-right social movements also calls for a better analysis of the interconnection between local histories and transnational theories and mythologies circulating on digital platforms today.

Conclusion

The frontiers between these three ideal-typical categories are blurred and groups may move from one category to another, change strategies and tactics, and adopt more or less extremist views. This in addition to the internal dynamics within a group that may give rise to a more radical or extremist faction within. That is why it is worth underlining again that each dimension must be taken as a deliberate simplification of multiple ideological strands, based on a limited number of core characteristics. Exposing any of these strands in detail would grossly exceed the confines of this book.

Our 3D matrix solves or circumvents the main difficulties presented by traditional definitions of the far right. First, the dimensions are wide enough to apply transnationally and across historical periods and make it possible to compare a large number of manifestations of the far right. Second, the matrix helps draw boundaries between objects which are right of centre but not quite "far" right and draws us away from conflating core far-right movements with their context or with entities and concepts in conceptual proximity but with an empirically different central set of characteristics. Third, it is based solely on ideological facets rather than group structure (including lone actors) or repertoire of action; this is important since both structure and action are mostly opportunistic in nature and are in no way persistent enough to be a defining feature of a far-right entity.

Chapter 2 draws the outlines of the Canadian far-right ecosystem and demonstrates how to apply this definitional matrix.

2 THE CANADIAN FAR-RIGHT NEBULA

Introduction

The history of the Canadian far-right social movements family has seen several periods of intense activity, particularly just before World War II and in the 1970s and 1980s (Perry and Scrivens 2019). Between these two periods, as in Europe, far-right movements were ostracized; those that survived did so by going underground, more or less. As Perry and Scrivens show, the far-right social movement family has deep roots in Canada going back to at least the 1910s. Embedded in the local–global dynamics, some were strongly influenced by developments in the USA or in Europe. Indeed, the appearance of chapters of the Ku Klux Klan (KKK) in Vancouver, Montreal, Ottawa, Toronto, Oakville, and other Ontario cities illustrates the expansion of the KKK north of the 49th parallel. US KKK members, often salesmen, were instrumental in propagating the Klan's discourse, recruiting new members, and creating new chapters in Canada (Bartley 2020). As Pitsula (2013) and Bartley (2020) convincingly demonstrate, the KKK discourse found a strong resonance within some segments of Canadian society, which expressed fear, incomprehension, and frustration at the massive influx of non-white immigrants. The classic combination of feelings of superiority and vulnerability fuelled an ambient xenophobia against non-white peoples, especially toward Chinese and Indian labourers, as well First Nations individuals and groups. This context facilitated the implantation of foreign white supremacist groups in Canada as well as the creation of local movements.

After a decade of glory and massive federation in the 1980s, for the last two decades the Canadian far right has been marked by a high degree of fragmentation and never-ending competition between ephemeral groups. Membership has also tended to fluctuate wildly over time, with individuals routinely associating with multiple groups at once. These factors generate enough underlying uncertainty and fuzziness for the movement to resemble a nebula more than having a clear, discernable structure.

One explanation for the persistent fragmentation and drift lies in the combination of ideological diversity and uncompromising rigidity that characterizes the movement. The set of ideological ingredients does not vary much and includes the usual neo-Nazi, supremacist, racialist, religious, anti-immigration tropes held together by all sorts of conspiracy theories (including some traditionally left-wing boogeymen such as "corporations," "neo-liberalism," or "globalization"). Though they drink from the same few fountains, group-specific and individual ideological discourses are unique arrangements with little room for the tolerance of competing discourses.

This chapter uses the previously introduced 3D matrix to offer a novel way to sort out the similarities and conflicts between the various groups in the nebula and to account for the constant tension between the desire to identify with, connect to, and eventually mobilize a wider movement and the attractiveness of local, specific forms of extreme politics.

A look back at our approach

In most countries, the far-right political constellation is composed of formal political parties that have been scrutinized by researchers and a plurality of non-institutionalized, informal actors – individuals and movements – that typically receive far less attention. In this chapter we focus exclusively on the latter. To account for the broadest possible array of far-right groups, no matter how insignificant (some show a group façade but in reality have only one member), we created a database from information obtained online, via interviews, from court cases, and in media reports. Our objective was not to produce a quantitative estimate of the number of groups or individuals that might be categorized as far-right – a seemingly impossible task at this point given the dynamics and fluidity of the movement. For the same reason we will not be offering estimates on the proportions of the various categories explored below. Rather we aim at illustrating the paradoxical combination of the variety that exists within the Canadian far right and its relatively few, narrow, root concepts and worldviews.

When we set out to begin our quest, we first visited skinhead groups and other far-right cliques and gangs. Composed of a small number of militants, they usually have minimal recognized hierarchy; their members have highly variable levels of commitment to or knowledge of skinhead subculture; and the actual content of that culture varies from one group to another. The degree of politicization is also considerably different from one group to another and sometimes from one member to another.

We then explored multiple, fast-growing, Internet-based organizations involved in online propaganda, recruitment, strategy, and fundraising activities. They run blogs, webzines, video channels, and social media pages in an attempt to directly or indirectly influence public debates locally and nationally. Some of these "groups" are composed of a fairly limited number of people who have computing, writing, and artistic skills and are very loosely, if at all, organized, with no hierarchy or membership criteria. Some of their members actually never meet. They rely on their supporters to contribute to the production and, especially, the dissemination of content.

We also looked at what we call operational groups, with a formal hierarchy as well as a more strictly defined membership. These see themselves as oppositional powers, and some of them function on the political scene much like other interest groups promoting specific agendas. Usually, these groups are also "digital activists" and use the Internet to spread their message, recruit members, and attract attention. Some are local, while others are chapters of transnational groups. Some seek visibility, while others elevate secrecy and marginality to core features.

Finally, we took into account "movement parties" that strive to attain mainstream status. They are "actors that are in transition from extra-institutional movements to partisan electoral competition" (Caiani and Císař 2019b, 12). In Canada none have achieved this status so far, though some have attempted to infiltrate official political parties as a shortcut to their goal.

Besides the entities that fall under the "group" category, we must not forget the role played by individuals within the far-right nebula. We are not referring here to the groups' members and activists but rather to atomized individuals who take on roles of agitators, pundits, and influencers and who actively troll, publish, comment, and garner a special kind of fame among far-right audiences. These microcelebrities are active contributors to the diffusion of far-right ideas. They are mostly active online, as we'll see in chapter 4, but can also be seen leading protests and pursuing politicians, journalists, and other public figures.

Six categories of far-right entities

Various writers have categorized the dazzling kaleidoscope of the far right in attempts to understand the links and gaps that characterize it. This is also a useful way to circumvent the highly dynamic field, where actors and groups constantly appear and disappear but can be recognized by their dominant traits. One common flaw of most of these attempts, however, is that the identified categories differ in their nature, which makes them difficult to compare and impossible to sort out because they are not mutually exclusive. For instance, sorting entities between "lone actors," "gurus," and "neo-Nazis" forces a comparison at incompatible levels of organization type, group dynamics, and ideology while allowing multiple entities to fit in multiple categories.

Our categories are based on the 3D matrix we presented in the previous chapter, with three facets: relationship to violence; relationship to political, social, and legal institutions; and the particular construction of otherness. We suggest that groups can be differentiated or associated according to a dichotomous rating on each facet (though in reality these dichotomies are really the ends of their respective spectrums, with infinite nuances between). Since our definition of the far right requires that at least one of the facets be present, this leaves us with six categories: entities that score positively on all three facets (1);

entities that score positively on a combination of any two facets (2, 3, 4); and entities that score on only one facet (other than violence) (5, 6).

These various categories are entirely focused on the ideology or worldview of the various entities (groups or individuals) we encountered. In each can be found groups, lone actors, gurus, and followers as well as a variety of repertoires of action. Understanding their commonalities can shed light on differential organizational dynamics, account for individual and group motivations, and explain why groups and individuals split, merge, cooperate, or quarrel.

1. The ultra-right

Our first category, which we label "ultra-right," scores positively on all aspects; they do not hesitate to use or encourage violence and explicit threats against persons or property. Members routinely believe they are engaged in a historical war for survival against either massive, quickly moving social and political tides or the slow but inexorable change brought about by demographics, careless policies, or the erosion of state sovereignty caused by international organizations. In all cases, violent responses are warranted, if not required, by the magnitude of the threat.

Various ideological discourses can be found in groups of this category, but most are characterized by the (mis-)use of history, an exclusivist view of the nation they defend, and the declassification/stigmatization of those they identify as their "enemies." Entire populations are dehumanized and presented as nuisances or outright threats. Both groups and their individual members refuse to take part in political and public debates, and their first priority is ingroup socialization and social control. In some cases, the intensive and sometimes aggressive use of the Internet aims at disseminating the message or marketing the group. Potentially sympathetic visitors to identified areas of the web (e.g., music discussion groups, especially in "death metal" and other such genres) are often approached for recruitment. Recruitment also takes place in person, via existing social networks (e.g., friends, family), or by calculated strategies to approach strangers in locations most likely to attract like-minded people.

Table 2.1 The ultra right

non-violent	violent
pro-institution	anti-institution
accommodates otherness	denounces otherness

The ultra-right encompasses many Canadian chapters of groups originating in the USA and elsewhere in the world. These include openly Nazi groups, racist skinhead groups, and the like. They are animated by a violent subculture permeated by Nazi rhetoric and symbolism. Many use symbols that are less recognizable than the traditional swastika, and Nordic runes abound, especially the othala rune, originally used by Waffen SS divisions, or the life rune; other archaic symbols like the Indo-European sun wheel are also common. Other codes include "88" (double H for Heil Hitler), the Celtic cross, etc. Most evoke either the near past of the Third Reich or the distant past of Aryan origins, both meant as illustrations of white racial purity.

These groups glorify violent means of action, sometimes because they are "needed" and sometimes also because they symbolize dedication to the cause, a masculine rite of passage, or a "warrior" social role for men. For the most part the violence remains in the realm of discourse (including in musical styles and lyrics), imagination, and illustration (with heavy reliance on ultra-violent memes, for instance), though occasionally it manifests itself through actual attacks on property and persons. Some groups also engage in violent enactments, in a form of play-acting through military-style training complete with weapons, fatigues, and survival or other field equipment.

Ultra-right groups are usually very limited in numbers and prefer to recruit individuals they already know. A large proportion of their activities occur in secret, with occasional splashes in the media when public actions are undertaken, oftentimes in legally questionable manners (distribution of hate material, banners, graffiti, etc.). The actual entities come and go but at the time of writing the Order of the Nine Angles, Aryan Strikeforce, and Atomwaffen Division were still active. Below we look in more depth at Atalante, the Base, and the Canadian Proud Boys.

Atalante

The name Atalante first appeared in 2016, mostly in Quebec City. The name is new but the group is not: its members were mostly taken from followers of the hate rock band Légitime Violence, which helps with finances through the sale of recorded music and concert tickets. Others came from Nazi skinhead gangs, especially the older Quebec Stomper Crew/Quebec Stompers.

Atalante is part of a closely knit network of Quebec francophone identitarian outfits, some dating to the 1980s, others far more recent. Some of its members have been published in the identitarian magazine *Le Harfang*, owned and operated by the Fédération des Québécois de Souche. It also has weaker ties to the considerably more moderate, and much larger, Storm Alliance, in part because of the latter's broader (white/Western rather than strictly francophone) identity politics. Using these contacts, in some of its events Atalante managed to mobilize about fifty sympathizers, which is rather large for this type of group. The main core of the group has fewer than a half dozen members, many of whom have criminal records for a variety of violent attacks, namely against leftist militants and immigrants, as well as drug trafficking and other offences.

Atalante explicitly draws from classic fascism but mostly takes aim at immigrants, fully adopting the "great replacement" conspiracy narrative. More broadly, it views the ideal society as populated by a homogeneous group, ruled by Catholic traditions in a strict hierarchical, non-democratic structure. The group has long sought to connect with international like-minded entities, among which are CasaPound in Italy, multiple entities in the USA, and the French neo-Nazi MMA club Pride France.

Though it glorifies war and combat, real and symbolic (its logo, a helmet struck by a lightning bolt, closely resembles the double S of the old Nazi Schutzstaffel), by and large Atalante is mostly violent in its symbols, propaganda, and lyrics but rarely in actual incidents. Acts of violence committed by its members are entirely spontaneous, disorganized, and usually prosecuted. As a group it has developed a modus operandi based on limited, low-investment actions designed to attract media rather than police attention. These have included the deployment of giant banners calling for the expulsion of immigrants, intimidating the media (a group of six members took over the offices of *Vice* in 2018 in order to noisily present a "prize" to one of its journalists for "trying to start a war"), and parading in public parks.

The Base

Explicitly named after al Qaeda, the Base essentially fell apart after having been infiltrated by *Winnipeg Free Press* journalist Ryan Thorpe in 2019. The group made the most basic mistake that gangs involved in clandestine activity can make: it recruited outside its immediate social network. Intrigued by leaflets, Thorpe simply got in touch with the group via its phone number, which quickly led him to the core of the organization – and eventually to an FBI investigation.

Contrary to Atalante, the Base's only public actions were the distribution of recruitment material. Its other activities, intended to be entirely hidden, involved mostly military-style and survival training. The group had acquired its own private land for this purpose, bought through an LLC named Base Global. Its ideology revolved around preparing for an inevitable "racial holy war," which white majority society could use as an opportunity to finally rid itself of its non-white elements. Part of the planning involved precipitating this war through various types of attacks (including false flag attacks) designed to increase racial tensions to a point where they would flare up and engulf Western countries into full-fledged civil wars. This "accelerationist" strategy is portrayed in various writings that are key to a large portion of the American far right, such as the novels *Hunter* and *The Turner Diaries* by William Pierce (under the pseudonym of Andrew Macdonald). It is shared by multiple groups and movements still in existence, such as the US Boogaloo Boys or the Diagolon movement, as well as moribund outfits such as Atomwaffen Division. It is also a reference book for many of the respondents we interviewed during field research.

Canadian Proud Boys

One action that helped put the Proud Boys, and specifically its Maritime chapter, in the public eye is their defence of now endangered colonial monuments. One of those particularly threatened is that of Edward Cornwallis in Halifax, who founded the town in 1749 but is also known for his bounty on "Indian scalps." In July 2017, a group of Proud Boys in black shirts appeared during a Mi'kmaw ceremony at the base of the statue and proceeded to bawl at the participants. Five of them were members of the Canadian military (four in the navy and one in the army), which helped generate media attention. A subsequent investigation was launched by the Canadian Armed Forces, eventually concluding that the disruption of the ceremony was not sanctionable conduct.

The last straw came in January 2021 when a large group of explicitly identified USA Proud Boys took part in the attempted insurrection in Washington (Campbell 2022). Weeks later, Canada added the group to its official "currently listed entities" list, established under the 2001 Anti-Terrorist Act (ATA), where it joined the likes of al Qaeda and the Islamic State. It also joined seven other freshly added far-right "entities": Combat 18, Aryan Strikeforce, Atomwaffen Division, Canadian Three Percenters, Blood and Honour, the Base, and the Nazi propagandist James Mason (the only individual on the list). The extent of what this means in terms of potential or actual state intervention is not clear and almost entirely untested in any court. Simple membership is probably allowed and individual Boys are unlikely to be arrested, though in May 2022 a man was arrested in Windsor by the RCMP for trying to join Atomwaffen Division and for multiple hate crimes (it is not yet clear whether the online application was a police trap). Group activities, financing, training, etc. are more explicitly forbidden and some such cases have in fact led to a few charges in the past, mostly in relation with Islamist entities. Distributing propaganda, especially on the Internet, might lead to the seizure of material and devices. Of course, one remedy is to change the group's name, as is already common practice. Atomwaffen Division has recently changed its name to National Socialist Order (NSO) and its discussion group to FashLash.

At the outset, the Proud Boys were "Western Chauvinist(s) [who] Refuse To Apologise For Creating The Modern World" (proudboysusa.com). Wholly structured by great replacement theory, their ideology fits very neatly into the alt-lite style of outwardly adopting widely held views about culture and politics. One example is the current anxiety, among the US right, over what is referred to as "critical race theory." It has become commonplace for conservative US politicians to call for bans on any teaching of recent history that might be associated with critical race theory. What this means is that any reading of history that shows the white majority as having had a morally wrong stance on race and slavery in particular is suspect. Unsurprisingly, USA Proud Boys were seen silencing protesters at Trump MAGA rallies and were given official licence by the president in his notorious 2020 pre-election "Proud Boys, stand back, stand by" injunction.

The Proud Boys simply adopt replacement theory wholesale and turn it into the personal politics of everyday behaviour, based on the conviction that everything they associate with civilization (science, technology, arts, philosophy) might disappear if no action is taken, both as a group and in their private life. This includes a glorification of masculinity, also under threat by feminism, diversity politics, and social movements such as #MeToo. Individual members are forbidden to watch porn or masturbate (more than once a month) or engage in other such activities because they "demasculate" men and because non-reproductive sexual practices threaten demographic superiority by lowering the birthrate of Westerners. Reproductive sex, on the contrary, also has the advantage of "encouraging" women to stay at home and care for a family, which is the natural order of things.

2. The radical right

Entities on the radical right tend to eschew violence, in part to avoid clashes with the legal system, and in part because they believe that the radical transformation of society and its institutions can be brought about by massive protest or increasing pressure from organizations and movements such as themselves. Some believe that government institutions will collapse from within, and direct action is not necessary. Others think that civil disobedience (for instance, not paying income tax) will mortally wound the state and result in wide-ranging reform. If the ultra-right questions the very principle of democracy, the radical right accepts it but judges it as severely corrupted by its most important institutions (governments, journalists, intellectual and media elite).

Over the years, multiple groups have espoused radical right ideas as a theme, a justification for other demands, or a rallying cry. In 2017–18

Table 2.2 The radical right

non-violent	violent
pro-institution	anti-institution
accommodates otherness	denounces otherness

Yellow Vests Canada grew out of the same widespread frustrations about gas prices as the French Gilets Jaunes who were their inspiration. However, the movement quickly veered towards typical anti-immigration themes including the carbon tax and the UN immigration pact (Yellow Vests Facebook page). The United We Roll convoy of 2019, ostensibly carrying a pro-pipeline and anti-carbon tax message to Ottawa, soon veered into the usual anti-immigration paranoia of many Western Canadian far-right groups. Both the convoy and the Yellow Vests episodes are typical examples of one of the new tactics of the radical right: the formation or takeover of popular, wide-appeal, and ad hoc protests, issues, or movements to exploit popular fear and resentment. In early 2022 the Freedom Convoy that paralyzed Ottawa was organized by the same people.

The Alberta Clann

The Clann is illustrative of one key aspect of contemporary radical right movements: their extreme instability. The reasons are multiple, among which is the desire to exploit current events in order to spread the message, which causes dissension between members who seek visibility and those who would rather remain hidden. The desire to hitch a fringe group to a wider, more popular, and usually more moderate movement or group also causes similar conflicts between those ready to (albeit temporarily) compromise in order to fit into the larger group and those who prefer to stay true to their core ideology. International connections can also generate ingroup conflict when some members disagree with changes in strategy imposed from abroad (or, conversely, if a change they would like to implement is rejected).

At the time of writing, the Clann is only months old but not because its members are new to the far right. Most of them were already members of the Soldiers of Odin, whose Canadian and various provincial chapters were founded around March 2016, a year after the original Finnish group was founded. Trouble brewed soon after: in November some Canadian members were already becoming weary of the relentless white supremist tack of the Finnish headquarters (Archambault and Veilleux-Lepage 2019). The Quebec chapter's founding member was kicked out and went on to form Storm Alliance, while the rest of the group happily took the supremacist step with a new leader. The Edmonton chapter essentially disintegrated into the Canadian Infidels, who were strictly Islamophobic, the Wolves of Odin, who sided with broader supremacist racism (and renewed ties with the original Finnish Soldiers), and the Guardians of Alberta, who quickly disappeared. The ideological issue is whether all immigrants are dangerous or if only Muslims form a threat – while, of course, each group claims not to be racist, since they don't *hate* Muslims or immigrants, they simply want them kept out of Canada. Beyond these nuances in racism, however, one issue was perhaps more decisive in creating the split: money. Canadian chapters started criticizing the racism of their Finnish counterparts when the latter demanded that membership fees be sent to Finland.

The Clann emerged from this patchwork, with most of its Clannsmen having been, or being, members of the other groups. The effort seems to be both to regroup everyone under the same banner and to erase the apparent splintering caused by the constant deluge of names. As of the spring of 2022 the Clann and the Infidels had the same "president."

None of these groups overtly recommends the use of violence to further their goals, though in January 2019 Infidels "visited" a mosque in Edmonton. They do believe that the federal government is complicit in a "Trojan horse" strategy to allow immigrants (or Muslims) to overrun Canada and that most (especially Liberal) politicians are traitors. For many, their solution is to separate from Canada, which is why they have close links with the Alberta Independence Party.

Front Canadien-Français

The Front peddles its own brand of "great replacement" theory, where French Canadians are threatened by multiple forces who want their language and, more importantly perhaps, their traditional Catholic religion to disappear. Though this has obvious similarities with Atalante's ideology, the Front's approach is distinctly more religious (and distinctively less hot-blooded) in nature. On leaflets posted in the spring of 2020 in Montreal it called for a symbolic holy war against the decline of the nation, weakened by its multiple departures from tradition, first among which is the adoption of Vatican II reforms. In that, the group shares views held by Catholic traditionalists such as the Society (Priestly Fraternity) of Saint Pius X or Fraternité Sacerdotale Saint-Pie X, a far older retrograde Catholic sect. Individuals move seamlessly from one organization to the other and beyond to other similar groups such as the Cercle jeune nation, the Mouvement tradition Québec, or the Fédération des Québécois de souche.

The group opposes LGBTQ+ rights, abortion, "Marxist" public education, etc., and explicitly rejects violence but vows to take over and entirely reform institutions according to traditional Catholic faith. Its entire lifespan can be counted in months, from its official creation in 2020 to sometime in 2021 (its Facebook page was last active in February 2021 and its website disappeared in the fall of the same year). One of its main figures appeared on multiple far-right and conspiracist outlets and even managed to co-sign a letter to mainstream newspaper *Le Devoir* in 2020, in which contemporary social science research and teaching in Quebec universities was accused of "anglo-saxon dogmatism," pluralism, and, of course, political correctness.

Interestingly, the Front's historical model is the so-called Duplessis era, named after Quebec premier Maurice Duplessis, who brought Quebec close to the fascist dictatorships of the 1930s with a heavily racist and sectarian brand of nationalism. In 1943 Duplessis denounced a conspiracy between his rival Liberal party and "international Jews" to increase immigration in Quebec (Rajotte 2007), a classic narrative that is still found almost unchanged in many corners of today's far right.

3. Xenophobic vigilantes

Racist supremacists do not give much thought to institutions or believe they are fundamentally good, if considered too lax or plagued with overly permissive laws, particularly with regard to immigration by non-white persons or Indigenous, LGBTQ+, and women's rights.

Table 2.3 Xenophobic vigilantes

non-violent	violent
pro-institution	anti-institution
accommodates otherness	denounces otherness

They are likely to think that institutions should be reinforced, militarized, and given free rein to "protect" the nation against invaders, either at the border or other entry points or by arresting and deporting those they believe should not be allowed to stay. Many dream of fashioning themselves into pro-state militias, police deputies, or assistant border guards – while criticizing the latter for their lack of responsiveness and inability to handle situations they consider of national importance.

Many are entirely disorganized, ad hoc mobs who gather to dismantle barricades or attack protesters when they believe police have not done enough to restore order.

Soldiers of Odin

The Soldiers of Odin (SOO) have fashioned themselves as social vigilantes, patrolling the streets to intimidate Muslims and other out of place, visible minorities while sometimes helping (mostly by distributing food items) those whom they see as deserving (i.e., members of the white majority) who are poor and homeless. We have briefly touched upon their inception as the brainchild of a Finnish neo-Nazi ideologue in 2015 at the height of the Islamic State wave of dread. They soon branched out to other issues, perhaps as the IS threat was waning. For instance, the Vancouver Island SOO attempted to dismantle a homeless tent city in Nanaimo in 2018; Storm Alliance, a Quebec City offshoot of the SOO, demonstrated against Haitian immigrants crossing at Roxham Road in 2018; again, in BC, in 2017 SOO disrupted an anti-racism rally by following some of its members, getting into fights, and finally throwing a smoke bomb to break up the demonstration. In most cases police gave free rein to the vigilantes, who tend to play at the margins of laws and bylaws, leading well-ordered protests clearly intended to intimidate. During the COVID-19 pandemic the

SOO fell mostly dormant; unlike other right-right formations it does not seem to have attempted to attach itself to anti-mandate protests, which may have seemed like a departure from their rather strict vigilante history.

In Canada, Soldiers of Odin have always publicly denied being racist, Nazis, or fascist in any way. As mentioned earlier, most chapters have distanced themselves from the Finnish neo-Nazis who founded the movement. Their original 2016 bylaws state that "'Soldiers Of Odin Canada' is a non-racist, conservative organization that seeks to keep Canadians safe in their daily activities and also uphold and protect our Constitutional Rights, by acting as a nationwide community watch organization." However, this must be read in conjunction with the next passage:

> Between the allowing of illegal aliens into this country and giving them the ability to vote and drive, accepting refugees from countries that hate us while Canadians are on the streets, releasing confirmed terrorists back to their organizations to cause more harm against Canada, and demonizing anything that has to do with European Culture to try and create racial tensions to turn citizens on one another; we as Soldiers Of Odin realize that it is time to take back our streets, provinces, and country. (SOO bylaws)

In short, the racist agenda is transformed into a matter of legality. Note that immigration laws are clearly not fully understood; however, the discourse relies on the explicit authority of the law, not its analysis. The legal details matter little and only serve to sanitize two important implications. One is that breaches to immigration law are indicators of vastly more threatening activity. The other is that both the official infractions and the more nefarious activities they enable are widespread enough to endanger Canadians and to warrant immediate, direct intervention. It is a nearly perfect definition of xenophobic racism.

The "Incel" movement

The "manosphere" is populated by a myriad of groups and individuals who espouse extremely varied causes that converge on the role of men and women, the structure of society, morality, and other topics, all viewed from patriarchal, male chauvinist, or squarely misogynistic worldviews. From the anti-masturbation "NoFap" to the "men's rights" and "fathers' rights" activists, most share a decidedly right of centre, if not clearly extreme set of beliefs rooted in the glorification of extreme patriarchy and hatred for "feminism" (i.e., non-submissive women). Most see women as a distinct group of humans that must be controlled and subjected to the authority of men, be sexually available, and be used for reproduction and childcare. One man was tried in 2022 for calling for a repeat of the 1989 École Polytechnique massacre in which fourteen women were murdered during their engineering classes – where the killer claimed they did not belong. His blog had 60,000 worldwide followers. At his trial he argued it was all satire, adopting the traditional alt-right defence. He was found guilty of inciting hatred against women in August 2022.

Few manosphere dwellers have been as present in the media as the "involuntary celibate" or "Incel" movement. Incels come in various forms of eccentricity, from those who are simply unhappy with their sex life, to those who believe that their lack of success in finding female sexual partners is entirely due to the structure of society, where unspoken conspiracies and illegitimate cultural constraints, all taking root in "feminism," reserve sexual gratification for a certain caste of privileged humans. We are of course especially interested in the latter. They are not opposed to legal and state institutions and do not target authority figures, but they do reject the laws that are meant to protect or empower women or are seen to diminish the power of men. On their various platforms, Incels discuss ways to reinstate maximal versions of patriarchal authority, to humiliate and disempower women and other men who support feminist ideals, to rape, maim, or kill women who do not make themselves sexually available and the men who are identified as sexually dominant (whom they refer to as "Chads"). Their rage appears to be unfocused at times, as in the 2019 Sudbury case in which a man used utility knives in an attempt to kill a female baby in a stroller.

Incels never act as a group; they are the purest form of lone wolves. This does not mean they are entirely alone: they use various Internet platforms as support groups, for reassurance, togetherness, and inspiration. Some use platforms to voice their problems in a sympathetic social context and be comforted by like-minded individuals, a form of interactive Internet recruitment and ideological engagement. Others adopt a more individualistic, passive form and simply scour the Internet for reading and viewing material that supports, broadens, and deepens their views. In both cases, the communications platforms are key since these men have worldviews so far outside the norm that they can only find peers by extending their reach globally.

4. Anti-state militias

"Anti-state militia" seems like a contradiction in terms, but such groups have a rather long history south of the border. The actual use of the term "militia" in the name of a group usually serves to connect it with history and to provide a varnish of legitimacy. Some lone actors also view and present themselves as part of an imaginary militia. The word "patriot" and its semantic variations are often part of the name these groups adopt or explicitly use to describe their program and members. Of course, it is a brand of patriotism that rejects most, or at least large portions, of the citizenry (the "left," the "elites," city dwellers, etc., depending on the group), all institutions and laws, and, in particular, any and all politicians and civil servants.

In general militias are medium-sized formations, somewhere between the thousands of members that social media groups sometimes boast and the restrictive cliques of racist skinheads, for instance. They like to meet in secret and engage in military-style training (sometimes with the help of a member who was or is in fact in the military). They tend to glorify organized, strategized violence and wear military, survival, or field gear, and idealize weapons (those that are edged, firearms, archery, etc.). Some groups adopt military ranks for their members and impose strict codes of conduct. Some, but not all, also follow a "survivalist" or "prepper" outlook and hoard supplies and equipment to prepare for the upcoming end of the world or major catastrophes.

Though many such groups are deeply racist (we categorized those as "ultra-right" above), in this category we want to account for the purer forms of anti-state oppositional movement, usually centred around the looming threat of economic, political, or agricultural disaster and, more importantly, around the notion of *freedom* (defined as freedom from "unjust" state laws).

Table 2.4 Anti-state militias

non-violent	violent
pro-institution	anti-institution
accommodates otherness	denounces otherness

Canadian Three Percenters (III%)

"Threepers" are mostly active in Alberta but have a small chapter in Quebec, often spotted providing "security" during events held by other, better-known groups. Their name is based on the myth that 3 per cent of US citizens were sufficient to win the War of Independence against their British rulers. Part of the Threepers' ideology is to fight extremist Islamists, which of course is code for "Muslims." We have nonetheless placed them in this category because their training is explicitly targeted at "defending" against the state rather than attacking individuals. Contrary to USA Three Percenters, in Canada attacks on Muslims have not taken place. Both the pandemic and their addition to the aforementioned "list of entities" seem to have slowed the rate of their activities, yet they are still a good illustration of a movement taking roots in the USA and later being imported to Canada, mostly in Alberta and, to a lesser extent, Quebec.

The group's main focus is military-style training and prepping. Members must be equipped with at least two airsoft guns (realistic-looking replica firearms) – a carbine or other long gun and a side arm – and usually appear in military fatigues, carrying typical expedition equipment. They emphasize military discipline and have often been spotted filling "security" duties at other groups' events, usually in full military field garb. But mostly their activities consist in training with weapons, tactics, and improvised bomb making.

5. Freedom conspiracists

Groups in the category we have named "freedom conspiracists" share very few links and almost never cooperate, in large part because they are so deeply involved in specific conspiracies that they no longer see any element of reality in the same way. They do share an utter rejection

Table 2.5 Freedom conspiracists

non-violent	violent
pro-institution	anti-institution
accommodates otherness	denounces otherness

of governments, albeit for vastly different reasons. Contrary to most other types of far-right movements, freedom conspiracists easily accept, if not welcome, non-whites in their ranks. Their discourse is entirely directed against legal authority and the various forms of state regulations that they denounce as tyranny, totalitarianism, etc.

Alexis Cossette-Trudel

Cossette-Trudel founded his online conspiracy business on the translation and light adaptation of USA QAnon material (chronic, vague statements referred to as "Q-drops" that only make sense with a hefty dose of interpretation), starting sometime in 2017. He has garnered thousands of paying subscribers in Quebec and in francophone countries (when he was shut down in 2021 he had more than 124,000 followers on his monetized YouTube channel). Eventually booted off every mainstream platform, he migrated to Patreon, which also eventually banned him. Undeterred, he now uses his own website, where he solicits funds payable by credit card, Interac transfer, or through a Bitcoin wallet (he is also present on Gab, Odysee, Gettr, VK, and Rumble, all famous for their far-right friendliness – Gettr was founded by former Trump acolyte Jason Miller).

Q-drops decreased and eventually ceased in 2021, after which the COVID-19 pandemic took a more and more central function in the Cossette-Trudel discourse. Anti-vaccine and COVID negationism are well spread and exist across the ideological spectrum. The special Cossette-Trudel brand, however, serves as a mere key – much as the Q-drops did – to the exploration of imaginary government corruption master narratives and lengthy descriptions of secret manoeuvring by so-called "deep state" operators and the world elite, including the often-mentioned George Soros and Bill Gates, as well as totalitarian countries like China. It also served to make the essentially USA-centric QAnon conspiracies relevant to his non-USA followers.

Unlike the cryptic Q-drops that usually referred to entirely hidden manoeuvring by nefarious forces and their opponents, the government response to the pandemic is a palpable, concrete manifestation of abstract, complex conspiracies piloted from distant lands. Any change in policies (e.g., tightening *or* relaxing vaccine or mask requirements) is systematically taken as proof of one or another aspect of the historic battle between a global elite authority and heroic resisters (led by ex-president Trump).

As the pandemic (or at least the response to it) wanes, Cossette-Trudel's revenue seems to be drying up quickly, and he is now quite literally begging for donations on his channels. No doubt events will soon provide a new focus for dedicated conspiracy theorists.

Cossette-Trudel reads the history of the world since World War II into a vast conspiracy among the elite that manifests itself locally through multiple threats to Canadians and French Canadians especially. The main danger, and the one most often mentioned, is the now infamous Great Reset. Initially promulgated by the World Economic Forum (WEF) as a way to reform capitalist structures towards increased sustainability, it was immediately recycled by multiple conspiracy theorists as a plan to dissolve national governments and impose a communist totalitarian planetary regime. Most mainstream critics have panned the Great Reset as an effort to do as little as possible while patching up its dwindling relevance by sounding environmentally conscious. Its originating organization, the WEF and its annual summit at Davos, is a perfect target for conspiracy theorists: it is elitist, funded by powerful corporations, and apparently secretive (in fact all its events are public though the complexity of the issues tackled may make it appear secretive). In Cossette-Trudel's version, the Trudeau government is advancing the Great Reset by increasing immigration and by being subservient to international laws and conventions. As such, it has become an enemy of the people, secretly bent on imposing a Chinese-style "social credit" surveillance and control scheme on Canadians.

Sovereign Citizens

Sovereign Citizens believe that the state has no legitimate power over them (or anyone else) and refuse to pay taxes, fines, licences, and the like. They rely on various historico-legal theories that claim that various technicalities in laws, the Constitution, or other statutory frameworks allow individuals to somehow (depending on the specific flavour of sovereignty) claim autonomy and independence from all levels of government. Some have declared their personal plots of land "free" and independent from Canada, as well as the province and municipality they happen to be situated in. These new sovereign entities are of course exempt from any law or regulation, including vaccine passports and mask mandates.

Many of those who identify with the movement go to meetings where "experts," usually for a fee, explain the details of the procedures required to declare sovereignty and the legal logic they are based on. In that sense, members of the Sovereign Citizens movement could be considered the victims of gurus who have essentially swindled them, only to then find themselves in extremely serious legal trouble, owing large amounts of unpaid income tax for instance and facing the courts with legal tricks that have no chance of working in their favour.

Variations of the Sovereign Citizen model include Freemen on (or of) the Land and Detaxers, who are more popular in Western Canada, while the USA-inspired Canadian Sovereign Citizens are mostly from Quebec. But the differences between the two groups are negligible. Each invent legal principles and rules that they claim to have found in doctrine, common law, natural law, the social contract, the Magna Carta, etc., and then use them as modern incantations: uttering the phrase "I do not consent," for instance, is supposed to nullify any attempt to arrest them or enforce any law or regulation wherever they are present or regarding their actions or omissions (Netolitzky 2016). The papers they file in court are replete with esoteric gibberish that is expected to coerce the court into finding in their favour. People claiming to be Sovereign Citizens or Freemen have used such tactics to attempt to cancel traffic tickets, to avoid paying divorce settlements or alimony, to refuse to pay rent, to contest citations for health code violations, and of course to protest against COVID-19 restrictions. Clearly, individuals who identify with the movement seem, at least at first, primarily concerned with their individual financial situation rather than with any particular ideology. Indeed, a few appear to be in rather dire circumstances and may be clutching at their last desperate chance to survive financially. However, almost all versions of the Sovereign Citizen movement attribute these difficulties to the state, its economic institutions, and the banking system.

They are also known to make intensive use of the courts and bureaucratic processes, usually filing bogus claims littered with invalid or nonsensical legal arguments (for instance, that their real name is spelled in capital letters and that any document or file that uses lower case letters refers to another non-person) and deliberately filing official forms and applications incorrectly. Another common practice is to repeatedly sue or place liens on the property of judges and other court officials, civil servants, and politicians, to a point where many have been officially declared "vexatious litigants" and subsequently must obtain special permission to initiate any further legal action.

So even if in most cases the original concern of the majority of Sovereign Citizens is money, things may quickly degenerate when the legal system doesn't comply with their defence and continues to press for back taxes, requiring licences and other such universal obligations. Central to this concept is that the individual is supreme and cannot be made to contribute or submit to even the most basic public or collective project. A few adopt increasingly extreme views of government authority, adopt guerilla legal tactics, and go as far as armed confrontation with police. In February 2021 a self-declared Sovereign Citizen was arrested near Quebec City with a cache of explosives and weapons in his home's basement. He was preparing a "great blow" against the COVID-19 response.

6. Nostalgic racists

Our last category contains various groups and individuals who denounce violence but wish legal means were taken to stem what they see as a tsunami of non-European immigration in European countries. This includes North America, which they understand as having been built from its natural, savage state into modern nations by white European colonists. Nostalgic racists long for a national identity and culture that is vaguely historic but mostly idealized from a particular reading of the past. They generally respect institutions and eschew violence but tend to portray themselves as permanent victims, whose "culture" or "ethnic group" or "race" is being debased or corrupted by

Table 2.6 Nostalgic racists

non-violent	violent
pro-institution	anti-institution
accommodates otherness	denounces otherness

constant interaction and mixing with persons and things that are considered alien (including *foods* in some cases).

PEGIDA Canada

Though it occasionally organizes in-person meetings and protests, PEGIDA is essentially a Facebook group. As such, it benefits from the instantly overinflated numbers of sympathizers that social media produces (a simple "like" is surprisingly easy to obtain but is a far cry from recruiting a new member), as well as from the low cost of a Facebook soapbox. The downside, as La Meute quickly learned, is that galvanizing the troops and mobilizing towards actual action is extremely difficult and invariably produces far more modest attendance numbers (one of its last events had fewer members than journalists present). Even the most dedicated will tire of the meetings and eventually limit their involvement to browsing the group's page and perhaps purchasing some of its merchandise.

The PEGIDA acronym was born in Germany in 2014 and roughly stands for "patriotic Europeans against the Islamization of the West." Neither its founder or members seemed to be concerned with the similarities between the concepts in that name and Anders Breivik's manifesto and the massacre he committed in 2011. The Canadian groups (mostly in Quebec and Ontario) seem to have few, if any, actual connections to Germany but have adopted its main claim in full: Muslim immigration is a danger to Western civilization in Canada – a conviction, as we have seen, that is shared widely across the spectrum of the far right (as well as the more moderate right, in fact). What is particular about PEGIDA Canada is, for one, the number of rallies it holds despite the generally low attendance (oftentimes members are grossly outnumbered by counterprotesters). The other particularity is its general respect for institutions, the rule of law, and the democratic process as a means of changing regulations.

PEGIDA's Canadian chapters have a relatively idiosyncratic agenda where they single out every instance of what they perceive to be multiculturalism and blame it for the weakening of civilization. The Canadian Broadcasting Corporation is a typical target, for instance. But, as has been the case with other entities discussed here, the pandemic has caused a temporary shift in the discourse, from the dangers of immigration and multiculturalism to the ways in which the state threatens civil rights.

Students for Western Civilisation

In YouTube videos advocating the study of far-right thinkers in universities, participants recommend a return to far-right readings of Nietzsche (popular with Nazi ideologues of the 1930s, encouraged by no other than Nietzsche's sister Elisabeth, who had republished his work with her own supremacist editing), a white-nationalist reading of Heidegger, and a rehabilitation of far-right ideologues in university curricula. The message is the usual need to protect Western civilization and the "interests and identity of European-Canadians," but with a slightly more intellectual-sounding mix of famous references and grad student grievances and a blog illustrated by art in the "heroic realism" style complete with portraits of the group's founder.

Having emerged at the University of Toronto, Students for Western Civilisation is attempting to garner a foothold in other anglophone universities by using legal and regulatory processes to attack various institutions and is striving to show relevance to everyday current events, especially those that might illustrate the dangers faced by Western culture. In Quebec it has filed a complaint with the Conseil de presse du Québec alleging that CTV News misrepresented its activities at McGill University; it has attempted to sue CBC News for its use of noncapitalized "white," when "Black" is always capitalized; it has also taken to Twitter to demand that the city of Hamilton protect its statue of Sir John A. MacDonald and that the Toronto police do a better job of finding those who vandalized Egerton Ryerson's monument in June 2021 (the university that owned the monument and bore his name has since been renamed). But its main recruitment tool is to accuse universities of quashing freedom of speech and silencing alternative viewpoints, in particular "white nationalist" ones, in favour of an exclusive Marxist approach.

Despite the grandiose discourse and imagery, the "Students" are, in reality, mostly the work of one individual, gaining very little traction on Twitter and other platforms (most tweets generating less than a half dozen retweets). Yet it is indicative of the atomization of the far right and the constant multiplication of would-be leaders who use social media platforms for propaganda, of course, but also in large part for self-glorification. On that it may be useful to point out that the central member of the SWC was at one point in a relationship with right-wing mega-star influencer Lauren Southern, whose shadow may have been too long for him to thrive under.

Points of convergence and divergence

Each group, and in some cases each individual, on the far right adopts its own cocktail of concepts, truths, ethos, and of course methodologies for the dissemination of its message and realization of its proclaimed ideals. Yet, as is obvious in the above, a few main themes tend to cut across group boundaries and manifest themselves, in one guise or another, in most discourses. Of course, other themes act in the opposite way and introduce lasting, sometimes explosive dissension. As we will see in chapter 5, each has a highly variable effect on recruitment, group cohesion, and group longevity.

Commonalities in themes and tactics

As will become obvious, commonalities are often the abstract base on which a specific group discourse is built. Its architects, however, are likely to have their own ideas about the specific shape of the construction. That is why the presence of common threads is not sufficient to compensate for group differences and, even in extreme conceptual proximity, groups never merge or even federate.

Victimization, resentment, and dangerous populations

The idea that the traditionally dominant group is under attack, weakened by "parasites," disappearing, or simply insufficiently respected cuts across almost every group and individual studied or interviewed for this book. What changes from one to another are the contours of the specific group being referred to, the nature of the threat, and the identity of those who are responsible. Positive discrimination is of course presented as anti-white or "reverse" racism; the removal of colonial statues becomes the negation of the glorious history of the early colonists and developers of Canada; the "critical race theory" rage that started in the USA is arriving in Canada and serves as a new target for those who already oppose any reading of history that "blames" the white majority for past wrongdoing. Of course, claiming victim status is not a new strategy; it is one that can be found in many political groups from anywhere on the left–right spectrum. What characterizes far-right groups is the intensity of the purported harm, where the worst kind of evil threatens the best in human nature with the most dreadful consequences.

Those held responsible for the dire straits in which the white population finds itself have changed with current events. One current is the traditional conspiracy-based antisemitism that eventually rears its head almost everywhere. A second layer, however, is usually added and serves several discursive functions. One is to maintain relevance by showing concern with broad popular apprehensions triggered by contemporary events and trends. The other is to present a more palatable face to potential sympathizers who might not respond well to traditional presentations of the age-old "Jewish question." So, in the years 2012–16, when the Islamic State was mobilizing Muslim youths in Canada and elsewhere, Muslims again became the target (as they had been post-9/11); for groups wary of accusations of racism the phrase in official use was "Muslim extremists" or "Islamists" or "radical Islamists." Later, as Haitians were fleeing the USA into Canada through Roxham Road in Quebec, immigration was identified as the new national threat. ("Illegal" immigration for the more scrupulous – needless to say, such distinctions quickly disappear in everyday exchanges and when solutions are suggested.) At the time of writing, as we have seen, the overarching targets of these groups were the various government responses to the COVID-19 epidemic.

Among the targets routinely denounced by far-right groups are, of course, those that encourage, support, or insufficiently oppose the group's perceived threats: government officials, the media, international organizations, and powerful elites. Each group or individual is likely to have its own priority, but extreme animosity towards politicians and the media is well distributed. Many groups have called for their members to perform "citizen's arrests" of media and political figures. (Prime Minister Justin Trudeau is often at the top of the list.)

Conspiracy theories as ideological bases and justification for actions

Conspiracy theories of various kinds have multiple sets of key functions in the far-right discourse. One essential point to keep in mind is the deeply Manichean, dualist view of the world that dominates all extremist groups, and of course those we have identified as far-right are no different. The entirety of popular right-wing literature, the very structure of the online far-right infosphere as well as the individual discourses of our interviewees rests on the attribution of blame on deliberately nefarious, or at least hostile, persons and groups motivated by material or political gain or by a thirst for social, cultural, and religious domination (or any combination of the above). This point will be illustrated in chapters 3 and 4. By contrast, those who are potential targets of wrongdoing are unequivocally morally righteous, oftentimes "ordinary" citizens and their dedicated representatives, who only seek (or strive to retain) power or global domination in support of morally sound reasons or "for the people."

The first set are narrative functions and serve to close the factual gap between the Manichean attribution of wrongs to limited, unique entities, and the vast complexity of actual life. The only way to blame a limited group or, even more so, an individual actor for some of the real or imaginary ills that plague an entire society is to concoct or to adopt a narrative in which multiple strings are being pulled in unison or from a central point. In the literature this is often presented in reverse: conspiracy theorists find simple explanations to complex problems by identifying responsible entities that can then be blamed. Having a human-scale account for the vast complexity of modern societies can be comforting, even if it involves nefarious powers bent on world domination – at least the source of evil suddenly becomes crystal clear. However, in our research it appears that the enemies identified vary little and in fact often throw back to conspiracies that, in the case of Jews for instance, were first hatched in the high Middle

Ages. Furthermore, many popular conspiracies are in fact *more complex* explanations of events, where rather simple stories are convoluted and contorted until blame lands in the usual place. September 11 was not caused by nineteen terrorists sponsored by al Qaeda; the invasion of Ukraine was not Vladimir Putin's fault; SARS-COV-2 is not simply (or at all) a virus; Donald Trump didn't lose the 2020 elections, etc. These events have in fact given rise to multiple Rube Goldberg–style byzantine intrigues with false flags, invisible hands, pulled strings, and sometimes supernatural intervention.

The second set has to do with the necessity to connect abstract, distant conspiracies, wherein the entities responsible have ultimate goals far removed from ordinary experience (some being aliens from outer space) or with actual developments in current events. The interpretation of the news with foundational texts (from the Bible and the Quran to *Das Kapital*, etc.) has always served the same function, commonly observed in sects: to maintain relevance in a fast-moving, evolving world. Its secondary function is to protect the current narrative from new facts that, without the proper interpretation, might seem to contradict accepted truths.

The final set of functions has to do with personal power or, rather, the feeling that one either has very little or deserves far more than others. Perceived disenfranchisement is often at the heart of conspiracy theories and contrasts directly with the near divine power wielded by conspirators, who control entire populations, institutions, states, and corporations. Disenfranchisement claims are also at the heart of most forms of violent extremism and political terrorism. Nearly all conspiracy narratives include components that aim at accounting for individual powerlessness, usually by attributing it to deliberate wrongdoing on the part of illegitimate forces.

Finally, for many conspiracy disciples, "knowing" the explanation for personal (perceived) powerlessness at least partially restores balance: knowledge is power. Unveiling and revealing the conspiracy is a form of esoteric exchange where those involved feel they are finally allowed a peek behind the magician's curtain where they discover his tricks. The more events, trends, people, institutions, etc., that are narratively tied into the explanation, the more powerful the feeling. While some are fine with leaving this knowledge at an esoteric stage, reserved for the few, others feel a vocation to enlighten the entire world:

> Now, this policy made a transition from European-based immigration, largely or 90 per cent to Asian and Middle Eastern and other areas of immigration. In, really, the transition was in 1967, this is generalizing a little bit or simplifying a little bit but, with the introduction of the point system to the immigration programs, right, which was in retrospect very impactful. And yet, how many people are aware of this or, you know, within general Canadian society, 1 per cent, 2? You know, these things are not exposed, right? (ED12)

> Basically I'm just trying to raise awareness ... [so] that Canadians have a more truthful understanding about World War II. The truth about Adolf Hitler, and National Socialist Germany ... also that Canadians become more aware of the extent of power of international Jews in Canadian society. (ED33)

White nationalism under many disguises

It should be noted that white nationalism is merely a more positive formulation of traditional hatred or contempt towards non-whites. It sometimes appears as "European nationalism" or "Christian nationalism," which sound more inclusive. "European" refers not to legal citizenship or physical presence on European territory, however, but historical lineage. The similar, preceding concepts of "white pride" and "white rights" were invented in the 1990s in order to "sanitize" the traditionally hateful discourse of the Klan in the USA. These and other euphemisms are more common among the self-styled "intellectuals" of the movement, the one time alt-right and alt-light followers who used it to counter accusations of racism, typically arguing that while racism is motivated by hate, pride in one's ethnic group is motivated by love: so, it is racism's *opposite*. It is also often argued that if there can be a non-controversial "Black pride" or "gay pride" there should be no problem with the symmetric pride of other groups. Whether that discourse is wittingly disingenuous or simply dense varies from person to person.

The more virulent actors and groups are likely to adopt the more assertive, confrontational language of white power and white supremacy and will enthusiastically agree that they are indeed racists. They are also the ones more likely to adopt explicitly racist iconographies, starting with the swastika of course, but including dozens of more or less recognizable replacements: Celtic crosses, reappropriated Norse runes, Third Reich military insignias and flags, round, triangular, or swirly variations on the swastika. They are also likely to elevate various historical figures or events to cult status with memes and speech codes (e.g., "14 words" for neo-Nazi ideologue David Lane's "We must secure the existence of our people and a future for white children," "88" for "Heil Hitler"). Finally, they will make heavy use of fiction and specific references to fictitious events, such as the "day of the rope" described in *The Turner Diaries* (on which day whites who reject white supremacy are hanged).

The multiple definitions of "nationalism," though they rest on the same basic foundations, soon explode in multiple, incompatible directions, however.

It is to be noted that being proud of one's lineage, culture, or religion does not automatically imply pride in all, or even most, others who are of the same population group or in that group. In fact, many of our respondents explicitly rejected their peers in general, condemning them as ignorant, lazy, timorous, or lacking values:

> I'm proud of being white and my convictions are [expletive] strong; today I hate [other] Quebecers more than I hate Blacks. Because Blacks have values, they support each other, more than us Quebecers. These days in Quebec everyone is snitching on everyone and no one has values. (ED38)

Like "patriotism" or "nationalism," pride does not in fact refer to an identifiable, measurable reality of which one might be proud. Pride in Canada does not refer to Canadian culture, physical territory, mode of government, politicians, institutions, laws, or people – on the contrary, it is usually evoked in *opposition* to most of those aspects. Pride in being white does not imply any knowledge in genetics and excludes most whites. Rather, all pride-related concepts are meant to corral a heterogeneous set of idealized, fantasized, and, especially, marginal values and beliefs that are utterly rejected, if not ridiculed, by the vast majority of those to whom they are supposed to apply.

White nationalism rapidly breaks down around this uniform core and takes a different face for nearly each group and sometimes each individual. There is no need to inventory every nuance and permutation, but a few main branches are clearly obvious. First, there are two general categories of nationalism. On one side, there are those who have adopted a form of nationalism that they claim to be based on a "European," white, or Western population and have taken a side in what they believe is a global clash of civilizations, Jewish conspiracy, or a plot to form a central planetary totalitarian government (multiple other variations exist). This form of "wide" nationalism is common everywhere in Canada. In that version of the world, immigration is either a deliberately used tool or the unwitting cause of the cultural genocide of those populations of Western European descent. Individuals who adopt this worldview usually report having first been introduced to it after having researched or expressed a concern with so-called "illegal" immigration in Canada.

In Quebec, this nationalism is present but constantly clashes with another, "narrow" version, centred around the concept of "old stock" (*de souche*) francophones, those who (at least claim to) have ancestry going back to French colonists. Under that vision, old stock francophones should be given unfettered sovereign political power over the territory since a) their ancestors developed it and b) they represent an endangered cultural bastion of French speakers in North America (the potential colonialist accusations of [a] being offset by the vulnerability in [b]). This is different from the dominant form of nationalism in Quebec that catalyzed the separatist movement from the 1960s well into the 2000s. The more popular form was partly based on the need to protect the French language as well but was also fuelled by the condemnation of the exploitation of underpaid francophone labour in the province and the "foreign" (i.e., Anglo-American) ownership of means of production. It had a non-ethnic, legal, and territorial understanding of citizenship and because of its inclusiveness, it tended to clash with far-right ideologies. Whether or not it has now broadly moved towards identity politics is subject to debate.

What is of interest for the purposes of this book is the right-of-centre "narrow" form of nationalism that claims to represent a "nation" or a "people" of white, Catholic, French-speaking citizens thought to be at risk of disappearance or "replacement." Its adherents oppose the wide version, which they associate with Anglo-Canadian federalism, aimed at the assimilation of francophone Quebec into a more general, and anglophone, Canadian nationalism. Under that view, "mass" immigration is decried not as an internationalist plot but a federal, Anglo-Saxon one aimed at drowning francophones in a demographic tsunami. These perspectives do not mix well:

> So we went to meet with a guy who ran an army surplus outlet in ... and, you know, he wanted us to train him and his crew in survival tactics and things like that. We had our Canadian flags out, like the army, you know, [expletive], we're Canadian. But these guys, they had their Quebec flags. Forget it, they boycotted us. They were like, "I'm never flying a Canadian flag, I'm a Quebecer." (ED38)

It should be noted that in one guise or another replacement theory is quickly gaining ground in the mainstream public discourse everywhere in Canada, and especially in Quebec, where the language question affords an additional argument.

Another important source of conflict between the wide and narrow versions is that the former supports the notion of a central government in the sovereign territory of Canada, while the latter recommends the secession of Quebec and the foundation of a new nation. From that point of view immigration is doubly dangerous, since immigrants are also thought to be less likely to support secession from a country they just landed in.

Separatist-identity nationalism is not exclusive to Quebec. Western Canada has its own brand of (quite marginal) groups calling for the creation of various forms of separate sovereign territories based on "Anglo-Saxon" culture. The Diagolon movement suggests linking

Western Canadian provinces (except BC) with central and south-eastern red states in the USA in a diagonal line to Florida. The new country would then be "ethnically cleansed." In February 2022, thirteen members of the movement carrying multiple small arms were arrested near the border crossing at Coutts, Alberta. Four have been accused of conspiring to kill RCMP officers (Grant 2022).

Nationalism is usually presented as a political weapon against globalization. Representations of fears of and solutions to the latter could fill a separate book, but suffice it to say that in general the central point is that there are forces that strive to further disempower local structures and citizens to the benefit of planetary elites. Globalization appears as the devil in many ideologies, across all spectrums, but in far-right variations its ultimate result is the disappearance of sovereign state power, accompanied by the fading of borders and border controls, leading to unfettered, wild immigration, and eventually the disappearance not simply of nation states but of the cultures they were meant to protect – which of course is taken as a disaster.

The concepts of globalization, degeneration, and disappearance are closely related themes in the discourse of most of our respondents. Globalization is not viewed for its economic or commercial aspects but for its perceived tendency to increase population mobility and migration. The arrival of new ethnic groups is thought to lead to degeneration, the loss of distinctiveness (and thus superiority in some discourses) for the group, and its eventual disappearance, at least in its present form. This closes the circle for this section, connecting us back to victimization narratives in which the group's survival is threatened by various forces that interact and become alarmingly stronger and stronger:

> We're below sustainability. That means in about thirty, forty years, we will be outnumbered. And we're approaching an Islamic state, Sharia law. It's a mathematical inevitability, here for Canada. Forty years from now, if you decide to have a family, and children, you're gonna be faced with Islamic culture. (ED25)

This is often accompanied by an overwhelming sense of emergency or impending doom, often requiring extreme action. The 2017 Quebec mosque shooter mentioned that the presence of Muslims made him afraid for the safety of his family. This is of course simply the evolution of primitive racism and easily connects with its more traditional forms. We were told many times that immigrants in general, and "visible" ones in particular, are dangerous for the reference group. Many of our respondents identified multiethnic adverts, the presence of non-white children in schools, and mixed couples in public as signs that society is decaying. A somewhat more nuanced and more contemporary-sounding version allows for the presence of other "races" but only if they choose to conform to an implicit, rarely unpacked set of national norms or "values" (usually symbolized by a trope as in, for instance, "if you come into my house, you remove your shoes" [ED37] or the classic "when in Rome ..."). When made more explicit, the most often invoked norms are those that have a visible component, like clothing.

Sources of conflict

Women and the glorification of "pre-modern" maleness

Early on, one of the basic justifications given for La Meute's existence was that Muslim fundamentalists threatened the rights of women. Among other things, Muslim women were forced to stay at home and to wear specific clothing while in public, especially variations of head dress (e.g., hijab, chador) and face coverings (e.g., burka, niqab). Like the Quebec chapter of the Soldiers of Odin, or the Ontario PEGIDA, La Meute gave prominent leadership roles to women. We will investigate the case of Lauren Southern in chapter 4 but suffice it to say here that she was at one time one of the most important political influencers in the international far-right infosphere.

Despite Southern's significance, the balance of movements, groups, and individuals inventoried here are ideologically far closer to the abovementioned "manosphere" and tend to promote views about women that are far from guaranteeing them equal freedom, to say the least. Many have extremely narrow views of the social roles that women should fulfill and most tend to revolve around the traditional raising of the family, usually meant to be as large as possible. Some, such as the Proud Boys, explicitly ban women from participation, while, of course, praising, if not glorifying, those who accept their appointed set of "natural" functions. This generates a conflictual understanding of the function of women as participants in the movement. Southern, for instance, was routinely contacted by male followers who accused her of being out of place as a powerful actor or propositioned her (Lombroso 2020).

It should be understood that though the anti-feminism that permeates this portion of the far right is primarily aimed at recruiting frustrated young males and older "men's rights" partisans, it also attracts some women. Here the most powerful version of the discourse is the "natural order" branch, where the roles of mother and homemaker are presented as essentially female, and for the women who forsake these, unhappiness and a lack of fulfilment are the results. Feminism makes women strive to become alpha male emulators, which leads to conflict with men and, above all, with other women. It also destroys the will to reproduce and multiply, a major factor in the reduction of the demographic weight of whites. One of our respondents celebrated the power of women who sacrifice everything for their family while disparaging the "feminists" who criticize his group (ED27).

At the far end of the spectrum, we find various groups and individuals who espouse entirely what we might term "pre-modern" visions of masculinity that are highly militaristic and exalt power in physical domination, hand-to-hand combat, edged weapons or other low-tech armament, sometimes inspired by medieval and especially Viking lore and its connection to (neo-)Nazi imagery and its use of Norse runes. Multiple martial arts clubs more or less explicitly themed around these representations have sprung up in France (Pride France), in the USA (Rise Above), and in Quebec (La Phalange). Most are short-lived and marginal outfits but constitute fascinating case studies of the combined obsessions with defence, physical health, purity and strength (including sexual prowess), strict regimens, a compulsive need to belong, and sectarianism that can be found everywhere in the far right.

One last related theme is specific to groups of far-right "preppers" or survivalists and consists in building up personal power and resilience in the face of various (and often combining or cascading) massive forces that may threaten entire civilizations: nuclear war, financial collapse, technological collapse, civil war (including its variant, race war), state overreach, and environmental implosion. Personally surviving, indeed dominating these disasters, of course includes hoarding supplies and weapons but also involves a specific brand of individualistic ideology that assumes that other (less prepared) humans will have to be fought off and neutralized in a post-apocalyptic, millenarian world in which only the strongest, fittest people will prevail.

The role of religion

For the time being, religion plays a far smaller role in the Canadian far right than it does in the USA. However, that is likely to change in the next few years, as Canada follows its southern neighbour and is taken by a storm of "Christofascism." Groups and individuals are increasingly galvanized by multiple highly publicized examples of backlash against LGBTQ+ and abortion rights, and the immigration of populations identified as representatives of opposite, if not conflicting faiths.

We have seen above a few examples of groups explicitly referring to Christianity within the core of their ideology. In Quebec the Fraternité sacerdotale Saint-Pie X (Society of Saint Pius X), a Catholic sect centred on the rejection of the Vatican II reforms of the 1960s (and founded by the excommunicated bishop Marcel Lefebvre), has inspired some individuals to adopt worldviews where conspiracies and hidden powers rule the world and must be fought in the name of Christ. Among other points, the Fraternité considers other religions to be mistaken and ultimately dangerous. Unsurprisingly, the religion most reviled is Islam and some religious extremists love to distribute "love Muslims, hate Islam" pamphlets inspired by the axiom "love the sinner, hate the sin" (wrongly thought to come from the Bible).

At the same time many other movements position themselves clearly *against* traditional religions, either because they have concocted their own supernatural contents to graft onto their ideology (often in a religious version of popular conspiracy theories) or because they explicitly present themselves as secular: "my religion, I'd say, would be the laws of nature. Like, natural law ... I look at nature for representation of our society ... Religion is the cause of the biggest problems in the world in my opinion" (ED20).

Of course, it should be noted that many explicitly non-religious groups focus extensively or exclusively on "critiquing" Islam and self-describe as defenders of their reference group, nation or country against Islamist depravity. In order to do so, some study the opposition in detail:

> But yes, I studied the subject! ... I was in jail for nine months, I read the Quran every day! For nine months! ... I took a pencil and paper and every day for nine months, I wrote the verses from the Quran. Because when you write something you understand it more than if you read it. So how many people have actually read the Quran three times and wrote out the verses? How many Muslims even read the Quran three times? (ED16)

That focus inevitably pushes their discourse into constant religious discussion, sometimes peppered with verses from the Quran and citations from the Bible, usually in an effort to demonstrate the calamitous nature of the former and superiority of the latter, as demonstrated in the media infosphere in chapter 5.

Finally, many groups and individuals camouflage their Islamophobia under the language of secularism, often unaware that some of the secular values they claim to prefer are specifically Christian (for instance, the idea that wearing visible religious signs is vainly flaunting one's faith).

The "system" as the enemy

Whether and to what extent existing institutions ("the system") are part of the problems identified by far-right ideologues and militants is a profound subject of conflict. We have seen that a clear break exists between ideologies that aim to use state power to attain goals, for instance to reinforce immigration laws and protect national borders, and those that consider the very structure of the state as the source of the problem. Of course, the first can morph into the second, as the "drain the swamp" discourse in the Trumpist USA eventually exploded into a full-fledged rejection of the democratic process four years later. Whether historians will view the flopped insurrection as a warning or a rehearsal remains to be seen.

The fundamentally populist stance against (ill-defined) "elites" also has different, conflicting flavours. The more widespread stance is that the current elites are malevolent, corrupted, or manipulated from afar by even more powerful global elites. The solution then is to replace them with a new group of legitimate leaders, politicians, and civil servants. Further contradiction then follows as to whether this replacement should proceed democratically or not. A notable minority consider, however, that any form of centralized political power is inherently illegitimate, a view that is also common in anarchist circles. This is obviously the case of Freemen on the Land but also of far-right "preppers" who refuse any limitations of their right to self-determination.

The system may in fact be many things. Many of our respondents had trouble with the justice system and found it corrupt and stacked against them. Many Freemen theoreticians have intricate conspiracy theories and damning accusations against the banking system. For many others the economic system is the central problem:

> Well, yeah, I think the National Socialist system was um, not the same as communism, okay, and not the same as capitalism. I think that National Socialism was more for the benefit of the people, the German National Socialism. Whereas capitalism is not for the benefit of the people, and communism is not for the benefit of the people. (ED33)

Money

Money can sometimes act as a catalyst and bring together various independent groups and individuals. This was the case, notoriously, with funds collected to support the February 2022 "Freedom Convoy." Promises of various forms of support covering fuel, attorneys, traffic tickets, and other expenses, for instance, were probably instrumental in motivating some of the participants.

Usually, however, financial matters tend to have the opposite effect. Losses, or gains for that matter, are a conflict flashpoint within many groups and cause splits and rivalries. Though originally the Freedom Convoy did well with promises of financial support, some internal conflict appeared once it became obvious that a large portion (42 per cent) of the funds and most donors (59 per cent) came from the USA (mostly from rich republican enclaves in Florida, Texas, and California; Cameron and McKay 2022). In all, the convoy project and its initiator collected around Can$24 million in funds: $10 million first accumulated via GoFundMe, which quickly refunded donors when the platform cancelled the project; $12 million via alternative platform GiveSendGo (whose database was hacked and leaked to the media); and $2 million via Bitcoin wallets. The accounts where the $14 million was to be deposited were frozen by the government of Canada after the Emergency Measures Act was invoked. GiveSendGo then suspended payments and seems to have returned a portion of the money. Over a million dollars in Bitcoin seems to have been distributed to truckers. At the time of writing, some $6 million is still being held in escrow by an injunction obtained by Ottawa residents suing the convoy's organizers (Fraser 2022).

In 2017 La Meute's leadership was shaken by the matter of how to use the proceeds of the sale of merchandise, including mugs and T-shirts, marked with the group's logo. Its main founder was left off the list of administrators when the group became an officially listed corporation. The new leadership then accused him of having badly managed and diverted funds from sales, and banned some four hundred unhappy members from the group's private Facebook page.

Conspiracy theorist Stéphane Blais collected more than Can$500,000 in order to protect and support those who resisted government-imposed COVID-19 sanitary measures. Two years later no money had been spent on those primary objectives and Blais's movement is imploding. He has also been collecting funds ostensibly to support his lawsuit against the government of Quebec, which he claims had no authority to impose emergency sanitary measures. So far he has simply obtained a series of delays, and since his high-profile lawyer left early in the process, no actual work is being accomplished. Blais eventually lost his licence as a certified public accountant, a process he unsuccessfully opposed by using pseudo-legal language similar to that of Sovereign Citizens.

Most groups find various ways to be active with very low to no funding, but large undertakings such as events, publications, or the need to have staff or technical expertise require money they generally do not have. Direct contributions, crowdfunding, and merchandizing are all greatly simplified and/or enhanced by various widely available and affordable technical tools: that is not where the problems lie. Rather, the dangers appear when money starts pouring in, causing conflicts and rivalries in groups that were not thought of, much less organized as, commercial enterprises. Basic bookkeeping skills are usually absent, and when they are available, they are not properly employed; responsibility and authority for expenses is unclear or disputed; planning is deficient or entirely nonexistent.

Conclusion

The far-right nebula has expanded dramatically in Canada since the middle of the 2010s. More numerous and more visible, groups have also diversified on multiple levels. This is why our categories of "ultra-right," "anti-state militias," "xenophobic vigilantes," etc., are more efficient in drawing the new map of the nebula. They are economical: accounting for a vast number of ideological nuances with the minimum number of categories, while also managing to cover the entire spectrum of the Canadian far right.

Part of this expansion is essentially virtual, as the multiplication of groups and sub-groups does not necessarily represent a growing number of individuals: it is common for most exponents of the far right to belong to several groups simultaneously or in rotation. Groups are also rarely exclusive and are more than happy to count each other's members or count their own more than once. Some count one-time visitors to their social media accounts as "members." As a result, it is extremely difficult to attempt to quantify the size, growth, or expansion of far-right groups and movements. This is also, of course, heavily dependent on one's definition of "membership."

One more clearly observable fact is that groups with a more explicitly violent discourse have contributed to legitimating the rise of the more traditional far right, such as our "radical right" and "nostalgic racists." The latter, because they mobilize registers of violence that are primarily symbolic, are able to present a more socially acceptable face by underlining the contrast with their less mannered cousins. As a result, they make their way into mainstream public space more easily, aided by the new mobilization opportunities offered by social media.

Intergroup dynamics vary from one province to another, and occasional alliances between groups belonging to different categories can blur the lines, during federating events for instance. Such a period of effervescence can also raise public awareness, but it is a double-edged sword: if higher visibility helps sell a far-right message, it also raises concerns and sometimes apprehension in large portions of the public. For instance, the COVID-19 pandemic has partially reshuffled the cards; it gave freedom conspiracists a higher profile and constituted a moment where far-right content and material circulated more widely in Canada. This culminated in the so-called "Freedom Convoy" in February 2022. Though it cannot be reduced to a far-right event, the Freedom Convoy gave groups that were almost dormant before and during the pandemic, like La Meute, a new visibility and gave newcomers, like the potentially violent Diagolon, a large forum. At the same time, it rang alarm bells among more liberal groups, in government, and in various policing organizations. The pandemic emergency is quickly fading from memory and in the next few years it will be interesting to reassess its longer-term effects on both the expansion of the far right and official awareness.

The next chapter explains how groups construct their discourse in order to fulfil three main goals: to recruit new supporters, to attain a sufficient level of public acceptance or tolerance, and to inspire and energize the troops.

3 MANUFACTURING SOCIAL PROBLEMS

With Rosalie Chevrette

Introduction: far-right activists as moral entrepreneurs

Beginning in the late twentieth century the two main interrelated building blocks of the far right's quest for broader relevance were immigration (those present as well as the dreaded more to come) and Muslim presence and influence domestically and internationally. Though scholars argue that migration policies have been dominated by elites (Geddes 2006), Mudde (2000) has provided several examples where right-wing radical movements, thought to be marginal in Western Europe, have influenced the drafting and implementation of immigration policies. In the Canadian context, where the far right is essentially extraparliamentary, some similar groups increasingly have gained public visibility by multiplying appearances in public, on the web, and on social media. The 2019 Roxham Road episode, when numbers of asylum seekers crossed the USA-Canada border by simply cutting through a narrow patch of lawn, has shown how the far right can affect the political agenda. In October 2019 several groups, including Storm Alliance and La Meute, organized a demonstration at the end of Roxham Road to denounce the massive arrival of migrants and call for the closure of this illegal crossing point. This demand, which they began making as early as 2017, aims to influence public debate on the subject, as it has become a point of contention between the Quebec and federal governments. Yet research on the far-right action repertoire and its influence on public debate is still scarce (Tanner and Campana 2020a; Campana and Tanner 2019; Nadeau 2020).

Many groups are quite content to remain secret and do not seek in any way to gain influence in the public sphere. The previous chapter showed that violent groups tended towards circumspection, if not secrecy. In the following pages we concentrate on the far-right public action repertoire, and we will show how its mobilization tactics focus on the construction of immigration, Islam, and Muslims as social problems.

Any group's repertoire of public action is shaped by multiple factors, among which are individual peculiarities, accidents, opportunities, and coincidences, the nature of the group and its ideological and organizational trajectory, etc. Groups that seek public exposure and influence can be found mostly in the "radical right," "freedom conspiracists," and "nostalgic racists" categories, which share a general anxiety about immigration and immigrants (the "relationship with otherness" dimension of our matrix).

Contemporary far-right movements tend to be populist and identify elites as internal enemies for putting their own interests ahead of the interests of the people (Rydgren 2007). In doing so, they seek to reposition themselves as the voice of the customary "silent majority," the "invisible" or the "forgotten" (Betz 2018), "saying aloud what everyone thinks." That is why populism is defined as a "political rhetoric appealing to the power of the common people in order to challenge the legitimacy of the current political establishment" (Abt and Rummens 2007, 407). It is an ideology "that considers society to be ultimately separated in two homogeneous and antagonistic groups: 'the pure people' versus 'the corrupt elite,' and that argues that politics should be an expression of the *volonté générale* of the people" (Mudde 2004, 543).

As a social movement, the far right has the capacity to form one-off alliances (though those remain fragile), marked by the explicit project of the protagonists to mobilize in unison, organized around a logic of claim, and the defence of a cause. In fact, when important events speak to their overarching concern with otherness, groups from otherwise different categories rarely hesitate to temporarily combine forces, for example, marching on Roxham Road or converging (physically and virtually) in the French Alps with the alleged "entire" far-right world, as we'll see in the next chapter. To the extent that social movements reflect existing social discomfort and cultural changes, they can gain the ability to (re)define and push certain problems in the traditional media and, eventually, on the political agenda, acting as "problem entrepreneurs" (Neveu 2002, 2015).

Once mobilized into movements, citizens who believe that democracy cannot be left in the hands of professional politicians may act as a source of interference, an alternative power in the political landscape (Neveu 2015). They attempt to establish authority on what they deem to be a "public problem": a situation or a behaviour that has negative consequences for a significant portion of the population and that needs to be addressed. To gain authority over the problem, they must generate public acceptance of their specific understanding of its causes and effects and, usually, the culprits that can be blamed, shamed, or elevated to the rank of public enemies. Almost invariably, those culprits are either non-majority populations or majority elites or both. In this perspective, far-right groups who mobilize to make their cause more visible participate in the construction of social problems and may be considered as "moral entrepreneurs" (Wilson 2009).

As such, they also identify and propose solutions, which soon morph into demands to the institutions or interlocutors deemed pertinent or considered to be "part of the problem" (Neveu 2015). For the most part, the solutions revolve around the exclusion or disappearance of the "other," defined in religious, racial, ethnic/cultural terms as distinct from an idealized community defined by its whiteness, Christianity, culture, or all of the above. The demands are framed in a moral imperative, oftentimes with a degree of urgency (Becker 1963), thus initiating a moral crusade aimed at the establishment of rules or laws intended to cast entire groups as deviants or strangers (Wilson 2009). In particular, this phenomenon has been observed in opposition to the Muslim community in Canada (Campana and Tanner 2019). The "disappearance" of the other, of course, can take different shapes according to the extremism of the group, from simple cultural assimilation to extermination, with expulsion ("re-migration") and sterilization in the middle.

Repertoires of opposition

To understand how far-right groups attempt to influence the debate and claim their legitimacy in defining immigration and Islam as a social problem, it is useful to look at the actions they undertake in order to construct a public problem (this is not a chronological order). First, they must try to reach and convince a sufficient proportion of the public – through perception building – that their concern is real and sufficiently significant for ordinary people to be preoccupied with it; in other words, to frame the situation as a public problem. This involves the production of stories and images and the mobilization of symbols that serve to define what is or is not part of the problem, in other words, the stakes that are involved. Always in view of gaining wider traction, this has to be accomplished in keeping with what happens to be the particular set of socially acceptable values in the wider society at the time. Second, the social problem must be popularized. Astute ideologues know that even the most convincing narrative can only be effective once it is widely disseminated, which shows the importance of having access to the media and other public forums. Third, it is crucial to build up the gravity, the exceptional nature of the problem. Throughout, it must be noted that in order to convince the target population that the goal is the public good, the entrepreneur must never be perceived as motivated by his own interests.

It bears repeating that these strategies should not be understood as a fixed set or as a sequence of phases always present in an immutable chronology. Moral entrepreneurs will choose their own set of actions according to their capabilities, their social and political context, etc., and will adjust when they deem it necessary (and may nevertheless fail). We are then in no way claiming that these strategies are successful, only that they are thought to be by those who employ them. Actual success is highly contingent on multiple contextual elements. But when it all falls into place, the entrepreneur can be said to have been successful if the actions have led to a public policy transformation, meaning that a significant takeover of the problem from powerful social institutions has occurred (Neveu 2015).

Strategies and repertoires

Studying the far right as a social movement allows us to take into account various types of actions that have broad social effects, especially in the way they influence the media, public opinion, and the political debate. These actions are not selected at random; as Tilly (1984) pointed out, they are taken from "distinctive constellations of tactics and strategies developed over time and used by protest groups to act collectively in order to make claims on individuals and groups." For Tilly, each social movement is confronted by a series of pre-existing forms of protest, unequally accessible according to the identity of the group and their context, the places, times, population, and the attitudes adopted by the authorities, the public, and the organizations with regard to past collective action.

In this chapter, we focus on what has been termed "unconventional" political behaviour (Marsh 1977; Barnes and Kaase 1979), meaning actions and tactics "performed" outside the realm of conventional political participation (i.e., voting, being a member of a political party, lobbying) but below the threshold of politically motivated crime (hijacking, terrorism, guerrilla warfare, etc.; Marsh 1977). This leaves a rather broad range of forms of action that can be used by collective actors, with various goals, from communicating grievances and claims to attempting to influence decision-makers or public opinion, to recruitment, group publicity, or financing. Strategies vary either in the logic that drives them or in the degree of radicalism they imply (Porta and Diani 2006). Moreover, as stressed by social movement scholars, the choice of repertoires of action is influenced by the political opportunities available (Caiani and Della Porta 2018). That said, political opportunities are not structurally given but rather culturally constructed: they are filtered through the perceptions that far-right movements have of them, which in turn help define their strategies, based on their appreciation of the potential support they can obtain.

As we will see in the next chapter, most of the actions described here have Internet components; some take place entirely online.

Many entities on the far right have become adept at exploiting every advance offered by information technologies, starting with the now defunct Bulletin Board System (BBS) of the 1980s (Atton 2006; Back 2002, Caiani, and Kröll 2015; Caiani and Parenti 2016; Daniels 2009). Besides making it easier to recruit and communicate, the Internet has also allowed far-right groups to develop new tools and techniques to enhance their visibility and legitimacy (Hawley 2017; Marwick and Lewis 2017, Nagle 2017; Scrivens et al. 2020) and make use of "participatory culture" (Jenkins 2006).

The development of the Internet, and social networks in particular, has profoundly upset the structure of industrial media, starting with its power to maintain and reproduce an intersubjectively accepted set of truths, values, identities, authorities, order, etc. By shattering the cultural oligopoly of the media, the "Web 2.0" provides moral entrepreneurs with new, inexpensive communication vectors that are highly reactive, widely accessible, and not easily censored. Thus, it seems that the Internet has profoundly altered the repertoire of actions of social movements in two ways: first, by facilitating existing forms of action, making it possible to reach more people more easily and within a time frame that was previously unthinkable; second by creating new tools for activism, leading to a diversification of mobilization practices (Van Laer and Van Aelst 2010; Lewis 2018) and the creation of a formidably powerful new infosphere.

Canadian repertoires

There are clear differences between groups to which our participants claimed to belong. For example, ultra-right groups, unsurprisingly, tended to give more space to violent actions within their repertoire. Their discourse was also more explicitly violent, thus relegated to the margins. We also looked at nostalgic racists, where most massive public groups are found, who enthusiastically expose their repertoires in various forums, online, on the streets, and in the media. We focused on the ideology, the online discourse (both public, such as official statements made by the leader of the group, and private, such as publication and comments posted by members on social media and forums), and the symbols displayed on the web (for a further reflection on methodological challenges posed by researching the far right on the Internet, see Crosset et al. 2019).

Protests, as messages addressed to sympathizers, decision makers, political adversaries, and the wider public, constitute important tools for social movements to attract attention, to appeal or to threaten, to make claims heard and visible, and eventually to influence politics and society (Koopmans and Rutch 2002). This is where groups manufacture – and package, as it were – the social problem(s) that they will attempt to *own*, or hold an authoritative discourse on, defining its contours, its consequences, and the proper solution.

Framing

Far-right groups often initiate actions through which they can frame a problem – that is, to define what is and what is not part of the problem, to suggest a way to perceive the issues at stake, and to articulate it within socially acceptable values. More astute formations opt to surf on populist waves triggered by current events to reap the same broad approval. This requires some reframing and adjustments in their discourse to make it look reasonable, or less marginal, to the wider public. That involves staying clear of their usual radical repertoire, such as demonstrative actions and expressive events that run the risk of giving off an aggressive, "extremist" image. For example, one of the framing tactics used by far-right groups is to organize public conferences where more conventional speakers are invited:

> The other thing was basically to bring in speakers and try and attract the public to come and listen to the speakers. Good speakers, not crazy speakers, but people who present, I would say, our message, certainly the message that is consistent with our approach. (ED17)

This demonstrative action is here used to mainstream a marginal worldview by associating with speakers who are not explicitly aligned with the movement, who have established authority or expertise regarding the issue at stake, and who share a compatible view of the problem. By associating with speakers who have a more mainstream audience, far-right groups benefit from their credibility (as previously noted by Lewis 2018). Also, this kind of activity offers several strategic advantages, such as having more control over the identity of the attendees and making it easier to find a venue that otherwise might not accept an outright radical political meeting.

Aside from organizing public conferences, far-right groups mainly push their worldview through the diffusion of contents on the web. In fact, as we will see in the next chapter, mainstream social media sites like Twitter (now X), Facebook, and YouTube are (still) heavily used by the far right to spread messages and news – "fake" or not – to large numbers of people with little to no investment of money, time, or other resources:

> I'm just a private citizen with a freedom of speech, I use YouTube, it doesn't cost any money, I make YouTube videos, I'm reaching over a thousand people a day. Okay. Okay. I'm just one person, with a very low budget. (ED32)

Despite the recent ban of extremist accounts and groups on Facebook, Twitter/X, and others, in an effort to contain misinformation and extremism, the platforms remain highly popular vehicles for rabidly reactionary news commentary and fake news. Facebook, Twitter/X, YouTube, and others still offer platforms for myriad conspiracy theorists and fringe groups who produce persuasive, engaging videos on outrageous topics (Marwick and Lewis 2017; Lewis 2018; Howard 2020; Marantz 2019). Mostly through trial and error, these users have learned to tone down the language and to avoid the red flags that can lead to de-platforming through calculated adjustments to the content they offer (more on these aspects in chapter 4). This, of course, is an overall improvement, since the general level of hate, polarization, denunciation, and incitement to violence has significantly declined.

Some entities choose to present themselves as news providers or current events commentators and usually specialize in fairly specific types of content, related to a single issue or a narrow range of issues. Their worldview is communicated through diversified vectors such as news articles, videos, photos, and memes. Usually the format is, deliberately or not, reminiscent of popular alternative media publications:

> People are happy, they consider our work ... you know, they thank us a lot for providing so much information they wouldn't find elsewhere. When you go on [our Facebook page], you only focus on that [illegal immigration, Islam, and Muslims]. We don't talk about anything else. (ED29)

Any one of these tactics, as many others, aims at placing the group, as well as the particular issue at stake, as non-marginal. Both are (re)framed as rational actors and objective concerns that touch everyone.

Popularize the problem: accessing mainstream media

Even if the problem and the group are legitimized and primed for mass consumption, presence on traditional media is still seen as both a badge of success and a necessary step for actual change, especially for radical right, freedom conspiracist, and nostalgic racist groups. With that objective in mind, organizing marches, drives, mass meetings, and other visible forms of mobilization remains an essential tactic for most of our interviewees – though they must be closely managed and controlled in order to avoid any flare-ups or open confrontation. Our respondents claimed it allowed for maximum gains in visibility and a powerful way to pop on the radar of traditional media. Yet only very few of the interviewees used it, for a variety of reasons. Some reported trying many times to organize a protest but blamed their opponents for blocking their efforts:

> Well, we tried. It's not because we didn't try, because we wanted to ... There were 500 people against us ... So that's it. We tried a first time. We tried a second time. The second time the police closed the subways. They took away the three leaders. I arrived 5 minutes late, 5–10 minutes late. I just arrived, and it was already over. So I asked, "how come?" "Because the police picked us up." (ED29)

Faced with the possibility of counterprotests or police presence (that is, when it is antagonistic; a few groups have maintained good relations with their local police), and probably realizing the nontrivial nature of the logistics involved, many invested in other propaganda strategies on the web. It has been proven unequivocally that engaging and interacting with participants online is much easier, and more rewarding, than trying to convince them to take part in physical action, where the personal investment is far more onerous (beginning with transportation).

One highly effective virtual approach is the systematic spreading of fake news and other alternative content, made easier by the massive amount of data on the web, including photos and videos, coupled with the increasing power of photo and video editing software. Always, the objective is to generate content that is sensationalistic and shocking, to make it "go viral" and overflow into the papers and nightly newscasts:

> Okay, say I see [a conference where French imams are invited to talk], and I post on that, and after there's a huge controversy ... Because what I did, I went looking for some excerpts ... I discovered iMovie and, for example, I looked for excerpts in conferences and lectures given by imams, and I sorted out the excerpts that, let's say, were the most outrageous or, if for example they talked about women, like "women should never go out without being accompanied" or things like "if your husband, at night, feels desire, you have to satisfy him otherwise angels will curse you all night long." I made things with that, and I know it caused a huge controversy and it really became viral. (ED22)

This is a rather standard practice in the far-right infosphere: fuelling moral panic about Muslims (taken as a homogeneous group) and their claimed conception of women. That type of content doesn't exactly qualify as fake news, but the framing of the video still provokes a clear distortion of reality where extreme cases are used to characterize an entire population, where context elements are excluded, and appalling aspects are emphasized in an effort to shock the public.

Of course, far-right groups also use time-tested low-tech tactics to get coverage from the mainstream media, such as the distribution of flyers, unrequested newsletters, postings, and the like. At first sight, posting and distributing flyers serve as recruitment tools and as means of local communication. But these actions also rest on the hope that the media might pick them up and cover them as stories, which is far more attractive for the groups. As Marwick and Lewis (2017) explain, that the media will probably report on the story to debunk the contents of the flyers or to dismiss the strategy does not matter – the media are already largely understood as distorting or hiding the truth to serve the elites. The only important thing for the groups involved is getting the story covered in the first place, since the amount of media coverage devoted to those issues gives them the impression of importance in minds of the general public. This phenomenon, which they refer to as "agenda setting," shows how traditional broadcast media is both influenced and influential in determining what people think about and how they think about it. When their issues are covered by the media, even if it's to debunk them, far-right groups succeed in pushing their viewpoint into the public sphere and in gaining increased visibility and influence over the public agenda. In fact, as explained by far-right activists, many tactics are undertaken on the street precisely to get media attention:

> Well, we need, we need both [street action and social media], but if you're out on the street, eventually, the media attention will come, eventually they'll come, eventually they'll pay attention to you, yeah, if you're out there in their face, yeah. (ED4)

> So ... there've been protests here in Mississauga ... with banners over the highway, about traffic gridlock and immigration. And there have been similar protests in Vancouver. So it's, it's a matter of trying to get, get people more aware. (ED5)

The ostensible claim is that gaining public attention serves to raise awareness and educate the population on immigration issues, yet the final prize is undoubtedly to influence policy:

> Political parties aren't ready to respond to, for instance, our call for less immigration or not any immigration. But we think we're bringing in far more people than we need if we made best use of

> our existing human resources. And we don't think that you're going to get political parties concerned about having levels of immigration too high, unless there's a fairly strong public opinion on the subject, which you now have in countries like the United Kingdom for example, where there is real pressure from the public to review immigration policy. And I think to get changes made in policy, for instance in terms of the levels of immigration, how many people we bring in, we need a public opinion that demands it. (ED15)

The popularization, or visibility, of the issue at stake is intended to mobilize the population and to engage a public debate on immigration, and particularly on Muslim immigration. It also provides a choice position for the anti-immigration groups who were at the vanguard and who can now capitalize on their newly recognized "expertise" and clairvoyance.

Demonstrate the gravity

The last category of tactics undertaken by far-right groups to elevate their issue to social problem status is to demonstrate the gravity of the situation. To do this, many groups have borrowed from the vigilantism action repertoire and, more specifically, from digital vigilantism. The objective is to generate intense and enduring visibility, through the relentless exposure of specific population groups as priority enemies – which also reinforces the cohesive strength of the imaginary community under construction (Tanner and Campana 2020a; Trottier 2017; Loveluck 2020; Fourchard 2018).

One typically used strategy is to highlight and exaggerate the deviance of individual members of a community. Websites will systematically inventory instances of deviance within a designated racialized population, such as Blacks, Muslims, Jews, Asians, etc., in order to make those instances appear representative of the entire group. The more horrendous the crimes, the better. If the exercise is successful, the targeted group is understood as intrinsically undesirable, suspicious, or outright dangerous because of its unique, foreign, incompatible biological or cultural characteristics:

> Our goal is very clear, it is to inform people. Properly. Because journalists, you know, they don't do it ... So we share a lot of information because [our] ultimate goal, [our] mission, is to inform people of Islamic radicalization around the world. (ED29)

Some groups also play on the perceived injustices that their community is supposedly subjected to, at once exploiting and stoking popular mistrust toward elites and traditional media.

> And then taking that to the people to show them: look, here's what's *really* going on. Here's why you don't know about it, okay, and ... our country is changing so profoundly and so quickly that ... it's an injustice for you not to have an understanding of the proper context and the broader implications of this entire dynamic! Okay? So ... we're not telling you what to think. We're giving you the option; we are raising up our consciousness and level of understanding. (ED12)

In many instances, the vigilantism is directed at a particular individual, perceived as a threat to society:

> I happened to check on him [a controversial public figure expressing sympathies for radical Islam] on the anniversary of Bin Laden's death, and I told myself, I'll go check what his cubs are saying about it, and it was a big thing. It was in code, but it was really clear: "Three years ago died a great man." After that I started to monitor him more closely and then he started to praise the use of violence against those who insult Islam, he said that it was necessary to fight the enemies of Islam, to legitimate what I perceived as a desire of violence. He quoted violent verses. So I flagged him on ... It's not usual for me to do that, normally I only flag people who speak in public. (ED22)

When individuals are targeted, either on a personal basis or because of their official or attributed role as representative of a given organization, they become vectors of legitimation for the group. Their speech, actions, or omissions are systematically analyzed and spun to support the ideological frame. If they should act in a violent manner or justify the use of violence, they become ideal cases of the exceptional gravity, emergency, and significance of the cause.

Once construed as the enemy, the "mark" may be subjected to doxing and see their personal information – workplace, screen shot of a private conversation or publication on social media, phone number, etc. – divulged in public. When phone numbers, email addresses, or street addresses are divulged, the implied threat is obvious (note that individuals associated with the far right are also often victims of doxing themselves; see chapter 6). But doxing also includes revealing apparently embarrassing information about the target. Some of our respondents reported creating false Facebook accounts to infiltrate groups and gain access to exchanges that could be portrayed as incriminating or otherwise deviant. Their potential access to sensitive information related to security issues sometimes led them to cooperate with the police:

> Police officers contacted me ... I don't hold any information. Whether for journalists that I trust, or for intelligence agencies ... my mission is that, in the end, I really work for civil society. So I don't want to be, to work for intelligence agencies, it's not something that I am interested in. So I will respond to their questions if they have any. But I will never try to contact them on my own. I do not serve the state apparatus. (ED22)

> He [the respondent's group leader] has been connected to the police, shared information with the police, which is about things going on ... We're not vigilantes, we don't take the law into our own hands, that's not what we're about. Our job, if anything, if we are aware of information that the police ought to be aware of, we will communicate with the police and let them know. (ED17)

As the extracts above show, respondents active in digital vigilantism justify their actions by claiming they are reducible neither to sectoral interest nor to selfish claims: they are simply endeavouring to "work for civil society" and "prevent national security incidents" by sharing and exposing information about their opponents. As such, and in line with previous work on digital vigilantism (Loveluck 2020; Trottier 2017), the justification is more powerful than the information revealed in showing the seriousness of the menace. Public charges on the Internet may be meant to challenge public opinion to evolve over a particular issue or to force police to seize an offence, a crime, or an injustice (Loveluck 2016).

Of course, as we'll see in the next chapter, the far-right infosphere is an ecosystem with multiple actors, goals, methods, and results, heavily reconstructed by the functioning of the infosphere itself. So, it should not surprise anyone that a few of its actors have unstated goals that evolve in parallel to the altruistic ones:

> As I explained to … you shouldn't sue or fight people like me. It's just going to make Islamophobia worse … We should get together around a table and talk, try to understand each other's agenda … because when people sue me, like … like, you know, I don't have a choice but to try and do the things that are going to please the extremists on my side. Why? Because they're the ones who support me and give me the cash I need, and who are best at generating public support for me. (ED22)

The use of techniques like digital vigilantism reveals a double purpose. First, it allows for the groups to enhance their legitimacy by reassuring their members and the public with noble intentions and with a demonstration that their actions are required by the situation. Second, in the case where information is reported to, or demanded by, the police or intelligence agencies, it implies the gravity and seriousness of the problem and therefore contributes to fuelling moral panics. Both are congruent with how activism, including for far-right actors, is shaped in the era of digital technologies (Tufekci 2017).

Some groups in the anti-state militias and the ultra-right choose to underline the severity of the situation by suggesting that more aggressive methods should be employed or allowed by the law. Violence and potential violence become part of a discourse where the preservation of society (as they imagine it) is blended with the non-institutional repression of criminal behaviour. The general theme is that the situation generates a need for them to "protect themselves." Actual activities include learning and teaching close combat fighting techniques and martial arts (Krav Maga, Systema, etc.) or organizing paintball weekends and firearm training. The legal status of some of these activities is unclear at best. In framing the problem as an emergency or by adopting a fatalist discourse about the future, many of our respondents appeared to feel deep anxiety, both about general impending doom and about specific threats to their person:

> And ... that is the central point here: we're going to lose everything we have. Okay. And it's going to be dangerous. So that's it. We want to avoid ... we warn people. That's all we do, we're not doing anything wrong ... We'll have been there for everyone, we will have made our way, we will have informed people, we will have warned people that they should be getting ready. This is not funny. Some have gone out and got themselves a rifle, and it's not for hunting. Yes, they're taking their hunting permit. But it's not for hunting. It's to defend themselves. That's where we're at today. (ED29)

While members generally justify their training with the necessity to be prepared to defend and protect themselves and their family, some groups organize forces (armed or not) and promote them publicly on social networks through accounts and photographs of the event, usually exhibiting a panoply of weapons and field survival tools, military-style fatigues, and warrior stances (often wearing face masks to hide their identity). The array of extreme self-defence strategies, equipment, training, and weapons is a manifestation, an enactment of the severity of the situation, of the need for decisive action, and of the group's pertinent expertise and readiness. This is only enhanced when some of the participants can be identified as current or former members of the military.

Though much of the semi-militaristic combat preparation (with highly variable degrees of actual competence) mostly takes place in closed forums with little exposure to a wider public, hints at the necessity of "protection" are constantly being used in more open contexts and/or by groups with a "sanitized" public face. One classic example is the designation of individuals or groups as "event security" during public rallies or conferences, ostensibly to protect against interference from leftist militants or "antifa" (whether or not they are actually present). Until their official designation as terrorists, Three Percenters' militias often took that role. In addition to the reiteration of the constant danger, such collaborative exercises also serve to show common cause between separate groups and a desire to federate (or at least to appear to).

The wolves guarding the gate: La Meute and "illegal" immigration

How the wolves of La Meute "guarded" the gates against immigration is a fascinating case study of a group and its members positioning themselves as authorities on a political issue, turning it into a social problem of epic proportions, and claiming the legitimacy to propose solutions.

La Meute's Facebook page claims to act as a discussion forum between sympathizers and organizers, a space dedicated to free debate, transparency, consultation, and interaction around the "problems" of "radical" Islam and "illegal" immigration (the qualifiers are usually stressed for public consumption but quickly dropped in actual exchanges). The overarching narrative is that political authorities and intellectual elites are either corrupted, inept, or both and acting against the interests of the majority by encouraging unfettered Muslim immigration.

A limited clique of organizers and managers holds the reins relatively tightly and, despite appeals to democracy and openness, tends to make unilateral decisions. The official "manifesto" of the group was written by one of its leaders. Yet one crucially important aspect of the platform is that the digital enclosure is almost entirely constructed with the free labour of members who provide content. Page content or group publications are almost entirely generated by ordinary members, vastly increasing the quantity (less so the quality) of interactions. Our discussion below is based on 232 user-populated threads collected between October 2015 and September 2016, and then from 30 January to 5 February 2017, following the Quebec City mosque attack. All are from La Meute's private Facebook page. The posts were analyzed and sorted into five categories: *description* (internal organization of the group, its rules); *discontent* (individuals reacting negatively to news about immigration, Muslims, or Islam); *commitment* (posts about engagement, keeping the fight against immigration and Islam as well as keeping the movement alive); *images* (pictures or symbols affiliated to the group); and finally; *profiles* (information about activists).

Watching the gate

La Meute was born on Facebook in October 2015, the brainchild of two former members of the Canadian Armed Forces. As documented in the US context, far-right groups created by former military personnel are not exceptions (Belew 2018). As put by one of its founders:

> La Meute's purpose is to gather those who worry about the Islamic invader who sneakily travels our land and quietly gravitates to the political sphere. It is imperative that our generation rise before our children and grandchildren become victims of our inaction against Islam for centuries and centuries ... amen. (CAP_001)

Concretely, the group aims to "eventually become important enough to exercise political weight in promoting the views of those who disagree with the present politics of the federal and provincial governments [with regard to immigration]." Firmly ensconced in the "nostalgic racist" category, it presents itself as a protector of the "nation against the Islamic invasion" (Rémillard 2015). As of January 2016, just a few months after its creation, its private page boasted 20,000 followers. The number reached 50,000 one year later. At the writing of this book, followers hover just below 28,000 (the group also has a public page with 15,000 followers). Of course, these numbers do not represent active contributors and contain many lurkers and observers (journalists, members of law enforcement, scholars). Only a small portion of members – about a hundred individuals – are active on a regular basis (Marcil and Rousseau 2018).

La Meute occasionally takes to the streets, but its protest activities and practices mostly occur online and specifically on Facebook. It provides a space for convergence, recruitment, meetings, and interaction where ideas and actions are being discussed and sometimes launched. To a great extent, La Meute's use of Facebook illustrates the de-intermediation enabled by digital activism. Its activists are engaged in participatory activities that consist in monitoring, or surveilling, the Muslim population (individuals, groups, organizations, mosques, etc., in Canada or abroad), to then raise general awareness of the threat of "Islamization." In members' eyes, their actions are needed to compensate for the inadequate handling of immigration by the authorities, who are usually perceived as corrupt, inept, or ineffective:

> For too long people have complained of the population's inertia. For too long, our society [has not done] anything when confronted with unacceptable decisions, or situations, such as corruption of our elected representatives. Today, LM represents a cry from the heart of a population that is fed up with [this situation]. It is enough. It is time for people to stand up. (CAP_112.2)

The group is a popular movement of autonomous citizens engaged in what they perceive as self-protection: "We want to protect our lands, our values, our founding principles, our liberty, our security, and the future of our children against the Islamic invader" (Rémillard 2015). Although La Meute carefully avoids physical violence, its constant, unrelentingly hostile discourse towards the Muslim community undoubtedly constitutes symbolic violence. Muslims are suspicious, devious, have hidden agendas and powers, threaten the general order of society as well as its basic values, etc. They are Cohen's (1977) typical "folk devils" and, at the very least, they should be excluded from the full rights and privileges of citizens. In consequence, members see the function of the group as a form of gatekeeping, to defend values, culture, and political ideas:

> Sharia is not compatible with modern society and will have to be stopped before it takes roots and destroys the founding principles of our nation. Let us take Europe as a crystal ball. Let us enjoy this chance that they did not have. The world is changing ... This does not necessarily mean that it is progressing. It is up to us if we do not want to see our world collapse. (CAP_112.2)

Of course, exchanges must keep within the boundaries of the applicable legal framework and the private terms of service rules; despite being private, the group is under intensive surveillance. Like most groups who operate at the fringe of legality, members and administrators must navigate potentially conflicting objectives. On the one hand, they need to be visible in order to attract the largest number of members and followers and, as a result, to generate media attention. On the other hand, they then must manage an ever-growing base of contributors which, inevitably, will include more extreme individuals who do not mind, or who do not realize, that they are crossing the threshold of social, political, or legal acceptability. Failure to do so creates multiple risks for the organization, from being "de-platformed" to having to respond to law enforcement and other authorities. Not to mention public opprobrium and sociopolitical death.

To avoid excesses, participants on the Facebook page are constantly notified that it may be under surveillance by journalists, members of law enforcement, or researchers. Administrators also warn against posting outright, explicit accusations or attacks, or in fact any language that would make La Meute look like a far-right extremist group. The far-right label is associated with infamy by such groups, conveying an image of extremists and radicals from which they are trying to escape. When required by the situation, the moderators intervene to preserve balance or exclude offending contributors from the page. In practice, however, despite the constant reminders to follow the rules and the direct interventions, loss of control is quite frequent. The reality is that, while explicit calls to violence are banned, the constant scorn against Muslims, the calls for their exclusion, and the general climate of hostility mean that conversations often become overly excited, as contributors get caught in a dynamic of "one-upmanship" that easily leads to excessive language.

Framing the "Islamic" threat

Getting followers and influence are the twin holy grails of digital platform users. This comes at the cost of maximal visibility and constant, prolific content production (Van Dijck 2018; Gerbaudo 2019). This activity not only contributes to the indexation and ranking of the site (through the algorithmic recommendation dynamic) but also builds loyalty among subscribers who feel they can get their information from a trusted source and that any absence from the page amounts to their "missing out" on important developments. This of course applies to any group that attempts to maintain a Facebook page. Administrators and organizers have to keep their followers "captive," and one strategy commonly used is to keep those followers entertained and to pique their curiosity in order to make them contribute to the page. The most effective way to reach that end is to constantly raise new topics depicting Islam and Muslim citizens.

One way to do so is to bring up themes that are proven crowd pleasers, especially in the form of "quizzes" that encourage engagement. They are meant to "combine business with pleasure and educate yourself while having fun" (CAP_174). Quizzes also reward those taking part by giving them the impression of participating in both the construction of the group (where they become La Meute) and the realization of its objectives. Finally, this process also strengthens the links between individuals who otherwise might never have connected. These relationships then encourage further engagement and participation.

One quiz asked, "Name one of the four types of Islamic veil." Followers then posted their answers in comment form and others responded, rather like a team playing a board game. Another question was, "Name one rule of the Sharia that is not compatible with our society. Three [La Meute] stickers are to be won in the draw" (CAP_054.5). Unsurprisingly, many – if not most – of the answers betray a lack of basic knowledge about Islam. They also convey degrading stereotypes, even fears, reflective of how commenters visualize, or frame, the community. A few representative examples of responses to the question include:

> In the Muslim faith, according to the Sharia, a man can marry a one-year-old child, and have a complete sexual relation with her when she turns 9. (CAP_054.6)

> The right to rape a woman if she commits adultery. (CAP_054.6)

> According to the Sharia, husbands can beat their wives as they please. (CAP_054.6)

> They have a right to tax those who are not believers so that they can stay in a land governed by Sharia. (CAP_054.7)

> Killing! … Murder seems to be entirely part of their way of life. (CAP_054.12)

As mentioned, such quizzes not only help shape a degrading image of Muslims, they also mobilize a "highly dispersed and individualised constituency" (Garbaudo 2012, 5) who can now connect and exchange their ideas in a specific place, regardless of its digital or physical nature. This collective process is a powerful way to frame Islam and Muslims, as well as the function of the group.

Quizzes sometimes succeed beyond expectations and launch lengthy exchanges. And though a distinction was initially made between Islam and radical Islam by the page administrators (with the first considered non-problematic, as long as Muslims integrate into Quebec or Canadian society), the difference between Islam and radical Islam vanishes quickly, as the following excerpt illustrates:

> As you may recognize, I am far from believing that Islam is a religion of peace. When we listen to talk from Salafists, or Wahhabis, who are often the most vocal, Islam claims to hate not only non-Muslims but also those who are not Muslim enough. That Islam, which seems the most radical at first sight, is still Islam. Do not become anesthetised by those who talk about Islam, because there is no such thing as a moderate or radical Islam … there is only Islam. And in that Islam, there are those who finance, make war, attack, think, disturb, and wait for the right moment. (CAP_174)

Other representations of Islam are imbued with conspiracism, as in the following example, which describes a grand organization believed to be directing Islam as a whole:

> Islam has very well-organized lobbies, it has a herd of attorneys and Saudi sponsors who pay in petro dollars. We are talking about fighting a multimillionaire politico-religious ideology. (CAP_025.2)

Claims that Saudi Arabia is behind nefarious Islamic strategies are frequent. Its government is seen as a sponsor of radical Islam, in a global plot to rule the world:

> Thanks to each halal item sold throughout the whole world, terrorism is subsidised by billions of dollars. Halal is a market that reaches almost 650 billion dollars per year. All that money serves Saudi billionaires, Sharia, and terrorism. Halal is the money side of Sharia. (CAP_091; CAP_094)

The string of comments launched by the quizzes enables all sorts of depictions of Islam, which the administrators then edit, add to, or erase. Most of the time the most controversial are left in place, provided they do not explicitly violate the rules. Controversy electrifies the atmosphere of the thread and mobilizes massive interaction. The more reaction, in the form of cheers and laughs translated by icons, the more the administrators are likely to ignore the potential rule breaking (e.g., borderline hate speech).

As put by Gérald Bronner (2013), we live in a universe where the "massification" of information, as well as the multiplication of its vectors, such as digital platforms, easily overwhelm the capacity of individuals to find meaning. This has generated a new division of knowledge and the rise of a knowledge specialist status. In times of pandemic, epidemiologists became the new priests for those worried about the COVID-19 virus. In other words, we *rely on others* to pre-digest the information and knowledge we need to understand our environment and act within it. To encapsulate this phenomenon, Bronner coined the notion of "democracy of the gullible," in the sense that we easily choose to trust those who claim to have the expertise we seek. Unfortunately, Bronner also notes that the massification of information is correlated with an increased risk of confirmation bias: the more information is available, the less it is manageable as a whole and the more we are likely to cherry pick whatever matches our preconceived ideas and our preferences. La Meute's Facebook page is illustrative of this paradox. It attracts citizens who clearly are preoccupied by vastly complex issues such as immigration, identity, security, and who have chosen to turn to "alternative" sources in order to get the clearer, simpler answers that are not available in traditional media. This makes La Meute's framing of the issue more powerful.

Leading the grassroots

The constant framing of Canadian authorities as inept, if not deliberately ill-intentioned, enables the La Meute collective network to frame itself as the legitimate guardian of democracy and freedom, as well as an embodiment of moral integrity, public order, and popular sentiment. This is the image it attempts to convey in the media and in its well-ordered, police-friendly street demonstrations. Its organizers always make sure to underline the high number of members on the Facebook page, often adding the (then) 50,000 of the private page to the 40,000 of the public one, despite the fact that there is obvious overlap between these groups of subscribers and that they are, in the vast majority, inactive. The message, always, is that La Meute is "the people" and that the media and politicians should take note. In fact, many commenters express their enthusiasm at being part of a large group whose members share their view on Islam and have a collective sense of purpose and a powerful way to account for modern social and political problems. They are no longer individuals who would otherwise feel confused, lonely, or isolated within society and who do not trust any of the traditional political parties or authorities.

> I am proud to be part of La Meute because I share its values, its objectives, and the means to fulfill them. With La Meute, I learn about what is going on at home or elsewhere. I share opinions; I sometimes react to what is going on elsewhere and here. More than this, I share with people who have the same preoccupations I do: to protect, to defend, my people. Also, I bond with amazing wolves. (CAP_067.3)

Some express a level of commitment that goes beyond signing up on the Facebook page or expressing their sense of belonging by getting a tattoo of a wolf's paw, the group's symbol (one member even added her children's names to the logo, displaying, for the whole group to see, the high position of the group in her hierarchy of priorities).

While most of the group's activities happen online, some of its members call for more direct gatekeeping enforcement actions, some of which are insidious. One woman complains about the supposed construction of a mosque in her neighbourhood, which she says happened behind the proverbial closed doors and without any public consultation. She then asks for advice on the Facebook page, though she remains vague about what type of advice she is seeking. Members then chime in with various comments and suggestions, which quickly escalate to ridiculous extremes, where one person recommends pouring pig's blood and putting a pig's head on the plot, arguing that this would then make the site "impure" for Muslims. These comments have a special resonance in the province of Quebec, because the Quebec mosque that was attacked in January 2017 by a far-right activist, killing six people, had previously been the target of a similar act in which someone put a pig's head on its doorstep. Needless to say, mosque goers were more worried about the intimidation and implied threat to their security than by the "impurity."

Clearly, La Meute's Facebook page contributes to setting "the scene and construct[ing] ... an emotional space within which collective action can unfold" (Gerbaudo 2012, 5) and thus to "reconfigure social spaces, (re)draw boundaries and redistribute meanings" (Amicelle, Aradau, and Jeandesboz 2015, 228). This phenomenon is strongly linked to the affordances of Facebook – and their appropriation by page administrators and activists – in particular the necessity to constantly generate interactions, comments, likes, and shares in order to build images, meanings, and "Molotov posts," channelling users into a reading of their environment that is not so much grounded on rationality and trusted knowledge as it is on emotion, prejudice, and beliefs. Clearly, that has been extremely successful at generating constant interaction, a quick, spectacular increase in the number of its members and intense, constant media attention (in Quebec).

Impending multicultural doom

The immigration of Muslims to Canada generates a doomsday scenario where "multiculturalism," envisioned as a political, social, and economic system, is deliberately devised to reduce or even neutralize the power of the "white working silent majority." That topic is also periodically revived through quizzes. Usually the underlying, horrifying "truth" is that non-white/European immigrants are deliberately invited to Canada and given multiple forms of privileged treatment once they get there. One corollary of that claim is that, either simply by having no access to these privileges or through specifically designed oppressive action, governments are depriving the white/Euro majority of their culture, history, religion, and values. Many comment threads start with expressions of fear and insecurity about immigration, followed by a buildup of increasingly angry or panicked responses, to the point where some fear the disappearance of their community:

> Be sure that we are not against different ethnic groups or cultures, but we have to understand that if we stick to the Canadian law on multiculturalism, as conceived by the Liberal government of Pierre Elliot [*sic*] Trudeau ... the multiculturalism may lead to the idea that the common identity of a society is defined exclusively by "political principles" rather than in relation to a culture, an ethnicity, or a history. It is essential, if we do not want to disappear, to put the dominant root culture, values, founding principles, and our history in the forefront while respecting cultural differences, as long as these differences respect the dominant culture and foster the building of a common identity. (CAP_174)

Some members express their concerns and reveal how deeply the presence of Islam affects their identity and grounding principles, while also revealing that they confuse Islam, Muslims, and Islamism. For many, the simple presence of Islam constitutes a threat to the future of the "nation" and the next generations.

Conclusion

As demonstrated by Marwick and Lewis (2017), social and participatory media enable those with marginal views to find each other, to cooperate on media production and knowledge dissemination, and to share viewpoints that it would be intolerable to air outside of the group's bubble. As we have seen, many far-right groups have colonized multiple popular communication platforms in order not only to recruit, organize, and collect funds but also to frame, justify, and popularize their particular construction of social problems (Tanner and Campana 2020a; Tanner, Crosset, and Campana 2020b).

In order to reach their members, prospective adherents, and, eventually, the public at large, far-right entities use especially adapted communications strategies in presenting both themselves and their issue. Sometimes effective approaches are discovered organically, through a series of trials and errors. At other times, actions undertaken by others and deemed successful are simply imitated or adapted. Always, the most important measure of success is the ability to reach the large number of "fence-sitters" who are thought to be more receptive to a particular message or propaganda:

> There's a lot of people in the middle who are not anti-immigrant, but they sense maybe there's something wrong with what [Canadian society is] doing, and somehow we're bringing in too many people or many of them are not integrating well in the Canadian society. But they don't know *exactly* what the problems are, how to connect them. And that was the group we were largely appealing to. People concerned about immigration but didn't know the issues well, didn't know how to put the case and so on. (ED15)

The main strategy is to tap into the vague feelings of insecurity or uncertainty that are a feature of late-modern societies and focus them onto a selected target, while acquiring authority on its definition and, ultimately, on the definitive, clear-cut response to the identified problem.

Efficacious frame amplification strategies build on existing opinions instead of attempting to induce a radical switch in interpretative orientations. Radical transformation of dominant ideologies would be next to impossible, but they are not needed. Large numbers can be seduced by a strategy that combines comforting the audience in some of their beliefs while channelling dissonances towards selected targets. They simply need to be shown how their beliefs, values, or emotional states are congruent with the particular set of definitions offered within the movement's framework (Benford 2016).

Groups then use social media and in-person actions in order to clarify, expand, maintain, and invigorate their interpretative framework, in an offer to align personal interests and support for the social movement (Snow et al. 1986). The massive amount of propaganda available to all in the far-right infosphere basically means that one could never consume anything else and still be continuously fed "new" material. Multiple variations of the main themes maximize the chance of alignment with personal preoccupations and emotions. Less extreme frameworks appeal to a broader audience and aim to channel and amplify various anxieties and insecurities and transform them into preoccupations about immigration, Muslims, Jews, elites, politicians, the mainstream media, etc. Once a sense of urgency, or gravity, is instilled, a call to action, through further participation or in the quest for more radical, extreme frameworks, is felt by many visitors, who will then involve themselves more deeply into the movement.

We have referred heavily to social media and information technologies in general, as vectors of communications strategies adopted by the far right. Indeed, they are key to the success of contemporary moral entrepreneurs at large, and the far right, when it adopts that posture, is no exception. But so far we have not touched on the question of how these vectors function and the nature of their impact on the multiple ongoing messaging strategies undertaken by groups and individuals. That is the subject of the next chapter.

4 BUILDING THE FAR-RIGHT INFOSPHERE

Introduction

The previous chapter showed that the repertoires of action of many far-right movements are centred on the dissemination of their understanding of various issues, trends, and events. In so doing they build their own legitimacy and appearance as significant experts in the identification and solution of what they consider problems. Some of the tactics employed come from the traditional "physical" sphere: demonstrations, the posting of signs and banners, or the distribution of flyers calling for the return of immigrants to their countries of origin (#remigration), for example. Others reside in the "virtual" realm and involve propagandizing through misinformation and the reframing of issues. This distinction between the "physical" and the "virtual" should not be taken too literally, as it does not reflect the reality of contemporary activism where hybrid forms dominate. Virtual or informational elements are best thought of as components of various tactics, present in nearly all forms of political activism and especially far-right activism. One example of this is the 15 March 2019 attack that took place in Christchurch, New Zealand, whereby a young white supremacist live-streamed himself on Facebook while killing fifty-one people and injuring forty-nine others.

This reliance on social media is by no means unique to the far right. A recent survey conducted by the Pew Research Institute (2019) shows that 73 per cent of the US population visit YouTube daily, followed by Facebook (69 per cent). These proportions are higher for younger people, as more than 90 per cent of those between the ages of eighteen and twenty-nine and 87 per cent of those aged thirty to forty-nine indicate using YouTube daily (79 per cent of both groups say they use Facebook daily). It is also worth noting that 74 per cent of Facebook users and 51 per cent of YouTube users say they visit the platform at least once a day, with 50 per cent visiting several times daily. Those numbers of course only represent a fraction of the popularity of social media platforms, where new applications constantly appear and quickly gain users.

The present chapter expands on the informatics of far-right activism. The quantity of available research on the use of social media by activists has grown exponentially over the last few years, and we will start with an overview of that literature. Curiously, while topics such as the role of social media in the recruitment, visibility, and diffusion of activist discourse or group coordination have been widely addressed, its actual impact on users, on their discourse (production and diffusion) and activism, and on the structure of the far right as a whole has largely been neglected. The reason is that for the most part the role of social media has been conceptualized as that of a neutral tool used by top-level, free-willed agents to ensnarl unwitting, techno-determined subjects.

It is now common knowledge that digital tools, and in particular social media platforms, have blurred the boundaries between producers, users, activists, politicians, ideas, and actions in contemporary culture. This is, quite simply, their main feature and defining characteristic: they are participatory. Of course, they can also be manipulated to some extent. In politics some of the most spectacular illustrations include the impact of social media platforms in the 2016 US presidential elections and the 2016 Brexit campaign (though the real impact on voters remains to be confirmed; Bail et al. 2020; Howard 2020). The January 2021 assault on the Capitol in Washington, DC, also showed that social media can play a role in the coordination and mobilization of a mob. In contributing to and fostering the spread of words calling for action against "the steal," social media was a factor in the normalization of the assault (e.g., its reframing as a political demonstration) and its violence.

It should be noted that recent content surveillance by the main social media corporations has introduced an important distinction between the services and the way they are used by extremists everywhere. Since the broadly used services such as Facebook, Twitter (now X), and YouTube are now likely to ban content and/or users for breaking speech rules, many entities have chosen or have been forced to switch to more tolerant platforms like VKontakte, 8Chan, Gab, Odysee, Truth, Parler, Rumble, MeWe, Voat, Hatreon (now defunct), or BitChute. In so doing, however, they have cut themselves off from mainstream exposure and the ability to reach the aforementioned "fence sitters" whom they seek to recruit. In order to solve this problem, many have elected to maintain sanitized, "vanilla" channels on the traditional, more popular platforms, eager to take advantage of their unequalled visibility. In Canada, anti-immigration groups and identitarian activists and "influencers" are still very active on Facebook and YouTube for instance.

Technologies, including social media, are not neutral and are deeply value-laden in their conception, function, workings, implementation, and practical use (Leman-Langlois 2019; Feenberg 1999). At the same time, actors do have latitude in the way they select and use technologies and are not entirely determined by them. Yet they do not master them fully and systematically, since technologies offer what we might refer to as "resistance." Users must develop strategies to lessen this resistance. They can 1) adopt them in whole or in part, adjusting to their features, failings, shortcomings, and requirements; 2) divert and subvert them towards unintended uses; or 3) resist and sabotage them (be it simply by infecting databases with false information). Also, one needs to account for the affordances that characterize technologies or "contextual relational properties ... which frame, while not determining, the possibilities for agentic action in relation to an object within a networked social environment" (Norocel 2022, 2).

The combination of these strategies leads to vastly diverse and complex, idiosyncratic (re-)configurations. That is why social media should be approached through the various ways in which they are appropriated by far-right activists rather than through their official description, their visible characteristics, or the way "the rest of us" use them. In our opinion the resulting complex and particularly dynamic interplay of users, contents, and technologies is best viewed as a system. Thus, in the section below, devices and platforms will be, perhaps provocatively, considered on an equal basis with actors, events, and ideas in the far-right activist ecosystem. More specifically, we will use the notion of actants, as developed by Bruno Latour (2005), when referring to elements of that political space understood as a network or collective of socially productive interactions, leading to composition effects generated by the interactions of the different elements and human and non-human actants of the activist ecosystem.

This will be illustrated in the third section when we focus on how a particular activist, Lauren Southern, has made practical use of a digital platform. We offer a vastly different view from most studies to date, avoiding their instrumental view of technology or their focus on the unidirectional influence of platforms on users. This is the case, for instance, in most of the "online radicalization" literature. This perspective is reductionist since, once again, it examines neither technology per se nor the ways in which individual practice transforms it. In contrast and following more recent and promising hypotheses (Munger and Philipps 2022), we will instead explore a "supply and demand" hypothesis. This suggests that we consider platforms as "brokers" that offer opportunities for individuals and content to "meet" and to give shape to symbolic communities gathered around anti-immigration or other identitarian frames.

The Canadian far-right activist media ecosystem

The Canadian far-right activist "virtual" ecosystem is complex, rapidly evolving, and similar on many points to the situation in the United States (Hawley 2017; Marranz 2019; Perry, Gruenenwald and Scrivens 2021), ranging from merely conservative "backdrop" sources to increasingly extreme channels. Those aimed at the public, presenting a genuinely moderate discourse or a deliberately sanitized or "mainstreamed" version of marginal worldviews, play the role of both gateways and vectors between the conservative and the diverse supremacist, nativist, neo-Nazi, and countless other flavours of far-right content. Multiple channels originating in the USA and Britain are highly popular in Canada as well, among both English- and

French-speaking audiences. Francophones also turn to French, Swiss, and Belgian far-right resources.

Digital platforms and far-right activism

Contemporary digital platforms vary in complexity and size but in all cases still rest on the twin paradigms of user participation and infinite interconnection. Initially gathered under the "Web 2.0" moniker, it was observed that with blogs, and later social media, the passive "1.0" user-browsers had morphed into user-producers and cooperators with regards to content generation. The engine of this transformation was of course extreme ease of use. However, this ease of use only applies to content generation and, as a trade-off, has made it essentially impossible for users to affect either the form, the quantity, or the contribution processes. This trade-off will be important in our analysis below. Infinite interconnection, for its part, is largely theoretical and users mostly connect to people they already know (school, neighbourhood, workplace, and celebrities). Its main impact has been on the marginal, who are usually separated by geography and find it difficult to congregate traditionally and physically. Far-right adherents, first and foremost, have used the participatory web to connect to one another. In so doing they have also developed new tools and strategies to generate, grow, and maintain both 1) their visibility and legitimacy in the wider community, as well as 2) group cohesion, fundraising, and organization.

For the public at large, digital platforms have made the contemporary "participatory culture" of crowdsourcing and grassroots political involvement possible. One of the consequences of this transformation has been to redefine media autonomy: moral entrepreneurs who might have struggled to draw the attention of traditional media can now mobilize inexpensive communication tools and vectors that are highly reactive, widely distributed, and accessible while difficult to regulate in a reliable manner. The trade-off, of course, is that the multiplication of soapboxes reduces both the forcefulness and the credibility of every single one. Furthermore, it must be noted that the traditional media now routinely recycle information that was first made available on participatory platforms. It also constantly places the platforms themselves at centre stage, quoting users, creating stories out of discussions or conflicts on one forum or another, criticizing specific platforms or the entire industry, etc., each time further increasing their power.

In other words, as an infinite series of semi-autonomous, semi-interlinked "actants," the Internet as a system has generated new tools for activism, leading to a diversification of mobilization and diffusion practices to "raise awareness" (Fielitz and Thurston 2019). It is a particularly powerful conveyor of anti-establishment and anti-government discourses since at the base the Internet has always promised a more democratic, free participation in public discourse, more openness to ordinary people, and to be more immediate and direct as well as more authentic and transparent (Lewis 2017; Gerbaudo 2019). Whether it delivers, of course, is an altogether different matter. In reality, more access also means more self-appointed gatekeepers, more exclusion, more bullying, harassment, etc. It has also encouraged both governments and industrial actors to introduce stricter content rules.

The relationship between fringe groups and the media has become a topic of growing interest in the literature on activism (Gerbaudo 2012; 2019; Foellmer, Lüneborg, and Raetzsch 2018; Fielitz and Thurston 2019; Knupfel et al. 2023). Some have focused on how digital media platforms have contributed to the visibility of such groups, helping the promotion of their causes, ideologies, and objectives (Schulz et al. 2022; Wolfson 2014). Others have adopted the connectivity paradigm mentioned above to look at how these new capacities are understood by their users as instruments of mobilization within social movements (Smith 2021; Bennet, Segerberg, and Walker 2014; Kavada 2015; Van Dijck 2013). Another path of inquiry has focused on measuring the actual impact of the Internet on the mobilization of movements, including far-right groups, for instance when transforming the COVID-19 pandemic into an "infodemic" (Bruns et al. 2021; Caiani, Della Porta, and Wageman 2012) or in relation to climate change (Knupfel et al. 2023). Finally, how media distribute content that provides "validation, momentum and legitimacy," thus helping to shape the preferences of social groups and foster their mobilization, has also been an important topic (Elinas 2018). In a nutshell, digital media platforms are shown as "important organisational agents" in the structuring and programming of social movements (Bennet, Segerberg, and Walker

2014, 233; Gaudette, Scrivens, Davis, and Falk 2021). For instance, in the far-right infosphere social media have helped provide an agenda and thus frame crucial issues such as "immigration and crime, helping legitimize a political space in which radicals can thrive" (Elinas 2018, 1).

Given the ubiquitous nature of digital platforms, it is easy to overestimate their role in collective mobilization and political activism and grant them complete power over captive audiences. This mechanical logic is often present in the media, where recruitment efforts are always taken to mean that persons are effectively being recruited, merely stating points instantly convinces audiences, and organizing protests means that protests will take place. The previous chapter has shown that the reality is vastly different. Digital media platforms must be considered within the context of political opportunities and resources available, as estimated by those who ponder the possibility of using them.

Product of the network: The alt-right, 2008–18

The phenomenon known as the alt-right has triggered renewed research on the far right and specifically on how social media and the digital interplay within such movements. The alt-right might be defined as "an amalgam of conspiracy theorists, techno-libertarians, white nationalists, Men's Rights advocates, trolls, anti-feminists, anti-immigration activists, and bored people" (Marwick and Lewis 2017, 3). Although some of its leading figures became known outside of the nebula, such as Richard Spencer (who coined the term), Mike Enoch, and Nathan Damigo, their popularity has proven to have a limited shelf life (Wendling 2018, Hawley 2017). Yet between 2008 and 2018 its presence and visibility in the public sphere and in political debates were considerable (Philips 2018).

Within the far-right nebula, some call for a distinction between those promoting outright white supremacy, for instance stressing the need for an exclusive white European ethnostate (the alt-*right*), and those proposing a "softer" line including a nationalist state based on citizenship (the alt-*lite*; Marantz 2019). These semantic distinctions never referred to any substantial difference in real life. The objective was to promote age-old identitarian, white-centrist views and policies, but with a contemporary twist, which for the most part consisted in the increased use of social media platforms and, more importantly, the style and aesthetics that they used (memes, trolling, sarcasm, symbols, expressions, keyboard-to-screen acronyms). In enabling this aesthetic, digital tools are consubstantial to these activists and central in their actions.

Those self-identifying with the alt-right had a limited repertoire that consisted mainly in trolling, shaping, and propagating "fake news" and conspiracy theories that reinforced their ideology or in making use of irony and (dark) humour to denigrate ideas, trends, or populations, notably immigrants, "normies" (those considered boring, conventional, mainstream), and feminists as well as conventional conservatives (Nagel 2018). The overall goal was to foster an online "culture war," that would result in a shift in the so-called Overton window, the boundaries of what is considered acceptable public discourse. The rationale was that this would then "red-pill" normies or make them realize that they are wrong to accept society as it is, which would trigger "massive radicalization" (Dovey and Ebner 2017). The number of necessary but uncertain causal steps between the trolling and the fantasized massive radicalization never seemed to be cause for worry.

The tactics employed by alt-right/lite activists include the diffusion of memes, easily "imitated and reiterated around the web" (Nissenbaum and Shifam 2017, 483) and used to capture "lurkers' attention and to win their hearts and minds" (Hawley 2017, 73). The term "Molotov JPEG," coined by Hawley (2017), captures this dynamic perfectly: memes can be used to set fire to public opinion. Effective memes quickly become mere templates, where the elements of an illustration serve as a basis for new messages, sometimes generating thousands of "descendant" memes, easily produced and instantly recognizable. As they shape the web, these groups are also shaped by the web.

Dovey and Ebner (2017) showed how the alt-right and its infosphere reinforce each other by analyzing the infamous 2017 "Unite the Right Rally" in Charlottesville, Virginia, which ended in violence and the death of left-wing activist Heather Heyer. According to them, the "narratives and incentives provided to encourage participation varied widely across different platforms, demonstrating the organisers' attempt to tailor their communications efforts to different target audiences" (Dovey and Ebner 2017, 15) and luring them into embracing their causes. Throughout the recruitment and organization phase, the main strategy was to tone down the rhetoric, sanitize the message, and reduce the use of language typically associated with far-right extremism. Dovey and Ebner also showed that the main target was the so-called "Generation Z" (those born between the mid-1990s and 2000s), among whom 58 per cent had voted for Trump in the 2016 presidential election (Avalos 2017). A few short years later, the alt-right momentum quickly evaporated, in part in the wake of the Charlottesville disaster, in part because it was recycled by the skyrocketing of the QAnon movement starting in 2017. QAnon essentially makes use of the same mechanics, however, and in early 2021 the attack on the Capitol in Washington again illustrated the necessity to account for digital media platforms in civil mobilization (Matthew 2021).

At its core, the alt-right worldview did little but reprise extremely conventional tropes on the far right, mainly that white people are under siege and a "white genocide," a "Great Replacement," or some other imminent disaster threatens their survival. This meant pointing their finger at the usual boogeymen: Black citizens, immigrants at large and Muslims in particular, Jews who pull the strings of global migrations, and of course anyone who doesn't accept the far right's "truths": the "liberal" media, academics, and politicians. Broadly speaking, QAnon is less openly racist but rests on the same fears: immediate dangers caused by immigration and the distant manipulation by nefarious forces, the nature of which varies among subgroups but almost always includes Jews (along with blood-drinking Democrats, aliens from outer space, etc.). For instance, the removal of racist confederate monuments becomes a manifestation of the accelerating destruction of a culture and, ultimately, of those who identify with it. Those immediately involved in the (official) removal or the (less so) destruction of the monuments are the obvious enemy, but their small number makes them unsuitable antagonists. The danger is amplified by imagining that they are part of "a wider conspiracy theory, arguing that 'the international Jewish system, the capitalist system and the forces of globalism' seek to erase the European people through mass immigration, hate speech laws and the removal of cultural heritage" (Dovey and Ebner 2017, 15).

On the Unite the Right Facebook page, the Charlottesville event was framed as a defence of free speech and the First Amendment against "a totalitarian Communist crackdown" (Dovey and Ebner 2017,

15), as well as the necessity to preserve Southern heritage. Within the new media ecosystem that promoted the event, the theme provoked a "movement of convergence" for many far-alt-right/lite extremist figures and audiences coming from all types of forums (Discord, Reddit, Gab, the Daily Stormer, the Right Stuff). That also spread to less polarized media sources, such as Rebel Media in Canada, now called Rebel News. The alt-right/lite echo chamber was continuously flooded with such grievances on race, in addition to constant attacks on over-inflated or entirely imaginary enemies like "Antifa," the establishment, normies, and communists, as well as complaints about freedom of speech or the threat to cultural heritage. These strategies "resonate[d] with different sub-movements through the strategic positioning of arguments" (Dovey and Ebner 2017, 17). The Unite the Right event and its capacity to galvanize a movement of convergence is rather exceptional in the everyday dynamics that characterize the alt-right/light nebula, which is usually a fragmented, conflictual space. When the dust finally settled, however, Unite the Right provoked even more fragmentation of the far right, as many tried to distance themselves from the violence (Marantz 2019). It is telling that the following year, the "Unite the Right 2" rally gathered just twenty supporters.

Human-machine activism

Much has been written about the role of social media and other newer communication technologies. Beyond our usual, but logically flawed, tendency to attribute new social trends to new technologies, the interplay between technology, perception, interpretation, intention, and action is a crucial matter for the social sciences. In the next few pages, we outline our approach to the question.

Alternative influence networks

A growing literature on the use of digital platforms and social media by far-right activists suggests they might be qualified as a subcategory of "influencer" (Lewis 2018). Having reanalyzed current general trends in social media use (Weeks, Ardèvol-Abreu, and Gil de Zúñiga 2017), Lewis redefines the alt-right/lite online nebula as an alternative influence network (AIN) and its central human actors as "microcelebrities." Influencers "shape public opinion and advertise goods and services through the 'conscientious calibration' of their online personae. They often develop highly intimate and transparent relationships with their audiences, which they then monetize by inserting advertisements for products and services into their lifestyle content" (Lewis 2018, 4). The sort of influencer active on the far right does not market goods and services, they build audiences and "sell them on far-right ideology" (Lewis 2018, 4). This is why Lewis refers to them as *political* influencers.

These influencers build up their alternative media sphere by using two powerful tools: 1) The utter rejection of traditional information media, including their contents, judged to be biased or incorrect, as well as the traditional standards they use for building credibility and trust. This is replaced by a participatory culture where their audience is called on to repeat, reinforce, and flesh out the message (e.g., by commenting on YouTube videos). Of course, critical, or even lukewarm, comments are not welcomed. 2) The creation of an alternative, oppositional social identity for themselves and for their (participating) audience, just as mainstream influencers who incessantly display and "sell" their persona, activities, apparel, possessions, and lifestyle. Mostly, political influencers offer a prepackaged culture for those who reject progressive values and feel like underdogs in contemporary liberal societies. That culture is grounded on *relatability* (a carefully calibrated image that combines the unique position of the celebrity influencer and his/her closeness to "ordinary" folks, "the people") and *authenticity* (the influencer appears to be utterly transparent or "real," is highly responsive to the audience, speaks at a personal level, and stresses emotions and affects).

The transparency and proximity being cultivated represent a deliberate departure from the distance and neutrality that characterizes traditional media, at least in the case of large industrial, national media. In that, as Lewis argues, alternative influence networks (AINs) "provide a sense of countercultural rebellion" for their audiences (Lewis 2018, 4). Within that sphere, information is consumed less for its factual value than for its power to illustrate, maintain, and propagate a collective social identity (Lewis 2018; McIntyre 2018; Munger and

Phillips 2022). In other words, information is deemed to be *true* if it illustrates a principle, a value, or an ideological preference, whether or not the actors or places involved exist, the events happened, or the reported words were uttered. This is of course the perfect environment for deep fakes and other AI-generated deceptive content to flourish. In line with Paolo Gerbaudo, we argue that political influencers create and maintain a symbolic space that provides a sense of identity, place, and belonging as well as social and cultural support for an audience: "they signify an identity of both social underdogs and a hip counterculture – courting young audiences looking for a community with a level of rebellion" (Lewis 2018, 20).

But AINs also have a "product" to sell. As Lewis puts it, "microcelebrities on social media develop highly intimate relationships with their followers before inserting advertisement and marketing items into their content" (Lewis 2018, 25). They adopt classic marketing and advertising approaches (Webster, 2014) to promote themselves and their ideology. For instance, far-right vloggers and bloggers use their biography (which, like the rest, is unlikely to be fact-checked by their audience) as an example of the personal growth they have experienced, much like run-of-the-mill infomercials. "By creating a 'publicizable personality' and displaying the way they live their politics as an aspirational brand – influencers are better able to appeal to a market of potential viewers" (Lewis 2018, 28), a crucial condition in the intense competition of the attention economy. The format – usually lighthearted, funny, and entertaining – stands in stark contrast with the contents, anti-immigration, nationalist, racist, and sectarian identitarian discourses, but contributes to normalizing, banalizing hateful ideology.

The bio-technical realm

Alternative influence networks cannot exist without communications platforms. Influencers need their information instruments in order to reach their audience. At the time of writing, the most powerful of these instruments were still social media. For that reason, the manner in which activists appropriate these platforms becomes a central factor in the creation and dissemination of political discourse.

Table 4.1 | Classification of theories apprehending technology

Technology is:	Autonomous	Human controlled
Neutral – Means to independent ends	Determinism (e.g. traditional Marxism)	Instrumentalism (human-led social change)
Value-laden – Means that generate a way of life that includes ends	Substantivism (Means and ends linked in systems)	Critical theory (choice of alternative means-ends systems)

Source: Adapted from Feenberg (1999, 9).

That is because social media are not merely tools "for" doing something, they also affect the way things are done and, thus, the goals of activists. For instance, the alt-right's plan to reshape the "Overton window" stems from its use of and close identification to information technologies.

According to Feenberg (1999), the variety of theories characterizing the relationship between humans and machines may be summed up by drawing a double-entry table. The first opposes conceptions of technology as autonomous or human-controlled, while the second contrasts theories that assume that technology is neutral with others that portray it as value-laden. Table 4.1 sums up the resulting four theoretical categories. Note that in all four categories, humans and their devices are assumed as rigorously exclusive categories.

The bulk of current research on far-right and other extremist groups fits in the top right corner, where technology is *under human control* and *value-neutral*. With few exceptions (Gerbaudo 2012; 2019; Tufekci 2017; Wooley 2020; Howard 2020; Norocel 2022), this premise also dominates in analyses of the interplay between digital platforms and far-right or anti-immigration activism. Such technologies are commonly said to be used by those who wield them to "influence," "produce convergence," "spread disinformation," or "radicalize" oblivious audiences (Ribeiro et al. 2019; Tufekci 2018).

It is indeed hard to deny that technologies have a performative effect, at the very least in the sense that they contribute to the gathering or the convergence of disparate individuals into a group or community with similar views regarding immigration, identity, etc. In this sense, as put by Paolo Gerbaudo, "what ... has possibly brought [social media] so much attention is their internal or local use: their use as means of the organisation of collective action and ... as means of mobilisation in the crucial task of gathering people on the streets" (Gerbaudo 2012, 3). In this sense, the author underlines the central role of what he refers to as "soft leaders," such as the political influencers described above, "influential Facebook admins and activist tweeps who become choreographers, involved in setting the scene and constructing an emotional space within which collective actions can unfold" (Gerbaudo 2012, 5).

Political influencers certainly attempt to instrumentalize social media platforms, but can they be impervious to the actions, reactions, opportunities, and requirements of platforms and audiences? We believe that social media should be considered in their materiality, not as solid objects of course but in that they "provide users with the capability to perform some action ... that the software-in-use does things that cannot be reduced to human intention or action" (Leonardi 2010, 3; see also Bourne 2012 and Feenberg 1999). Software, firmware, and hardware influence users as they attempt to influence each other and, in a feedback loop, they are influenced and modified by how they are used. In other words, AINs are the outcome of a composition between social media platforms and the activists that use them and cannot be reduced to any of their elements.

Alternative concepts are thus necessary to grasp these dynamics, and one that seems promising is the Actor-Network Theory (ANT) (Latour 2005; Latour 1994; Law and Hassard 1999). One of ANT's central notions, technical mediation, suggests we should be looking at far-right activism as a program of action, as a series of objectives, decisions, and intentions staging or bringing together digital media platforms, far-right activists, and audiences. The value of conceptualizing activism through the ANT lens rests on the presupposition that none of the elements of the AIN can be considered as having a decisive weight in outcomes. This means, for example, that social media cannot act by themselves in radicalizing audiences. That activists alone cannot be considered responsible for the diffusion of their ideology. That audiences are not passive vessels being filled with hate. If we consider AINs as networks, then their elements, or actants, are not interesting for their nature, essence, or individual characteristics but, rather, for their interactions, since the evolution of the whole depends on the interplay between all its elements (Latour 2005).

Four main concepts are useful to understand technical mediation. The first is translation, "which does not mean a shift from one vocabulary to another ... but the displacement, drift, invention mediation, the creation of a link that did not exist before and that to some degree modifies two elements or agents" (Latour 1994, 32). Note that agents can be human or nonhuman but, since it is uncommon to refer to nonhumans as agents, ANT prefers the term actants for both humans and nonhumans – "a borrowing from semiotics that describes any entity that acts in a plot until the attribution of a figurative or nonfigurative role" (Latour 1994, 33). Human and nonhuman actants exchange properties, characteristics, and competencies, giving one another new possibilities, new goals, new functions (Latour 1994, 35) that need to be accounted for to understand how the technical mediation is unfolding. Understanding the network implies accounting for any obstacle that may arise during the composition process and analyzing how actants negotiate them. Introducing the idea of technical mediation makes it possible to provide a microanalysis of how far-right activists, digital media platforms, and audiences interplay in the production and diffusion of discriminatory and harmful speech.

The second concept is composition, in which action is understood not as the exclusive property of humans (or objects) but rather as belonging to an association of actants. In compositions, "actants are in the process of exchanging competences, offering one another new possibilities, new goals, new functions" (Latour 1994, 35). The final product of this composition is a black boxing "that makes the joint production of actors and artefacts entirely opaque" (Latour 1994, 36). The network has now identified what counts as knowledge and truth and what is rejected as falsehood. To the outside observer, the analytical challenge is to open the black box.

Of course, this translation process is fraught with obstacles and constraints that the actants must overcome in order to align with each other. The assemblage that successfully overcomes obstacles then offers new modes of functioning and capacities. In this perspective, technology and society are co-emergent, they are configurations of power relations that have become fixed, invisible, and logical.

Convergence refers to network outcomes; in our case, the technical mediation shaping far-right AINs that involves activists, social media platforms, and a participatory audience (though activists and their audiences are not exclusive categories). Simply put, all actants are modified by coming together, thus relocating agency between several actants rather than reducing it to one of them, usually human. The activist is not "captured" (Bourne 2012, 156) by the will of a Facebook page or a YouTube channel; yet her intentions are clearly affected by the nature of the chosen platform. As put by Bourne:

> humans are not in complete control – the non-human does more than express the will of the human, it affects it ... Ideas, norms, and values do not exist in isolation from or prior to a material world that they act upon. Ideas are often not strong enough or durable enough to sustain action. Rather, they require materialisation. (2012, 161)

Lauren Southern: YouTube activism as technical mediation

The staging of Lauren Southern, soft leader/political influencer, her YouTube channel, and her audience is representative of the interactive and participatory character of digital media platforms. It shows how "collective images" and "forms of actions ... or scripts" are proposed to the audience, which is invited to perform. "YouTube, even more than television, is a particularly unstable object of study, marked by dynamic change (both in terms of videos and organization), a diversity of content (which moves with a different rhythm to television but likewise flows, and often disappears from, the service), and a similar quotidian frequency, or 'everydayness'" (Burgess and Green 2009, 6).

To understand the technical mediation staging Southern, YouTube, and audiences, we analyze a video available on Southern's YouTube channel. It was recorded by Southern while actively taking part in what will be referred to below as the so-called "Alps Mission." The event, organized by Génération Identitaire, took place in April 2018 in the French Alps. A few hundred people took part, claiming to protect the White Christian identity of the European peoples. A makeshift blockade was erected to prevent migrants – mostly from the African continent – from entering French territory from Italy. The crowd soon unfolded gigantic "CLOSED BORDER" and "NO WAY" banners on a mountain slope, as well as orange security nets symbolizing physical barriers. Militants presenting themselves as the defenders of Europe had come from various European countries as well as the United States and Canada.

We selected a video from among the (at the time) 141 videos Southern uploaded on her channel, for its "raw," unedited character (it was live streamed). It is nevertheless representative of the whole. After extracting and converting the video into an MP4 file, we made a complete transcription of its content, capturing not only the audio but also the setting (such as people around Southern, actions unfolding nearby, interactions she has with individuals off camera, etc.), the live comments, and, finally, how the message is staged.

Dramatis personae

In Latour's "disinterest" phase, communication has yet to take place between actants. Lauren Southern was born in 1995 in Canada and is a central figure in Canadian – and North American – anti-immigration and far-right activism as well as an internet personality and influencer. At the age of twenty, she ran as a candidate for the federal Libertarian Party in a district in British Columbia, getting 0.9 per cent of the vote. Until 2017 she worked as a journalist for Rebel Media, founded in 2015 by Ezra Levant, another important figure of Canadian far-right activism, and a copycat version of the USA's Breitbart. She was active as a YouTube vlogger until the fall of 2018 and is still followed by about 650,000 people. On 14 August 2018, she announced that she was changing course and would stop posting on her channel, moving on to produce "documentaries." After a two-year absence, she started to post videos again, mostly commenting on the news. As of late 2022, she has produced and posted more than 220 videos between two and ninety minutes long, with viewing metrics between 21,000 to 3 million, for a total of almost 60 million views.

Southern presents herself as a journalist, and her videos consist mostly of monologues or interviews with figures expounding far-right, anti-immigration, white supremacist, racist views as well as various conspiracy theories or heavily prejudiced and generally misleading reports on events denouncing the far right or promoting multiculturalism, civil rights, or the LGBTQ+ cause. In the latter case, Southern adopts a provocative or trolling style for trick interviews with activists or militants involved with such causes. In a video posted in 2015, she holds a sign saying "There is no rape culture in the West" at a Slutwalk demonstration in Vancouver. In another, shot during a demonstration by LGBTQ+ activists in March 2016, she argues that there are "only two human genders." In response, LGBTQ+ demonstrators empty a container of urine on her. On two occasions, Southern was banned from entry into the UK and New Zealand, allegedly because of the risk she presents when stirring up ethnic and religious tensions. In May 2017, Southern was involved in Génération Identitaire's attempt to stop the NGO ship *Aquarius* from leaving Sicily to rescue migrants off the coasts of Northern Africa. She and her co-activists were arrested and detained by the Italian Coast Guard. They justified their actions by stating, "If the politicians won't stop the boats, *we'll* stop the boats" (Claxton 2017).

The second entity of interest is YouTube, the primary mission of which, as stated on its site, is to provide a channel through which "everyone can make their voice heard and discover the world." YouTube's mission statement fits with the classic rhetoric emphasizing the Internet's potential for democratization and enthusiasm for the medium's most popular characteristics, namely its "User Generated Content" (UGC) (Gillespie 2010) and the "participatory culture" that is generally held to be central to the "Web 2.0" (Burgess and Green 2018). According to Burgess and Green, YouTube may be thought of as a "patron," enabling – but also constraining – collective creativity by fostering the participation of a large number of actors in the creation and broadcasting of content, while maintaining control of the conditions under which "creative content is produced, ordered, and re-presented for the interpretation of audiences" (2018, 60). The content shared on the platform can thus be thought of as the result of the interplay between the platform's architecture – its affordances – and user tactics (Cardon 2008). It is important to note that YouTube, in addition to providing a sharing platform, also offers – much like networking services such as Facebook, Instagram, or Twitter/X – the possibility for users to build links between themselves, to interact and to communicate directly. The combination of watching and interacting maximizes the time spent on the platform and, consequently, increases revenue for Google as well as for users who monetize their channels.

While YouTube as a platform depends on a business model, in terms of use and legal restrictions (such as rules about content), its existence is also dependent on a large technical network. In other words, the materiality of the platform is produced by a series of interdependent systems. These include the end user devices (phone, computer, etc.), the transport systems of the Internet (including servers, routers, switches, antennas, metal, and optical fibre cables, etc.), as well as the appliances used for conversion, storage, analysis, and editing at the centre of the platform. They also include multiple sets of software, from operating systems to user tools to indexing and advertising bots, some directly visible to users, some whose existence is unsuspected. Not to mention the firmware residing on millions of devices.

YouTube leads us to our third actant, the audience. Years ago, Gross was already underlining that "the top-down tyranny of the media has been effectively challenged" (2009, 67). In the "Web 2.0," the distinction between producers and consumers is reduced and audiences participate in content production: "the practices of audiencehood – quoting, favouriting, commenting, responding, sharing and viewing – all leave traces, and therefore they all have effects on the common culture of YouTube as it evolves" (Burgess and Green 2009, 57). In contrast to the traditional model of broadcasting, the audience participates directly, in part wittingly and in part not, in increasing the popularity of a video, a person, or a channel and, in turn, the attention these generate. Through its Most Viewed, Most Responded, Most Favorited, and Most Discussed metrics, YouTube makes it possible to create a "simplified and atomized model of audience engagement – based on the raw frequencies of views, comments, response videos, and additions to users' favourites" (Burgess and Green 2009, 41).

Interest and the appearance of new goals

There is no information on why Southern chose YouTube as the way to achieve her goals, but it seems reasonable to think that the platform's affordances and popularity played a role in her decision. YouTube provides a valuable way to diffuse ideas since the costs related to both production and diffusion are low, while the potential to reach a wide audience is enormous. While vlogs are not exclusively hosted by YouTube, the platform is widely recognized as a way to encourage social participation and is a crucial tool for those looking for visibility (Burgess and Green 2018, 53).

On the second day of the aforementioned Alps Mission, Southern used the YouTube app on her smartphone to live stream for a little more than sixteen minutes, providing her update on the situation. From the beginning of the livestream, which is of poor quality due to a bad network connection, Southern appears in "selfie mode" and lets the audience know that she is broadcasting live. She is seen outdoors, near the demonstrators, with the mountains in the background. She varies the shots by moving her phone, at times showing some of the other demonstrators or those present to protest the "anti-program" (i.e., anyone attempting to disrupt the Alps Mission or Southern's live streaming, including representatives of the mainstream media as well as the police). Her live broadcast also contains informal conversations with other far-right figures and activists. Among these are US activist Brittany Pettibone and Martin Sellner, a German citizen whom she introduces as the "mastermind" of the Alps Mission. At the time of shooting Pettibone and Sellner were well-known identitarian activists and avid YouTubers themselves. Pettibone (who married Sellner and has since taken his name) still has 139,000 followers and her sites contain 119 videos. Sellner has 127,000 followers for his channel's 602 videos.

Just seconds after Southern launches her livestream, the audience starts reacting via YouTube's "live comments" function. Livestream comments are numerous and appeared very quickly, showing obvious interest in the activists' actions. A few comments are sceptical or even critical of the mission; others include insults against Southern, but the great majority are supportive of the cause in general and the action specifically. Some positive comments include known far-right symbols. For the most part the negative comments refer to the bad quality of the broadcast but tend to blame the device and the network rather than the operator.

The interaction of the main actants produces a new actant, the livestream itself. It is best understood as carrying a new goal, one that is not simply a mirror or a combination of the goals of the other actants. Southern's explicit objective in live streaming the Alps Mission is to prevent the entrance of illegal migrants and call attention to the wider problems they create for society. She chooses to achieve this objective via YouTube livestream and a portable device, with a poor connection in the Alps. She is also faced with unexpected events around her and has to adapt in real time. Meanwhile, as YouTube's algorithms are affected by the presence of political influencers or soft leaders such as Southern, they begin to suggest and promote similar anti-immigration content. This system plays a central role in the management of the platform. Already in 2016 Covington, Adams, and Sargin explained how YouTube uses "deep learning" to feed its recommendation algorithms. The system is grounded on two neuronal networks: the first deals with "candidate generation" and the second with "ranking." The neuronal networks are fed by diversified criteria, such as i) the user's record of use of the Internet; ii) "collaborative filtering," based on the similarity between users ("expressed in terms of coarse features such as IDs of the videos watched, search query tokens and demographics"); and iii) "data impressions" accessed via "a desired objective function using a rich set of features describing the video user" (Covington, Adams, and Sargin 2016, 2). Once these filters have operated, a list of videos, sorted by score, is promoted to the user. However, to make a final determination of the efficiency of the algorithm or model, YouTube uses live experiments: "In a live experiment, we can measure subtle changes in click-through rate, watch time, and many other metrics that measure engagement" (2).

YouTube's algorithms require the presence and participation of an audience that leaves traces of its activity and behaviour online. The audience, by clicking, watching, commenting, and liking Southern's video, coupled with the record of its past Internet activities, contributes to the promotion of the Alps Mission video, as well as other videos with similar content, by the recommendation algorithm. The algorithm engages and both assembles and reassembles a specific audience by overvaluing and favouring some content over others. On Southern's channel, it recommends Breitbart's and Brittany Pettibone/Sellner's channels, among others. That recommendation process is the outcome of an interplay, which is a property of associated entities between the user and YouTube's algorithm. While the user's track record and habits on the Internet modify the code, they allow for the continuous fine-tuning of the recommendations.

Given this, the new actant is born, with its own objectives: the livestream "wants" to be watched and engaged with and reacts in consequence.

Obstacles and passage points

As the livestream continues, even more new actants appear, disappear, and reappear in the frame. The audience is dynamic, changing. As a group, it is active throughout the live broadcast and sometimes draws or requires Southern's attention, and she takes the time to read some of the comments posted by her viewers. The mediation, translation, and composition processes are characterized by friction, resistance, and even opposition between the actants, each of which is potentially capable of putting an end to the livestream. This passage point must be negotiated for the composition to hold. For example, Southern struggles with the bad quality of the stream, which makes it difficult for the audience to follow the message and increases audience discontent, which is expressed numerous times. At times Southern also struggles with the use of her mobile phone, as her hand shakes, possibly revealing anxiety, the cold weather, or both.

The audience is part of the translation process and is an important actant that Southern has to adapt to in the ongoing streaming process. It collectively serves to interpret and make sense of the stream, and Southern adjusts her message in response. In this interaction, the platform's practical characteristics have a direct impact on Southern's program and how she reports on the situation. For instance, she repeatedly moves her phone, positioning it differently in physical space while asking if the image is better. She also reads comments out loud and often responds to them, addressing the audience directly, sometimes apologizing for the bad quality of the sound or image. Despite these efforts, some still complain that her engagement with the audience is insufficient. One user comments, "literally no reason to be live if you're not actually going to talk to chat and just pretend this is a prerecorded YouTube video."

Once all actants have successfully negotiated the constraints, alignment finally takes place (Latour 1994). The resulting collective effort is now capable of providing maximum visibility and cogency to the anti-immigration argument. Southern also counts on Pettibone and Sellner to offer more details about the Alps Mission, particularly about the support they received from the local population, the concrete actions taken to reach the mission's objectives, their experiences of violence from antifascists, and the inaction of the local authorities, including the failure of the police to protect the territory. This ideological and practical "alignment" in effect produces an alternative media frame on the mission, one that serves to contradict the one offered by mainstream media. According to Pettibone, "[we] will paint [the Alps Mission as] something else."

In the end, the Alps Mission livestream strives to fulfill the same functions as Hawley's "Molotov JPEGs" in setting public opinion on fire. The extent to which it might produce convergence in the public or influence democratic processes is beyond the scope of this chapter. Suffice it to say that within a year Southern's video had been watched more than 141,000 times and received 7,700 likes, 404 dislikes, and 1,382 comments. The latter include mere manifestations of presence, critiques, insults, and trolling as well as approval of Southern and Génération Identitaire's position. The video was also massively shared and developed a life of its own, well beyond YouTube, through its circulation across other platforms. In that, it is one among millions of similar compositions.

As Southern delegates the action of "seeing" to her cellphone and YouTube, she introduces one final displacement. According to Latour (2007, 197), this displacement is at once spatial and temporal: spatial, in the sense that the Defend Europe and Alps Mission now includes a new actant – Southern's video – broadcast and archived around the world and temporal as it remains accessible through the passage of time. A series of object-institutions continues to perpetuate the visibility of the mission, although the action itself is over and its protagonists are now involved in other activities. Note that to the visitor in the infosphere, all of these activities, to the extent that they are recorded, now appear to exist in the same seemingly hyperactive timeframe.

Conclusion

In this chapter, we have seen how a network of information co-creators produce and maintain a discourse about the status of the frontier, identity, and illegal immigration, some of the few unifying themes of the far right. We have sought to analyze that online activity from a different point of view in order to avoid the unsolvable conflict between socio- and techno-determinism that continues to plague research on extremism and technology. This is why we have largely avoided the "echo chamber" or "information bubble" tropes when speaking of the far-right infosphere, as those would throw us back into a techno-determinist approach.

In part of the literature reviewed above, Southern's Alps Mission stream is simply a technologically augmented capture of events and political discourse, produced and watched by individual, rational actors who merely make use of one of the most ubiquitous tools of the information society – their phone. In this narrative, actors are in control of technologies and use them to suit their objectives. That is, obviously, also the perspective of those actors themselves. Another portion of the literature takes on the opposite approach and represents individuals as psychologically or socially determined "non-agents" who coincidentally happen to use tech tools – only to be radicalized by them. Platforms and information ecosystems, as information-shaping machines, then directly modify the thoughts and actions of their users. This is the well-worn "internet radicalization" trope, in which unsuspecting subjects are caught in an inexorable, machine-led (de-)socialization.

We have tried to demonstrate that these approaches, including more nuanced variants, are not fully able to account for machine-mediated activism and its impact on the far-right infosphere. Of course, to the human actors involved, as well as to most observers, the above interlinked processes appear seamless and homogeneous, like the proverbial black box. To use a particular range of processes as an example: as technological tools become more transparent, intuitive, and immediate, they consistently appear to users as simpler, more uniform, and unequivocal in their objectives and function. (I use my phone to text; the text is then received and read by another user on their phone; tracing, analytical, archival, identification, etc. processes can be ignored.) Yet in actuality this simplicity is the product of increasingly complex hardware and software, involving countless providers worldwide, as chip speeds, wireless and wired connection power, and the number of network nodes and lines of code skyrocket. The same phenomenon is at work in the human–technology–ideology (information) composition as a whole, where the breadth, depth, and immediacy of interactions entirely obscure the work of the multiple actants involved. The massive number of intricate, globe-spanning links and lightspeed computations feels like simply "being there."

This artificial social, temporal, and spatial proximity favours human exchanges in a way that appears fully natural (give or take a few limitations and glitches – but direct, in-person interaction is not magically free of shortcomings either). This power has been effectively mobilized by far-right groups, individuals, influencers, Facebook page administrators, and other organizations, who have made good use of the power of information technologies and, in particular, of social media. They are quite deliberately, "rationally," building the infosphere they need (while learning to need the one being built) to recruit, grow in power, influence, and profit, build social capital (as influencers, for instance), etc. The mainstreaming of radical views, the widening or shifting of the "Overton window" is, for most actors, a calculated power strategy.

This chapter has offered an insight into the operation of contemporary radical right groups and the repertoire of actions they use. Most of the actors we found here belong to the "radical right" category of our matrix: they tend to eschew explicit violence, in part to avoid clashes with the legal system and in part because they believe that the radical transformation of society and its institutions can be brought about by massive protest or increasing pressure from organizations and movements such as themselves. Much like Lauren Southern, some believe that civil disobedience (for instance, calling on the public for action against immigration and fomenting fear about immigration, organizing peaceful/ordered protests) will destabilize, affect, and weaken the state and result in wide-ranging reform.

If the ultra-right questions the founding principles of democracy, the radical right accepts them for the most part while arguing that democracy is severely corrupted by those who occupy central functions in its most important institutions (governments, journalists, intellectual and media elite). They have wholly adopted digital platforms as the crucial tool in their new repertoire of action in order to raise public awareness and watchfulness and, eventually, call for participation and action in order to counter state inaction. In this sense their message is fully compatible with mainstream platforms and allows them to be weaponized towards the promotion of their oppositional discourse. Its basic blocks are virulent opposition against organizations and laws, as well as against those who are responsible for them, and the denigration of otherness. As a result, of course, citizens' confidence in social and cultural relations and toward their institutions can be shaken.

That does not mean that the ultra-right refrains from using digital platforms to organize, recruit, elaborate, and diffuse their violent propaganda. Simply, they prefer to use more secretive, private platforms in order to do so, with a different set of goals. When they use open-access platforms, it is only to open a very narrow, sanitized window on their discourse and activities. Anti-state militias and xenophobic vigilante groups adapt their practices to their objectives: they usually make use of open-access resources to disseminate their discourse but fall back on restricted-access platforms for everything relating to their internal organization and actions.

In all cases, the platformization of the message, however, is not accomplished without profound transformation. From the very beginning, they cannot reasonably be said to even "choose" freely to use YouTube, Facebook, or whatever their next platform happens to be. The technical distribution of their reference infosphere is, in many ways, a global social construction project, led by a myriad of varied actants, and where much of the work is already done. Further, technical mediation causes transformations and adaptations in the substance of the discourse, in what is shown and not shown, what becomes important and what is dismissed, what is commented and what remains unsaid. If Southern had used another platform (or, as the participant complained, had she simply recorded a report with none of the hurdles of live capture), her objective would still have been part of a process of translation, albeit a different one, with potentially different outcomes (nature of the contents, dissemination, engagement, etc.).

The stream, with countless other compositions, like posts on Facebook, then becomes one of the new building blocks of the infosphere, part of the practically infinite flow of information that serves as an environment for thought to those following the breadcrumbs of the ever-amplified message.

In the next chapter we will explore what happens to those who follow the breadcrumbs all the way to the streets and suburbs of ordinary, physical reality.

5 RECRUITMENT, ENGAGEMENT, DISENGAGEMENT

Introduction

While the previous chapter showed an entire world of influencers and information producers, consumers, and participants, almost always carefully remaining at arm's length from crime and violence, a short exploration of the far-right nebula quickly reveals multiple groups and individuals who are less scrupulous about making use of more extreme means of expression. They are a minority within the far-right minority, but well worth a chapter in this book, where we seek to understand how individuals find and follow one of various paths leading to behaviours harmful to others. Most of these paths involve group participation, via the powerful benefits groups offer to their members, which may present themselves in different ways to different observers and may contribute to "recruiting" them. To sort these out, this chapter focuses on engagement and disengagement factors and processes. In doing so it tackles issues related to recruitment, encouragement, and amplification.

Note that rather than using the contested and overused term "radicalization," we choose to make use of the two concepts of engagement into far-right groups (interaction) and commitment into these groups (actively taking part in illegal activities). In so doing we discuss the diversity of individual trajectories and analyze the role of the main factors of engagement and commitment, such as ideology, peer influence, resentment, fear or anger, the need for protection, longing for a sense of community and personal identity, sensation-seeking translated into a desire for excitement and violence, etc. The nature of the group and its objectives can influence trajectories of engagement. The symbolic and material retributions it offers can also partially determine the degree of investment within the group. These issues can only be understood through the prism of the intrinsic motivations of individuals and a series of contingent events.

Who is in the far right?

We start this chapter with a detailed description of individuals who have taken part in activities motivated by far-right objectives or worldviews. Our approach is not quantitative, as the number of cases we have at our disposal is relatively low. With this data, we also cannot reliably distribute personal biographies within our matrix of categories, which is why we will largely leave that aside for the current chapter. The analysis that follows is based on some fifty interviews and 125 criminal and civil cases. Information from these cases is often partial or not entirely trustworthy, for the usual reasons. Interviews and court transcripts were processed with multiple manual and automated techniques (we mostly used the Nvivo and QDA Miner text analysis packages). In addition, we rely on our direct experience arising from participation in psychosocial and criminological intervention in a violence prevention program in the province of Quebec. Though this program is aimed at all forms of radicalization where violence is a risk, nearly every case treated between its inception in 2017 and the time of writing this chapter (2023) has been related to ideologies, concepts, and goals typical of the far right. Many stem from the initial identification of children, often by their school or by various social service providers. For obvious reasons they are highly confidential and will not be individually described or discussed in order to ensure anonymity.

Types and profiles

Two clichés are common in the literature on radicalization. One is very old and considers that extremists and terrorists are, in one way or another, "not well." Terrorists resort to unusual actions, therefore they must be unusual or abnormal themselves, plagued by some mental condition, the severity of which is assumed to be proportional to the gravity of the terrorist's actions. This observation sometimes comes from trained psychologists and psychiatrists and, in those cases, includes various diagnoses such as paranoia, schizophrenia (e.g., Gottschalk and Gottschalk 2004), and extreme forms of dependency or need for individual validation (e.g., Kruglanski et al. 2014).

As most of these models failed to account for the diversity of many datasets, the purely psychological models have been in steady decline. Multiple studies have in fact concluded that, on the contrary, extremists and terrorists are essentially "normal," meaning that their psychological makeup is indistinguishable from that of the general population. For some writers, that has morphed into an argument that terrorists are fully "rational" actors, continuously weighing the costs and benefits of joining violent groups and partaking in their activities. The rationality theory is well illustrated by Wintrobe (2006) and Pape (2005), the latter arguing that even suicide attacks are strategically calculated acts, both for the organizers and for the bomb deliverers, albeit with a different arithmetic. After all, every definition of "terrorism" is organized around the twin concepts of (political) goals and (violent) means and thus implies rationality through intentionality.

However, in our opinion the "rational extremist" hypothesis, if taken to mean that individuals reach objectively strategic decisions in engaging in acts of violence, grossly overpredicts the number of terrorists and terrorist acts. If it is entirely logical and efficacious to deliver bombs to fulfill political objectives, it would be done far more often than is observable. It would also occur in a predictable frequency, regardless of chronology and geography, and yet the opposite is true. We suggest that a narrower definition of rationality is in order, one that is both subjective and local, instead of objective and universal. Yet, while this fits the data much more closely, it has very low explanatory power and (re-)opens the door to psychosocial, social, and cultural factors.

Carefully reviewing the literature helps resolve some of the contradictions between explanations based on mental health and those based on rational calculation. Though often present, it seems obvious that personal psychological factors can be given too much causal weight. They should not be presented as sufficient to cause terrorism, and context needs to be given more importance, at all levels: from current events in geopolitics to the micro traumas of everyday life such as divorce, death of a loved one, bankruptcy, etc. In a way, violent extremists are inescapably rational: they have aspirations, they analyze their context, and they set themselves immediate, strategic objectives as well as long-term political, group, and personal goals (which may conflict; more on this later). Further, if we accept that the overall prevalence of mental conditions is roughly equivalent for most human populations, we are inevitably drawn to the conclusion that the primary engine behind the observable geographic differences in rates of political violence must come from local political, social, economic, and other factors – some of which are explicitly identified by extremists themselves – as well as others that are structural and un-problematized but no less powerful.

At the opposite end, mental conditions are often used as straw men by "rational actor" theorists, who portray them as debilitating ailments that would render their sufferers useless or dangerous to groups, incapable of conforming to the parameters of a collective project; therefore, successful terrorists cannot be mentally vulnerable. Yet human rationality is, put simply, not opposed or in any way incompatible with most, or even multiple, coexisting psychosocial troubles. These do not extinguish one's ability to pursue goals or plan strategies. In fact, we should all be thankful that political, economic, or scientific goals can be reached even if all actors involved are not models of rational efficiency.

The second cliché is more recent and is found in the mantra that "there is no single type" or even a typology of terrorists: they come from different social, religious, political backgrounds, have highly varied levels and types of education, etc. In short, they are found "all over the map." One of the faulty premises supporting this conclusion is the assumption of categorical homogeneity, when in fact extremism and terrorism are politically designated dustbins in which have been thrown vastly different objects. The same is also true for the "crime" category. In criminology, the original nineteenth-century project of finding the natural, or born, criminal was eventually abandoned when the fundamental differences in the "crimes" became impossible to brush under the scientific carpet. The error now seems obvious, even when focusing on a specific crime: it is pointless to try to identify the unique type of "murderer" who, for example, either kills his children and then himself or members of organized crime groups for money. Put simply, there are many different criminalized acts and many different reasons, causes, or factors involved, and this is also true of extremism and terrorism.

That said, when the wider categories are unpacked, types do tend to appear – though they require a high tolerance for exceptions. Our interviews with members of the far right, as well as what we could gather from our other sources of information, do reveal a level of diversity in personal characteristics. But they also reveal some clustering around "types." This is quite short of a proper, state-of-the-art typology, not least because it is not numerically adequate for statistical analysis, but it still offers extremely valuable pieces of the puzzle.

A human mosaic

A mosaic is made of a number of uneven, uniquely different pieces that, together, form larger patterns and shapes that can be interpreted by observers. In much the same way, the personal characteristics of the members of our sample group are rather diverse, which is consistent with other research on the topic. They also show clear groupings around a few narrow, central, or typical points. One in particular cuts across the near entirety of the sample: the vast majority is male. Here we must introduce a caveat, as we encountered major difficulties in recruiting women in our population: they do exist, we have spoken to them, but all declined to be formally interviewed. Despite this collection bias we feel comfortable claiming that women are in a clear minority. Consistent with this hypothesis, more than 90 per cent of the defendants in the 125 court cases we reviewed were men. The reasons for this will be obvious below, when we look at the factors that influence engagement. Among others, the yearning for power, personal authority, and superiority, the call of violence, and the attractiveness of the warrior ethos continue to be far more likely to be instilled in men than women in Western culture at large (Tomsen and Messerschmidt 2020).

Age at time of involvement

Among the criminal cases, two populations stand out. Those involved in "terrain" activities such as deploying hate banners, getting into fights, desecrating cemeteries, destroying property, and being arrested for excessive alcohol consumption or drug possession are mostly teenagers and young adults, almost exclusively clustered in the sixteen to twenty-four years bracket. This population tends to become less involved in group activities starting in their mid-twenties. The two main reasons offered by our interviewees are those usually given for desistance from crime: finding a reputable form of employment and beginning to raise a family. "It was probably the birth of my daughter ... which started that, that process. Before then, you know when I was twenty, twenty-one, twenty-two ... I would've said, I'd be dead or in jail by the age of thirty. But once I had a daughter, it's a very selfish decision to make" (ED13).

The second group comprises individuals arrested for, or involved in, the dissemination of hate propaganda and various types of threats, harassment, and the like, usually on the Internet, and they tend to be older (in our crime database the oldest defendant is eighty-three; our oldest interviewee is seventy-three). In that group the beginning of hate-related activities is inconsistent and varies from individual to individual. One respondent (ED16) reports having "realized the dangers of Islam" in his late twenties, during the Sharia for Ontario movement of the 2000s. He then started harassing Muslim organizations and individuals, serving time in jail on at least two occasions; he still maintains an Islamophobic YouTube channel. Another (ED11) started with small demonstrations and was then involved, for decades, in the organization of political parties, marches, concerts, cross-burnings, and hate-themed conferences.

Education

Of course, education varies with age and teenagers won't have been to college. That said, most of our young adults involved in violent activities, those who were members of skinhead and other street groups, had quit school early. Most saw it not as an educational setting – they often report having "learned nothing" in school – but rather a site of latent, manifest, or explosive confrontation. School is where their social group is engaged in chronic conflict in terms of educational success (ED10 says he was frustrated with members of other ethnic groups having better grades), perceived lack of respect for dominant culture (ED4 repeatedly deplored the disappearance of pork items on the lunchroom menu; ED2 is exasperated by what he sees as the privileges given other ethnic groups), or physical dominance of the premises. It is also a site where individual bullying takes place, and some of our respondents originally claimed to have joined violent peer groups for protection (ED10). One of our propagandist respondents explained that he played along in the educational system in order to obtain diplomas, but he had to educate himself independently since his teachers and the take on various subject matters was too far to the left (ED7). He now imagines himself educating others online.

Politics, religion, and ideology

The biographical stage at which individual respondents acquired viewpoints associated with the far right, how they developed them, and how they acted upon them varies in the extreme. In many cases, respondents were incapable of sorting out events, processes, or interactions, mainly because of the incrementality of their personal evolution. A few spoke of encounters that set off a series of events, but profound, cascading, or instantaneous transformations never happened. That is why we list politics and ideology along with other more mundane aspects of life. Of course, they are at the very centre of our investigation into the far right, but in functional reality they constitute components that only become explosive when combined in particular ways.

The key question is whether those involved in far-right groups and/or activities were drawn in that direction because they felt an ideological affinity or if they joined first and were socialized later by the group. Unfortunately, there is no single answer: though many youths did join groups (via peers or family or independently) after becoming interested in politics, some joined for the partying, the drinking, and the music: "forget politics there was nothing, it was anarchy, getting high and drinking." "White laces, red laces appeared. We had

Totenkopf tattooed or, SS bolts, you could even have a swastika tattooed, it didn't mean you were fascist or Nazi or anything. We were outlaws" (ED10). One of our propagandist respondents explained that he did not necessarily believe everything he published, but that mattered little if the publications were effective at raising money from the more gullible (ED22).

As can be expected, a rather clear distinction is visible between the propagandists and the violent in terms of the complexity of logic. Most of the skinhead and other "street" group members have great difficulty in sorting out the details of their claimed political position. For the most part their discourse amounts to a series of itemized factoids aimed at focusing hate on visible minorities. By comparison, the theorists of course are more likely to have read many (sometimes countless) texts from history, sociology, religion, and, of course, conspiracy literature, including online literature. The resulting ideological concoction varies but is usually built around cherry-picked facts, fictitious events, esoteric theories, and outlandish hypotheses strung together to form far-reaching conspiracy theories involving Illuminati, Jews, the Rothschilds, secret laws, coded passages in national constitutions, hidden history, the new world order, George Soros, environmentalist David Suzuki, and, of course, the "liberal-biased" media. Many saw a concrete manifestation of their elaborate narratives in the COVID-19 epidemic and especially in the responses of governments. The main blocks of the mythology are all present: a global menace, invisible and of nebulous origin; an equally global official response, led by suspicious international bodies such as the WHO and the UN; a popular panic leading to some shortages; a drastic increase in police surveillance powers.

Family and peers

The post-9/11 wave of network analysis applied to terrorist groups (most famously illustrated by Krebs 2002 and Sageman 2004) has shown at least one thing: the foremost determinant for joining a clandestine or marginal group is having a friend or family member who is already involved. The power of this is probably due to two separate aspects: first, friends and peers can relate to a set of common perceptions about the world, both in the way they make sense of it through a particular language ("ethnomethod") and through shared experiences; second, the key element of dark networks – trust – is already in place.

The connection operates in three main ways. The first one is when the peer or family member is actively inviting or "recruiting" into his or her group. In this case it is deliberate and calculated to increase group size or capability. Recruiting may also be incidental or casual, for instance, when the individual is invited to take part in a "secondary" type of activity, typically a concert or a party, where he will come into contact with the group and begin to be introduced to its ideology and, eventually, to its illegal activities. One recruiter told us, "[I] just sorta went through the crowd, voiced my opinion everywhere I went and ... most times it worked out for me and sometimes it didn't" (ED28). The third one is when the individual seeks out like-minded peers after having heard of their activities or propaganda; needless to say, that search is greatly facilitated when a family member or a friend is part of such a group. Parents, of course, play an important role at this level, and a few of our cases reported or were reported to have been brought up by openly racist parents. Though we have no control group of individuals who are the product of racist families, and thus cannot make precise predictions, upbringing has been shown to be a powerful predictor of racist attitudes elsewhere (Maxwell and Schulte 2018).

One strikingly common characteristic in our "street" population was a heavily dysfunctional family unit. This is also depressingly prevalent in the youths referred to the violence prevention program. For the most part our "terrain" extremists have known absent parents, family conflicts routinely escalating to open violence, threats, demeaning language, constant humiliation, and contempt. Individuals in that situation are likely to build far stronger emotional ties with their peer group. Our "prevention" sample is also heavily afflicted with poverty, as well as local social polarization and conflict. The balance of the sample falls into two types. One had an essentially "normal" family and broke with it for various reasons including the usual identity crisis or generational conflict or under peer pressure. The other happened to fit rather well in their family unit, where a racist or xenophobic discourse prevailed.

A sizable number of our respondents, as well as many offenders, are in fact autonomous actors, the now proverbial "lone wolves."[1] They research and/or develop extreme political views and act alone. That is the case of a few who were convicted of disseminating hate propaganda on the Internet, for instance. Though gathering and interacting with followers may galvanize and encourage, the propagandist lone wolf is self-motivated and needs no help to engage in extreme political activity. Some even fancy themselves as leaders of entire movements, when in fact the structure they describe or allude to is vaporous at best (ED20, ED33; the latter is also convinced he is channelling Adolf Hitler). Violent lone wolves are of course rarer but do exist: 2017 mosque shooter Alexandre Bissonnette acted alone, using the internet to do his "research" and to build up his worldview but without significant live interaction with anyone else on- or offline and no accomplices before, during, or after the massacre.

Other encounters with the criminal justice system

About half of our violent population have also been convicted of multiple types of offences unrelated to their ideology, including assault, sexual assault, and various drug-related activities. Interestingly, a sizable portion of the hate-motivated crimes recorded (assaults, murders, firebombings, attempted murders) were directed at fellow racists or rival extremist groups. One freshly recruited prospect killed a member of his new group with a baseball bat on the first evening. Another helped rape and kill his own sister, later helping dispose of the body. Aryan Guard members attempted to firebomb the home of a member

1 Though we are cognizant of the ideological problems that plague the expression, since it is found in a broad section of the literature it is convenient to continue using it. That said, it should be noted that the expression is used in white supremacist/genocidal literature as a way to glorify individual violent actors who trigger massive civil unrest and righteous civil wars resulting in salutary ethnic cleansing. In the mainstream media "lone wolf" has often been reserved for terrorists who were white, while liberally applying the label "terrorist" for racialized individuals.

of rival Western European Bloodline. Though recourse to violence is quite common in our population, it is often not directed at the realization of a political project or the advancement, incarnation, or "staging" of an ideology (see chapter 4). We consider these to be hate crimes even if they were not primarily directed at an ideologically targeted victim, since they took place during hate group activities. Of course, most of the violence did target groups and individuals linked to anti-racist activities, visible minorities, First Nations peoples, and homosexuals as well as attacks on various monuments and installations. Our propagandist population also commonly had had previous trouble with the law but for hate speech violations in criminal court or defamation in civil proceedings (ED9). A few had made threats or engaged in harassment and intimidation.

Psychosocial vulnerabilities

It is difficult to ascertain, from a medical standpoint, the exact mental state of individuals who join or participate in extremist groups. Some of our respondents reported having seen mental health professionals, but most did not (it must be noted that our interviews did not have a diagnostic objective). Some defendants had a psychiatric diagnosis attached to their pre-sentence reports (paranoid delusion, conduct disorder, psychosexual dysfunction), but most did not. One observation is unavoidable, however: those with a diagnosed mental health problem were those who engaged in acts of physical violence, while no such mental health issue is reported in the group of those convicted for hate propaganda (note that this is different from verified absence). This is another area where we can discuss, in general, the clientele referred to the aforementioned prevention program: the vast majority of the cases presented at least one but usually multiple rather acute psychosocial vulnerabilities, an observation also made by Rousseau et al. (2023) on a different population sample. Those include repeated and oftentimes ongoing childhood traumas (parental rejection or abuse), stress-related disorders, delusional disorders, narcissistic personalities, excessive alcohol and drug use. Many of those who did not seem to suffer from an addiction problem were nevertheless drunk or under the influence of drugs at the time of committing their offence.

Context factors

The individuals described above live in particular environments. Previous research has already narrowed down the number of contextual elements that are more likely to drive individuals towards the margins of what is generally considered socially acceptable behaviour, the most serious form of which being violent crime. Usually, these factors are deemed to be sufficient explanations for extreme behaviour, but they once again overpredict the incidence of extremism. Our dataset reveals the presence of the same usual factors but also that they must be combined with the individual characteristics shown above, and that the result is heavily dependent on the peculiarities of individual "trajectories" (in short, the sequence in which they appear; more in the next section).

One common way to sort out context factors is to categorize them in terms of "push" and "pull" factors. Pull factors are contextual elements that hail individuals and attract them to a particular cause, method of (re)action, or social group. They can take various forms. It may be that an ideological or religious worldview offers sought-after knowledge and understanding; for others it will be a group of friends that provides a sense of belonging; yet others find a charismatic leader who communicates a valued personal identity or place in the world. Push factors, on the other hand, are those that convince the individual that his current situation is lacking, morally wrong, or simply boring and that significant change is in order. The impression of rampant corruption, material, cultural, or political injustice or disregard for suffering are quite common.

Vergani et al. (2018) analyzed the literature on extremism and inventoried and ranked every factor deemed contributive to individual participation in violence. Though we disagree with the way the authors categorize and compare the factors, the paper remains a cogent overview of the main stimulants of ideological violence, and we will make use of the same categories.

One typical problem when listing "factors" is that they are firmly set in an etiological paradigm, where only objectively measurable causes can have objectively measurable effects. Both push and pull factors are then usually seen as psychosocial "causes" that have direct impact on individual and group biographies. Our general theoretical position throughout this book is not entirely compatible with that outlook. Though we accept that the "real world" has felt effects on individuals and that objective contexts matter, it is obvious that individual "readings" of the world must be taken into account. This was particularly obvious in our discussion of conspiracy theories, for instance. Each of the factors below must be understood as a multifaceted object with completing or competing sets of objective and subjective aspects.

Context factors: Push

Poverty or relative deprivation has been identified as a cause of multiple behavioural problems. The most common must be crime and acquisitive crime in particular: it has always seemed obvious that stealing is a logical, deliberate ("rational") response to deprivation. Needless to say, the relationship is a bit more complex, and it is accepted in modern criminology that poverty mostly generates crime if it is accompanied by other factors, such as joblessness or community dysfunction (Laub and Sampson 2003). The working poor in communities that have functional social interaction do not commit more crimes than average.

In the case of ideological extremism, the working theory is in part different. Of course, joblessness generates a large supply of young men who have a lot of time on their hands and little to lose, a prerequisite for crime, gang violence, and many types of violent extremism. However, with the latter the motivation is not (primarily) the acquisition of legally unattainable goods but the practical application of ideology. And because most of the ideologies that have accompanied political violence are social projects, their individual partisans are best described as "altruistic" (O'Gorman and Silke 2015). They do not choose to act for their personal benefit but for that of a select group of others (given the underlying racism or xenophobia this group is usually rather strictly defined). Given this aspect, our push factor becomes group deprivation, where individuals self-identify with a downtrodden, unjustly treated, defrauded, or otherwise mistreated social group – though they may not experience this injustice in their personal life. In other words, this discourse can appeal to both the deprived and the well off, since it does not refer to their own, personal situation. In the case of the latter, it only makes involvement seem more altruistic, or it can be presented that way as a form of justification. Note that group deprivation includes the fear that the group may be mistreated, even if it is dominant at the moment.

In clarifying this factor, we have gone from "poverty," which can be measured through various empirical means (e.g., income), to "group deprivation," where a clearly subjective and political aspect is introduced: the definition of the groups being compared. Let us then call this first push factor "group relative deprivation." It is an ideologically powerful mix of actual discrepancies in measurable buying power, employability, and economic weight with a peculiar understanding of the wealth of other groups and of who deserves better.

In the case of jihadists, one commonly identified push factor has been the policies of the West in the Middle East or in the Muslim world in general, which are deemed to be sacrilegious, unjust, etc. Far-right extremists point to multiple conspiracies to form a "new world order," a "great reset," or other items on the infamous "globalist agenda" meant to strip white Westerners of their rights. From the age-old Jewish conspiracies to more current claims that (white supremacist) "free speech" is being quashed by "international Marxism" or globalized modern culture, far-right groups almost invariably refer to supranational or foreign forces bearing on their group of reference. Here again is a vast system of belief that recycles a number of actual trends in geopolitics and global economics, like globalization of industrial production, massive migrations, etc. Some of these trends manifest themselves in everyday realities that have a direct impact on everyone, for instance, when the COVID-19 pandemic disrupted the crucial but vulnerable interconnections between the global supply chain nodes that make "on demand" production possible, with disastrous consequences.

A third push factor commonly identified is state oppression. Interestingly, it so happens that one stated objective of many terrorist groups is to trigger an intensification of state repression/oppression, which, it is hoped, will cause a mass uprising, revolution, and eventually political, ideological, economic, or religious change. This is the Marighella theory of terrorism – from Carlos Marighella, the Brazilian terrorist who developed it in his *Mini-Manual of the Urban Guerilla* in 1969. It is also an important strategy of the white supremacist genocidal group depicted in William Pierce's neo-Nazi utopia *The Turner Diaries*. It is the logic adopted by Canadian extremist Patrick Mathews, who fled to the United States and was finally arrested by the FBI in early 2020. He had been plotting, with accomplices in the USA, to attack gun rights activists in a false-flag operation designed to trigger regulatory overreaction, followed by a revolution, the collapse of state and federal governments, and an ensuing race war (the "boogaloo"). This is typical accelerationism, where small-scale actions set off a cascade of events resulting in the desired end state.

The actual role of repression in the genesis of politically violent movements remains ambiguous, at best (for instance, in India, Israel, and Egypt). But despite the immediate risk of being the target of the increased repression, the idea has wide traction among groups and individuals who invoke felt, feared, or past oppression as an important justification for their actions. The rationale is that there is a mass of like-minded individuals who would join their movement, if they only could be made to see and feel the same oppression and, in particular, the claimed loss of "rights" by individuals, groups, or "the right" as a whole. During the COVID-19 pandemic, the freedom discourse was transferred to more tangible matters such as masks, vaccines, or restrictions on travel or gatherings. Since then, the protection of freedom of speech has returned as the most frequent argument made by extremist groups, especially in more mainstream forums or public recruitment drives.

> Guys like myself, there's many others. I have a lot of other people that, that, that I am in contact with, that are, that are fighting at the highest levels. Sacrificing their lives, to make sure that we can keep some of the freedoms that we so dearly cherish. But are fading quickly if we don't do something about it. (ED32)

Objectively, many legal and regulatory doors have closed on several themes central to the far-right discourse as a whole; it is now more difficult to harass, threaten, or humiliate groups whose freedom (or mere existence) has traditionally been seen as dangerous such as women,

LGBTQ+ people, immigrants, Aboriginal communities, etc. In that sense, freedom of speech has indeed been limited, and severely so for those whose main form of expression revolved around those topics. In this area ideology and reality are intertwined in a paradox where the banning of a form of expression becomes one of its strengths.

A variant of oppression, especially in liberal-democratic countries, is disempowerment. In this case the state is not actively victimizing a group, but it is perceived to be structurally incapable of accommodating its goals, grievances, or claims. It has long been identified as an objective factor in pushing individuals or groups towards violent action, most specifically since Gurr (1986). There are many variants of this theory but, in general, it involves the realization that the legal mechanisms available for political participation and change are out of reach for a particular group or individual or simply do not exist. Individuals may then either abandon the participation project or adopt an oppositional stance against the system.

The purely causal approach breaks down in front of a fundamental contradiction: democratic indicators are positively associated with terrorist violence. In other words, objectively higher empowerment, as measured between different nations, leads to increased feelings of alienation and disempowerment. The story of the Front de libération du Québec illustrates this well. While society was gradually adopting many of the FLQ's key demands (protection of the French language, autonomy from the federal government, progressive labour laws), group members became more radical, more violent, and more desperate for even greater radical change (Leman-Langlois 2018).

Western political systems are widely criticized and said to be undergoing a crisis, but also at play in this particular case are various far-right amplifications of the concept of disempowerment. For instance, the idea that non-representative groups or individuals hold key positions within government and pursue a hidden agenda:

> Canadians should be aware that we live in an oligarchy. We don't live in a democracy, we live in an oligarchy, and oligarchy is defined as a tiny majority which holds the majority [*sic*] of power in Canada. So I would say the 1 per cent Jewish population of Canada controls most of the power in Canada ... My ideal goal is

> to topple Jewish supremacy in the world. To uh, eliminate the international ... the power of international Jews, to ... to topple Jewish supremacy. To have it contained by a, a gentile ... world. Gentile. It's a non-Jewish form of government. (ED33)

Of course, the most common is that institutions or individuals in power deny rights to certain groups:

> If you want to read a really frightening document, read the Supreme Court's decision in *Whatcott* ... he was charged by the Saskatchewan Human Rights Commission and ... Supreme Court and they just nuked him. They basically said that you can't hide under freedom of religion, political discourse, freedom of speech, what you've written is likely to expose the people to contempt as a vulnerable minority. You'd think they they'd bought in to the complete cultural Marxist view of the world, that there are oppressive groups (being white males, mostly) and vulnerable minorities (being homosexuals, sometimes women, people of colour, and so on)! (ED5)

It should be obvious that the local interpretation of objective factors is as important as their empirical content, or even more important. Furthermore, this interpretation can be, at times, vastly different from what average Canadians tend to hold true about the world. What is held as momentous on the far right may barely get a mention in the mainstream media (in 2018 the signing of the UN Global Compact on Migration set discussion groups ablaze; 2023 saw an explosion of frantic opposition to drag queens reading stories to school children) or may simply be completely fabricated (e.g., that ethics courses in Quebec primary schools promote Islam).

Disempowerment works simultaneously on three separate levels. On the first level, it is simply a fact that the far right is not represented in party politics, and most of its extreme discourse is banned in public and mass private (social media) forums. If right-wing political parties have flirted with conspiracy theories and anti-government ideologies, by and large they have, so far, kept those at a sanitary distance. On the second level, as a self-fulfilling prophecy, oppositional movements will be, by definition, *officially* disempowered. It is difficult to measure whether or not they get traction in the population or on the political agenda and groups benefit from that uncertainty when they claim to "speak for the people." This leads us to the final level, where "disempowerment" signals the righteousness of the group's demands for *equality,* as well as being a means of positioning the group as a representative of the far wider disempowered masses, whose needs are systematically disregarded by the elites in power, and whom they are attempting to recruit.

In short, individuals must learn to interpret reality and the information available about it in a way that makes cogent the weight of supranational forces, the oppression of the state, and their disempowerment, as well as the nefarious plans of hidden powers. In a continuous feedback loop, new current events then reinforce the interpretations and flesh out the truths held about the world. Engagement with influential individuals or groups further reinforces the constructed worldview and, conversely, the strongly held worldview reinforces group relationships. These practical "ethnomethods," or ways to account for the world, are not less real or more constructed than the dominant ones; they are only more marginal. This marginality, however, is not a weakness: on the contrary, it tends to cement bonds (while distancing group members from society) and to justify opposition and marginality. It also bestows unique (esoteric) insights that gives adherents the impression of having access to powerful truths and authentic contact with "what is going on." It is a form of privilege that many have been denied in other aspects of their life.

Context factors: Pull

The functions of symbolic, verbal, or physical violence within the far right are crucial in understanding group cohesion and evolution, as well as individual engagement and commitment. Also common with other forms of political violence, this aspect is especially salient with far-right extremists. Many individuals experience their first contact with the far right through the explicit, extreme, racist violence of Nazi punk, Aryan black metal, white power Oi!, and other music concerts. The martial demeanour, the explicit language, the military garb, and the obsession with weapons present in many groups symbolize the need for radical change, perhaps through violent armed struggle. They also represent the coercive application of authority and power, packaged to be especially attractive to young men.

Some groups on the "ultra-right" or "xenophobic vigilantes" deliberately seek spontaneous, haphazard clashes with opposed or competing groups, glorifying the skewed masculinity conveyed by physical domination: "I've been in, I can't even count the number of fights I've gotten into, it's all, it's, it's incredibly violent. I've been stabbed, I've been shot at, I've been, err, beaten with a bottle, I've been in those fights where I've used them on other people, it's, it's a very, very violent lifestyle" (ED28). Sometimes, however, violent clashes are sought for their propaganda value, presented as proof that the group is being unjustly targeted, and mistreated while simply attempting to exercise their right to free speech or to use public spaces.

Symbolic violence is also conveyed by the imagery shared by group members, for instance, in the form of memes on social networks. Far-right groups have different ideological or philosophical relationships with various historical figures but of course Nazi images and symbols are common, when allowed by the platform. At a more cryptic or symbolic level, one will find more socially acceptable images of crusaders and Vikings with slogans presenting war or less specific forms of violence as necessary or inevitable. "War," of course, can itself be symbolic, as in the "war against poverty" or the war against cancer, for instance, but the gory swords and pikes held by blood-soaked, exhausted, but proud medieval knights in full armour may lead to more literal interpretations. In the case of identifiable crusaders, the Islamophobic symbolism adds an implied justification for the violence. "Everyone wants to be a pacifist; nobody wants to sacrifice themselves. I'm ready to sacrifice myself. I'll probably die before I'm thirty" (ED3).

Vergani et al. also identify the availability of propaganda and other forms of information contents that purport to explain the world in whole or in part, usually as a hostile, unjust place (a push factor identified above), but also offer pre-established roles that aim to "hail" an audience, which usually consist in preventing, repairing, or avenging grievous harms, cultural, social, or existential disasters, or attaining individual and group actualization and the exaltation of having rightfully fulfilled their purpose in human history. It is easy to see how profoundly seductive this is to the populations described in the previous section, who are struggling with multiple intractable problems at the margins of society.

From a sociological point of view, propaganda is a form of communication that offers an appealing identity to a roughly targeted audience; this identity is the combination of a particular worldview (an ideological representation of history, society, humanity, etc.) and an appealing personal role to play within that worldview. In that, propaganda is an ideological invitation to see oneself in a new role or a new life. Note that this should not be understood as the opposite of rationality, pragmatism, or realism. There is no non-ideological, absolute, or *right* way to understand and interact with the world; thus, any explanation of the workings of humanity conveys or participates in an ideology and may then be deemed to be propaganda. The conclusions of Vergani et al., as well as much of the literature on this aspect, then, must be adjusted slightly: what calls individuals to extremist groups or action is *oppositional* propaganda. Individuals are being recruited into an identity, worldview, and/or ideology that is explicitly and deliberately designed to glorify marginality and conflict with dominant discourses about the world. Of course, as shown in the previous chapter, the far-right infosphere is key to the dissemination of propaganda, through memes, fake news, discussion forums, and the distribution of a few central works of fiction and nonfiction:

> As I started hanging out with the guys they would be going along with the ... their ideas and beliefs, and I'd be picking it up. And then they had books to read, and "oh here read this book," "here read that book," and you just kinda fill in the blanks ... George Lincoln Rockwell wrote the book *White Power*, and uh, it was uh ... *Silent Brotherhood* which was ... written by ... I can't remember who wrote that. Then there are the *Turner Diaries*, written by David Pierce [*sic:* William Luther Pierce]. (ED28)

Group dynamics, and especially the opportunity to belong, to be accepted within a group, are another commonly identified pull factor, often at the basic "engagement" form of participation. This aspect of togetherness, security, fun, adventure, and partying with peers is a particular manifestation of group membership that can also be found in more common crime networks. It is particularly salient within oppositional groups, who specifically represent themselves as excluded from more broadly socially acceptable activities or as explicitly different from the rest of the population (even if they claim to speak for the masses).

One easily overlooked aspect of group dynamics is that they do not indiscriminately absorb any and all potential recruits or admirers. Contrary to popular belief, and as noted by Hegghammer (2013), many recruiters and organizations choose their members:

> Yes, [Internet forum] Stormfront is a good place [to recruit], but we ended up staying away from that 'cause it started attracting a lot of kind of looney, really far out you know, extremist kind of strange types and we didn't want that type in ... because it's very lone wolf activity, we don't know what they're gonna do, right, so that's risky to have some members like that in the group ... you know like these guys can't socialize, like they have, they're unable to socialize in real circumstances ... but they, online, they're really active. And it's scary because those are the types of guys that would be like lone wolves and then blowing something out or just shooting somebody, because they're self-radicalizing at home, and getting feedback online like on Stormfront like they're getting told oh it's an amazing idea and whatever. (ED34)

This selectiveness is more important to clandestine and semi-clandestine groups who know that at least some of their activities are not socially accepted (whether illegal or not) and want to manage the manner and intensity in which they present themselves in public. Soldiers of Odin want to be seen distributing food to the (white) homeless but not to be seen intimidating (non-white) passersby. The group split in part because expectations of public behaviour became a subject of conflict. But even public groups such as La Meute (see chapter 3) manage membership and participation and exclude dissonant forum entries and members who choose to ignore the rules. Refused applicants and rejected members are then on alternative paths: they start looking for a new group to engage with, form a new group with fellow rejects, become lone actors or desist entirely.

When fulfilled, the hope of finding a "true" peer group is a key factor in individual and group identity building. This ingroup/outgroup difference can easily be exaggerated, not to mention entirely fabricated by the group leadership, in order to strengthen the feeling of belonging in the members. That is in fact the main function of ideology, to identify the boundaries between groups, the proper way to be, to speak, and to act, as well as point out everything that is wrong with society at large. Charismatic leaders or group members can also be seen as facets of this pull factor, as they draw in members to adopt a new specific identity:

> The guy is probably thirty-two to thirty-three years old, and he recruits kids who are looking for excitement, like eighteen to nineteen years old. They become his crew, like dogs, like a dog pack. They go on the hunt, around, like, poorer city blocks with pseudo-immigration in Quebec City. When he finds some [immigrants], they try to cause trouble. If they don't react, they might be ok; if they do, in the least way, they get knocked around. That's all they want. They want confrontation. (ED8)

Most members are ready, indeed eager to adopt these new identities, giving this pull factor its power. Kruglanski et al. (2014) refer to this as a "quest for personal significance": "the fundamental desire to matter, to be someone, to have respect." Note that this works whether the individual thinks he matters to a group, to a larger-than-life charismatic leader, or both. But Kruglanski et al. then proceed to label *all* factors leading to political violence as variations on this quest, which of course is essentially a semantic exercise permitted by the vagueness of the concept. Taken in a narrower sense, however, the active "quest" or more passive longing for a satisfying identity or image of the self is widely recognized as an important pull factor. It is of course more salient for some and in particular for adolescents and young adults, which explains why this population is disproportionately represented in most forms of political violence (as well as in multiple other crimes). Being accepted and eventually promoted within a peer group is extremely gratifying, sometimes well beyond ideological considerations:

Q: What did it mean for you to join this group?
A: Well, it gave me a sense of pride, more so than did the belief system. To be like a leader of the group, that was a big thing for me like it was, because you know, people all across Canada, like white power guys would be kind to me, to ask what could we do, should we add this concert, you know, how are we planning this or whatever, and I was also on an international board for people for ... so anything that would happen internationally and in our group, I had a vote on. (ED34)

At the same time, wanting to belong or to be significant is without doubt one of the most widely distributed human characteristics discussed in this chapter. As such, it may be a common ingredient in many forms of extremism but, taken as an explanation, it would grossly overpredict membership in extremist groups.

Contingencies

Aside from these commonly observable factors of engagement and commitment, there are also several individually experienced events and coincidences that can push or pull individuals along a path towards extremism. In fact, it is quite possible that for the most part, the phenomenon we are trying to describe is contingent, thus unique and unpredictable.

The main category of these coincidences is, as noted above, social network peculiarities. As first noted by Sageman (2004), the fact that an individual we have a connection to joins an oppositional group or introduces us to an extremist ideology (as parents tend to do with their offspring) is a powerful incentive to follow in their footsteps. This is only more powerful if network members engage in deliberate or unwitting (for instance, when aggrandizing their own engagement) recruitment strategies among peers. Network effects may operate in a vastly different way and, for instance, include iterations of the "state oppression" factor listed above: when, for instance, a family member or close friend is selected for governmental reprisal (i.e., is prosecuted or sued).

The unpredictable unfolding of global current events is another such contingent factor in engagement and commitment. People do not join the Islamic State if there is no Islamic State. They do not join militias to protect their gun rights if a politician associated with gun control does not win office. They are less likely to be introduced to far-right ideologies in places and times where right-wing populism has not gained a foothold in the public discourse.

Of course, current events and, in general, knowledge about the wider social world are not objectively and directly observable elements in an apolitical world. They are conveyed by various types of media, with highly variable reputations for trustworthiness. It is common for oppositional groups to identify some or all news media as part of the "mainstream" or the "elite" and thus as one of the sources of what is wrong in the society they oppose. In that case they may resort to alternative media offering versions of reality that are more in line with their existing worldview. At that point the actual content matters far less than the symbolic meaning of following and approving a particular far-right propaganda vehicle. More than ever, the medium has truly become the message. The decade-old but rapidly increasing state of turmoil most traditional media find themselves in today is only accelerating that phenomenon.

The mushrooming alternatives to mainstream media, usually located within the wider social media category, operate under vastly uneven reporting standards, if at all present. What is being offered by these outlets is likely be quite different from widely accepted facts or widely held, intersubjective interpretations of reality. Consequently, it has been shown that the far right is particularly vulnerable to manipulation via strategically produced and distributed fake news (Badawy, Ferrara, and Lerman 2018). It is no surprise, then, that the Canadian far-right groups we have been following have sometimes redistributed fake news of Russian origin,[2] for instance a 2017 trolling

2 According to the list of three million tweets from Russian trolls compiled by Darren Linvill and Patrick Warren of Clemson University, available at https://github.com/fivethirtyeight/russian-troll-tweets/.

fake news tweet from the "Internet Research Agency" (an equally fake body created by Russian intelligence) announcing "Canada FORCED to take DRASTIC Action to Stop Illegals From Flooding In." The number and dissemination of such tweets spike during signal events for the far right in Canada, for instance the January 2017 Quebec City massacre and the Canada–USA border crossings "crisis" (Rocha 2018).

Engagement and commitment

The sections above have described in turn the main individual characteristics in our sample populations and the main context factors that we identified as having been important in their biography. It is worth repeating that, taken individually, none of these characteristics or factors is either sufficient or necessary to explain why or how individuals begin to commit reprehensible acts. In other words, pieces of the puzzle are still missing. Now we must look at the particular ways individuals attempt to navigate contexts.

Extreme rationalities

First and foremost, it is important to repeat that, overall, individuals who join far-right groups or espouse extreme worldviews are no less "rational" than the vast majority of those who do not. With the caveat that we are not clinical psychologists, we define "rational" as "goal-oriented," with the implied presence of a basic, functional grip on reality. This covers a rather broad spectrum, one that we will not attempt to sort out from a psychological angle, which tends to be less than productive. Indeed, most studies of the psychology of extremists to date have shown that extremism is not a disease (Sommier 2012). That said, human rationality is by definition limited, not only by the objective realities of context but also by individual and group definitions and interpretations of this context, of individual and group objectives, and of what course of action is ideologically correct or, more pragmatically, most likely to succeed. Members of non-violent and violent ideological groups are simply agents who learn to navigate the complexities of their context in a specific way.

This approach is at once constructivist and realist. Individual perceptions of context are socially constructed, and dominant constructions or discourses about them are produced within specific social groups. This is why we have adopted an ethnomethodological approach to best account for the deployment of agency and action in the social context of a group (virtual or physical). From that point of view, individuals *perform* membership through participation: they are actively involved, through collective and individual action, dialogue, deliberation, in constructing the specific version of the world that they believe they live in. At the same time, though they are perceived and understood in variable ways, there are material conditions to be accounted for in the way individual and group action unfolds. Many of the tangible push and pull categories discussed above are specific manifestations of such material conditions. And barring a few exceptions, they are present in most of the individual biographies of our target population, in various combinations.

Under this "ethnomethodological realism," individuals under the influence of various arrays of push and pull factors do not become (radicalized) puppets devoid of agency. Nor is it simply that their rational decisions are modified by their particular context, where they attempt to play or optimize the hand they are given. We must sharpen our analytical tools a bit more if we are to understand the dual phenomena of engagement and commitment. At the very least, it is important to note that material, objective, factual, or empirically verifiable information, realities, phenomena, etc., do not present themselves to human experience in an un-theorized, natural, apolitical, or non-ideological state. They only appear under multiple, temporary, dynamic layers of conflicting interpretations. At the same time, if voluntary, rational (again, in the restricted sense of goal-oriented) action depends in the first place on the salience of one of these interpretations for the individual actor, it also depends on the way in which the object reacts or interacts. One may attempt to levitate but gravity will invariably choose otherwise. Not all bomb makers actually know anything about making bombs. In 2018 Cesar Sayoc sent fourteen parcel bombs to political targets in the USA (including one to the home of George Soros) but none exploded. Of course, whatever its material characteristics, this reaction is then subject to interpretation, where successes may become failures and vice versa. In the context of this book, this aids in the understanding of why individuals and groups engage in courses of action or strategies that almost everyone else would find unlikely to succeed, illogical, or even idiotic.

In sum, when studying the gateways that first introduce a person to a far-right context and the trajectory they followed prior to and following that introduction, we are touching on a process of rationalization and construction of meaning by individuals who must decide how to "go on" from moment to moment. This involves an unending series of everyday, small decisions – as well as some more momentous ones – that lead to their becoming part of the far-right nebula and, eventually, to committing illegal and/or otherwise controversial acts that both fit in and strengthen a particular worldview.

Beyond radicalization

A process called "radicalization" has often been used to explain how ordinary persons become extremists. For more than twenty years this has in fact been a clearly dominant concept, even though it has wildly different meanings and definitions in the literature. In this book we purposefully eschew using the term and associated concepts for a number of reasons. Of course, the variation in definitions suggests that the term has been used to account for extremely different objects: sometimes a (sociological and/or psychological) process; sometimes a mental defect that causes the individual to no longer respond to rational discourse or action; sometimes a change in opinion, sometimes in behaviour, or both, under variable representations of their interaction; other times it is a black box that simply marks a significant change in an individual.

What is more, radicalization implies not only a process but a clear pivotal point, or threshold, where the observer will note a passage from "normal" to "radical" behaviour or (expressed) thoughts. Yet there is no objective way to locate that threshold. It is heavily affected by the context in which the behaviour is observed and the normative judgement of the observer. We are quite willing to restrict the context for any concept linked to political violence to that of peaceful liberal democracies, but even with this reduced focus, the observer's own ideology and perception of normalcy is difficult to circumvent. One traditional solution to this problem has been to introduce the use of violence as a marker of radical thought/action, as in "violent radicalization" or "radicalization leading to violence." This semantic workaround bogs down another issue because the dependent variable (involvement in politically motivated violence) is now used in the definition of its own causal process, leading to a tautology. More pragmatically, it also does not account for much of our data, where violence is not only an important pull factor (where it would be a driver of radicalization) but also commonly explodes before any form of radicalization. Horgan (2008, 2014) also abandons radicalization, for similar reasons, and replaces it with the twin concepts of involvement, where the individual first starts to interact with an extremist movement, and engagement, where direct participation in terrorism occurs. The importance of these twin concepts is that they focus on action within groups instead of personal mental processes. On the other hand, Horgan defines the threshold between involvement and engagement as the commission of a legally defined terrorist offence (2014, 104–9), which we find both limiting in scope and too closely bound to legal definitions. We aim to account for a much wider category of deviant behaviours, sometimes with very limited overlap with the Criminal Code (and often with the vague and contentious articles bearing on hate crime and propaganda).

In its stead we have devised two categories meant to identify the proximity of actors to an ideology, to a political group, and eventually to the antisocial behaviours that the actors might associate with the ideology and political group. The first one is engagement, where the individual begins regular, deliberate interactions with an oppositional group or ideology (more precisely, with the materials associated with it). Group and ideology of course are likely to come together as a package, but we do want to account for lone actors who become captivated by their readings or other mediatized forms of propaganda. It is also important to distinguish, as already mentioned, between the mere consumption of a group's discursive production and actual interaction with its members. We must also be open to the possibility that some lone actors formulate extremist ideas entirely independently,

Table 5.1 Classification of forms of individual connection with the far right

		IDEOLOGY Absent	Present
Group members	engagement	1) familiarity	3) socialization/social learning
	commitment	2) common crime/deviance	4) hate crime/terrorism
Lone actors	engagement	(N/A)	5) self-socialization
	commitment		6) hate crime/terrorism

without any access to extremist content. The second one, commitment, is a deeper form of participation in that it involves the commission of deviant (socially unacceptable but not necessarily illegal) actions as well as clearly illegal ones.

Intuitively, commitment appears to follow engagement chronologically. This is not, in fact, true: this is why we illustrate this classification with a table rather than a figure such as a series of steps, a funnel, etc., which imply progression. For reasons that we will explain below, individuals can move back and forth between positions in the matrix, and entirely out of it, at highly variable intervals, according to the fluctuations in the personal and contextual factors listed below, to which we will soon add the particularities of group dynamics (when applicable).

Table 5.1 lists some of the possible combinations as a matrix between ideological and practical aspects: 1) Individuals may engage with far-right groups for a variety of reasons outside of ideology that usually have to do with a sense of belonging or familiarity with members of the group (family, friendships, etc., for the purposes of excitement, partying, security, etc.). In that sense, far-right ideological groups resemble youth gangs and their gang culture (Fredette and Guay 2014). 2) When the individual willingly participates in clearly illegal or at least deviant behaviours with the group, he becomes committed to the group: his level of personal investment now includes the risk of social or official reaction. Absent ideological underpinnings, such participation often results from a desire for thrills, "action," domination, or, as previously discussed, violence itself. 3) Individuals may also, of course, engage with a group primarily because of its politics. The resulting process can be understood as social learning, where group perception, understanding, definitions of context, and opportunities are absorbed by the individual, who learns to interpret the world through social interaction. Under differential association theory one learns from others a new way to perceive his or her social environment, in a manner that makes deviant behaviour acceptable, if not required. Independent, pre-existing knowledge of the ideology still requires familiarization with group interpretations through social learning. 4) When such individuals commit to the group by participating in deviant actions and/or illegal actions, their behaviour may quickly escalate to meet the legal requirements for "hate crime" or "terrorism." It is important to note that though "terrorism" evokes enormous mega-crimes, in fact most of these crimes are unlikely to be more severe than the common crimes committed by non-ideological offenders (destruction of property, intimidation, harassment, assault). The difference is that in this context they acquire the political motivation required by the Canadian legal definition of "terrorism."

For lone actors the possibilities are not as wide, as they, by definition, do not interact with existing groups or other individuals with whom they might constitute a new group. This lack of active, practical interaction with peers and, therefore, any form of encouragement, support, or inspiration explains why lone actors are less often encountered. Note that this is also true of ordinary street crimes, which are also most often committed in groups. 5) In these cases, engagement has sometimes been referred to as "self-socialization," through mediatized content such as books, websites, YouTube and other social media, etc., as long as no sustained interaction – as in a discussion forum for instance – with the authors of the materials occurs. Lone actors may also adopt extreme ideas and behaviours without contact with extreme contents. For instance, continuous mainstream media accounts of immigration "problems" may lead to non-mainstream interpretations. With self-socialization, the subject essentially joins an imaginary group that is in fact entirely reflexive, in other words where other members are constructed from elements taken from the individual's own identity. When actual interaction and communication occur, the individual shifts towards a process of group engagement, with its particular peer group mechanics. 6) Commitment, in these cases, closely resembles group commitment – barring the absence of accomplices before or during the act.

Some remarks must be added about engagement with or commitment to a group. Much analysis of political violence or terrorism simply assumes that group and member objectives are in sufficient alignment to make any differences insignificant. We have found this to be deeply untrue. Both explicit and implicit objectives and rationales exist within the group, and of course when individuals "engage" with the group it is safe to assume that at least some overlap exists between their personal goals and those of the group. But this overlap can be quite minimal. It is also dynamic and changes with time, as individuals and groups evolve with various factors such as current events, economic realities, ageing, etc. Members who find themselves increasingly at odds with group priorities may leave or attempt to transform the group. In fact, most of the far-right groups we have inventoried are under such pressures from within constantly and evolve, split, or disband in a rather short timeframe.

Dynamics of commitment and engagement

Looking at certain datasets, it can appear as if the reasons why individuals engage with or commit to far-right groups or ideologies are simply too varied, that their trajectories within the far right are infinitely diverse, and that, therefore, no single model can be identified. This is especially true of international datasets where extreme, but ultimately artificial, heterogeneity exists (in reality, most extremism and political violence is local, and international comparisons, though widespread, are problematic). When examining a limited population sample, in a more homogeneous geographical, cultural, and historical context, a few typical trajectories or pathways towards or away from violence do appear, albeit with some caveats:

- Incompleteness: it is important to accept that though we try to fit most cases into the smallest possible number of trajectories, a sizable remainder of unique cases will remain. This also means that our approach cannot lead to specifically targeted preventive interventions or to the identification of "at risk" individuals. In practical terms, to the extent that we want to prevent a specific set of undesirable behaviours (including speech acts), an exclusively generalist intervention might be more fruitful (and often for a set of ethical justifications that largely exceed extremism prevention, like the proper development of children).

- Political "causes": for the most part (again, with many exceptions), our sample population is composed of individuals who have adopted a worldview and are trying to align at least some of their activities with it. It also includes others who retroactively account for questionable behaviour by invoking specific rationales in what Sykes and Matza would refer to as a form of classic "neutralization." In both cases our starting point is that our subjects are rational, political individuals who are trying to make sense of the world. They are not determined by unique or interacting factors; rather, they engage and disengage because of self-reflection. Of course, peculiar forms of political engagement may make more sense to them because of their personal characteristics, their particular social context, at a particular time. Conversely, engagement helps them sort out, analyze, and account for the personal and social situation they believe they are in.
- Multiplicity of pathways: even barring unique and exceptional cases, it is not realistic to expect that such a complex set of behaviours could fit in a single explanatory model.

One additional problem in looking for commonalities in a diverse group is that most individual characteristics are dynamic: education, employment, status in a group, etc., can change quickly with time (that is also the case for other characteristics that are traditionally considered fixed, such as gender or sexual preference, and since those tend to be focal points in far-right discourse they probably have more weight in group dynamics; more research is definitely needed around this question). As we have seen, the individual is also thrown into a dynamic environment that includes, for instance, unpredictable but impactful developments in local and international events, the shifting structure of personal social networks, and the interplay between the dominant public discourse on societies, governments, and populations, and emerging worldviews – including those that quickly become viral on the Internet. We believe that context effects are a crucial component of engagement towards political violence and hate crimes.

The challenge set by this set of dynamic interactions is to identify some commonalities. One way to think of the problem is that individuals who choose to engage with extremist groups or to commit extreme acts find themselves at a key junction, or nexus, of factors that may or may not be deemed classically "criminogenic" taken separately but, when combined, become powerful catalysts towards violence – just as randomly moving spotlights sometimes meet and create a much brighter spot, perhaps only for a short period of time. For instance, the most talked about of these spotlights is the presence of radical ideology, but in reality, it is one among many, neither necessary nor sufficient by itself. It may or may not be present in violent individuals, even if they are members of an ideology-centred group. A few in fact engage in violence and only later rationalize it with a political discourse made available inside the group; others hold extreme, radical views but never act accordingly. But when combined with a personal crisis, a particular incident in the news, or the actions of a close friend or family member, a powerful convergence of forces emerges. Our most important point, then, is that it is the *interaction* of forces that leads to violence.

Gateways to engagement

What we refer to as gateways are the combinations of factors that first "hail" individuals into the far-right universe, the path to engagement with ideologies and groups. They are particularly difficult to identify and sort out since they are often fuzzy to the members themselves. Some of our respondents identified a special event or situation that constituted a turning point (such as the already mentioned Sharia for Ontario movement in the 2000s) but most had difficulty locating a single or central key or a threshold where they clearly began moving in opposition to society. Some simply reported having always been "that way." Of course, this may have simply been used as a justification or normalization by our respondents.

We have begun to underline a first line of demarcation in our population of interviewees, court cases, and prevention cases: those involved in classic street crimes or direct interaction with victims and those who concentrate on hate propaganda on the Internet or in public spaces (distribution of literature, installing signs and banners, etc.). For simplicity's sake let us refer to the former as "scrappers" and the latter as "propagandists." While in many respects this is a gross simplification, it does represent, with exceptions, the most important observable distinction within our population. The categories are not entirely mutually exclusive but in practice few cross from one group to the other.

To these first two categories we add "soldiers," who fancy themselves as paramilitary units preparing for armed conflict. They do not engage in wanton violence and protect their identity as disciplined and rational, having an all-important mission. Many have sought or achieved actual military training, and the Canadian Armed Forces have recognized the problem (CAF 2018). Of course, we also have a large group of simple amateurs who engage in one exceptional act of physical or verbal violence, often without fully realizing that they have crossed the line into officially sanctioned hate crime. They are often caught by the authorities because they do not have the necessary skills or experience in hiding their identity before, during, or after the act. They do increase the visibility of the far right but they are not linked to any network and are not particularly interested in far-right ideology.

At the bottom of the pyramid, we find an unmeasurable reservoir of knee-jerk haters who will drop racist comments at the bottom of news items, for instance typing "good riddance" following an article about an immigrant family who died in a fire, or who repost xenophobic memes without realizing these were concocted by a hate group (this includes trolls, who do the same for the sheer shock value). In this chapter we do not focus on that population, but, as we have seen in previous chapters, it has undoubtedly interesting and highly consequential characteristics as it serves to enlarge and solidify the echo chamber of the far right.

Scrappers include most skinhead-type members but also unidentified, incidental groups of co-offenders. For the most part they enjoy getting into fights and like to leave traces of their presence in the physical world. They tend to fit the usual cliché: they are undereducated because they did not fit in at school or in most adult-led organized activities. They often do not join for the ideology, which they have low interest in, and lack the critical skills that might protect them from the most bizarre theories about the world. They come from dysfunctional families and seek group membership not simply for belonging but also for role models, which makes them highly vulnerable to charismatic leaders and gurus. They are introduced to the far-right universe in essentially two ways: some seek out violent groups for protection, action, and excitement.

> That crowd, they'll take people who are ... emotionally weak but who want to show how strong they are. That's what they're looking for ... someone who is down and who feels that the group is taking them in with open arms, and look, it's going to be ok, no one will mess with you anymore. (ED10)

This fits with entry 1 in our classification matrix. Another one of our respondents illustrates this perfectly. After having been part of a gang in high school, "for protection," he engaged with more political groups in early adulthood. His politicization clearly followed an engagement towards violence, to construct meaning, and harmonize identity with behaviour. By his recollection, after having been part of the violent gang for five years, he met more ideological peers, whom he recognized as such because of media attention to similar groups, moving from entry 1 to 3:

> And uh, there was not, a heavy integration, and uh, in the community, and in my school. So, I mean, it was uh, off-the-cuff remarks. You know how it starts, uh, an offensive joke ... and uh, I, I, uh, people just, through casual conversations and, um, I ... learned of the skinheads in the, in the school. And I was seeing them at that time on *Geraldo* [television talk show hosted by Geraldo Rivera]? And, all those talk shows, that were pretty big around then. And uh ... and you just, as I started hanging out with the guys they would be, uh, going along with the, with uh, their ideas and beliefs, and I'd be picking it up. And then they had

> books to read, and "oh here read this book, here read that book," and you just kinda fill in the blanks. (ED28)

As he grew more mature, the exhilaration of the fight for courtyard dominance was replaced by broader social concerns – but with the same basic practical consequences.

One important gateway to engagement is high-contact concerts and events, where violent, hateful, and frustration-relieving music is played. Audience members soon begin to embody the violence and turn to explosive, mostly unplanned, and unfocused aggression. As discussed, most times this violence is in no way ideologically motivated: "someone would grab someone else's beer by mistake and a fight would start, five on one side and five on the other or five on one side and ten on the other and tap-tap-tap, right in the face" (ED10). This form of aggressive but unfocused violence is an overwhelmingly common manifestation of entry 2 of our matrix, where members strengthen their investment in the group through common deviant and illegal acts.

Finally, a few of our respondents did join a group directly for ideological reasons, as in entry 3:

> I was watching movies with Steve McQueen and Nazis and I liked the Nazis. They were better than everyone else and I like to stand with the best. Later, I learned about the politics of those Nazis when watching documentaries on TV and it just fit my way of thinking. Not to the point of going to war but just before he started the war, what he did with his country. (ED 37)

The politics referred to boil down to an extremely basic version of white supremacy:

> scientific studies were done on some races that are less evolved than we are; it's not an insult, a put down; it is what it is ... Everything that was ever invented was invented by Whites. ... There are Blacks who are more intelligent than me, who go to college, but to learn from whom? From Whites ... That is in no way racist, it's just the way it is. (ED37)

For their part, propagandists do not simply post a few messages or videos to social media; they are hyperactive media publishers, some with thousands of pages of writing and hours upon hours of video or audio under their belt. Most first appear in the public sphere by reacting to highly mediatized events such as the Sharia for Ontario movement of the 2000s, the trials of holocaust deniers such as Ernst Zundel or schoolteacher James Keegstra in the late 1980s, or the signature of the UN global compact for migration started in 2017. Many start by criticizing new laws or court decisions they see as unjust or threatening to the security of a population group with which they identify. Most are extremely knowledgeable and consume high levels of information about the topics they write on. They also feel very confident about their own expertise.

> I've been an activist easily for thirty years. In justice ... People have told me that ... you're a person with a ... like a ... great concern for justice. Some people view what I believe into, organizations, as injustice. But, I hope that I've articulated why ... what I do ... is not an attempt at injustice or supremacy or superiority, anything like that, okay? It simply comes from a deeper understanding of the issues and the legislation than, perhaps, or really, the average Canadian. (ED12)

Propagandists come in both group-based and lone-actor types. The former love to interact, online and in person, and thrive on the admiration of their followers. Social media platforms are ideal for this dynamic, with a constant tally of "likes" and subscribers. But this dynamic was present in the older static websites that some administered in the past and in the pre-internet days of print media and group meetings. The latter tend to become group founders and leaders when their publications begin to attract attention, a form of self-socialization that becomes socialization for followers:

> So, this was my own study in, in, developing the faiths and beliefs this church is founded upon, the ... was first of all founded on, deciding, well am I a person or am I man? And, according to

these scriptures, if I'm a person, or show respect to persons, I'm a sinner and I get no respect for God. (ED25)

Engaging and committing

The initial introduction to or hailing towards far-right circles – whether virtual, on paper, or in person – may or may not lead to further engagement: that is, a sustained or repetitive interaction with materials or persons. Lone actors will continue further on their own, consuming quantities of information and acting out accordingly, either in verbal or written form (internet postings, leaflets, and stickers) or through individual action against property or persons. A few will actively and continuously prepare for action that they will never undertake or for a world-ending event they probably will never see. New group members will start navigating the culture, language, and behaviours prevalent in their newly found peers. Ethnomethodologically speaking, they will learn how to enact their identity as members of the group.

In much of the literature on radicalization it is assumed that all violent actors are part of a larger group or network. Group membership is in fact part of quite a few definitions of terrorism and political violence. This requires some unpacking. Group effects are obviously enormously important in many facets of extreme forms of behaviour, but there is an entire rainbow of possibilities in group structures. Some are formal, durable, and structured networks, while others are largely coincidental, with far vaguer contours. Internet groups are the best examples of the latter, where "membership" can simply involve following or "liking" a group page on social network services. Membership affords access to group discussions and invitations to further involvement, nothing more. At the other end of the spectrum, groups that fancy themselves as secret paramilitary or clandestine networks can have interviews and trials for selecting new members. That was the case of the Base (Thorpe 2019), whose members were arrested by the FBI in early 2020. Interviews and other access rituals are commonplace in so-called dark networks, which strive to remain secret and quickly run into trust problems when trying to recruit at large instead of staying within the boundaries of family and long-term associates. As to be expected, less secrecy-conscious groups may have spectacular rites of passage, which immediately pushes them into the commitment phase, entry 4, of the involvement matrix:

> Yes, definitely you'd have to ... you know it's still criminal, like these groups are criminal, most of them ... so you had to fight ... like, I know, like I got in a big fight with a BMNE's gang, it's one of my personal stories, in downtown Toronto and I almost died. So, I got stabbed in the head and broke both arms and whatever, but that was sort of a rite of passage, like I went to a party next weekend and everybody was giving me more respect you know, because I put myself out of the line right against this immigrant gang right so. (ED34)

Once inside the group, new members will find that the rules, structure, and activities vary to the extreme; some are loose knit, opportunistic, and polymorphous (with clearly politicized activities being in the minority), while others have hierarchies, duties, explicit rules. Many have a dress code and patches that signal official membership. Violence tends to dominate, sometimes in actual practice:

> We knew there was a gang of Latinos, mixed with an Arab ... we didn't bring any weapons, no clubs, no knives, because we knew that if there was going to be trouble, and the police got there, we didn't want to be accused of premeditation ... When we got there ... the guys on my side mostly took off and when I stayed behind to help one of my friends I was stabbed with icepicks and letter openers from all sides and the police arrived and I was lying on the ground, knocked out by a club to the head, and I wound up in hospital. (ED37)

But for the most part, the violence is enacted through speech and narratives about what might occur in the future or in the constant reminiscing about past fights, including remote historical ones. As noted in previous research (notably in McCauley and Moskalenko 2008), the threat of violence increases group cohesion through the increasingly felt need for protection. We could add that it also strengthens the ties between members who collaborate in the preparation, commission, or hiding of criminal assault. Finally, it constitutes an important reinforcement of trust between members, who constantly imagine, re-enact, or narrate their need to rely on each other for immediate protection, much like soldiers in battle or police officers on patrol. Conversely, those who appear lukewarm or insufficiently enthusiastic during discussions of violence may be filtered out of further group activities. This is an important factor in transforming mere engagement into commitment.

Here the distinction between scrappers and propagandists is extreme. Scrappers are typically found in skinhead groups, marginalized, and self-identifying as such by attire, demeanour, and language. Propagandists form groups of like-minded individuals who often make great efforts to appear as ordinary citizens simply "concerned" with immigration, free speech, etc. When events are organized, propagandists also tend to present themselves as average members of the public. Demonstrations and public meetings by La Meute or Pegida Canada are illustrations of that mindset. Violence and talk of violence are explicitly prohibited:

> So ... no talk about violence. Because most of the time, it's really just a form of masturbation. The people that talk about it are not actually going to do it. It just relieves tension, pressure. But it doesn't accomplish anything. And also, it scares the intelligent people off. That's why I'm working quite closely with ... He's the man behind this ... And he says, you know, people ... we gotta be able to appeal to young couples, to soccer moms, to people who hold a job. It shouldn't be a pissing contest to see who's the meanest toughest skinhead. That may impress a very tiny number of people, but it isn't going to win the middle class we need. We're not going to win them by talks of violence and boots and braces and a body full of tattoos! I mean I don't have anything against that per se, but I just know that ... that's not the way we're going to win people. (ED5)

These groups make entry 4, ideological commitment, essentially impossible. They continually navigate the boundary between extreme discourse and explicit hate speech or illegal acts. Though some of their language might seem deviant in their immediate social network, they are free to take it to new heights on friendly forums. There, the discourse usually revolves around symbolic threats of physical violence, usually on a grand scale:

> what we have is a movement of cultural assassins, okay, who are hypocrites, okay, and using our country and our legislations and the naiveté of our policies of immigration refugees and we haven't even spoken about refugees at all, we don't have to, but ... And multi-cults, all non-democratic legislation and ... and ... completely rewriting ... you are rewriting our history, you're pushing us out of government because we're white, you're pushing us out of leadership positions and business because of the crime that we're white and you're doing it through reverse racism. Instead of what you deem racism, okay? This is what I'm about. (ED12)

This emotionally felt sense of mission explains why many propagandists are hard at work disseminating information about the themes they most believe in, whether they think this is practically efficacious or not, and remain firmly set in entry 5 – engaging but never committing. However, in doing so they may face a certain amount of frustration. After three brief periods of incarceration, ED16 chose to be more prudent:

> Depression. Hopelessness. Simple, hopelessness. I look around and I say fuck! I've been doing this for ten years, I mean I've been studying Islam for ten years, I've gone to jail three times, I spent lots of money, sometimes I feel like a fool! Like, *un clown*! And nobody cares, and everybody keeps building mosques. (ED16)

While preaching in vain may not discourage, explicit forms of motivation can consolidate the feeling of having a role to play in society: popular and media attention are highly sought after.

> But ... that [flyer] thing was a bomb. It was like putting a bomb under a Parliament. You should've seen what ... most of the reaction came from the area around there, you know, from the

> Toronto area. We got about 500 ... 500 emails just in a reaction to that. And all kinds of interviews. You'll see some of them on the ... on the Internet. If you look around. But the one that I did with the CBC was probably on the Internet. (ED14)

The thrill of the deviant but impossible to prosecute act is obvious. Though many propagandists have been in trouble with the law, either accused of hate crimes or sued for defamation by various parties, most are skilled – or experienced – in navigating the very limits of legal public discourse. This is in part due to the lax guidelines on what constitutes hate speech or the relative difficulty in mounting a successful prosecution for what often appears to be a minor crime. Occasionally, they are the ones suing journalists or anti-racist activists for what they perceive to be slanderous accusations. Those who are members of groups they perceived as insufficiently committed to the cause may eventually leave for more extremist groups. Some elect to set up entirely new formations, for instance from anti-immigration to explicitly white supremacist anti-immigration:

> I had a falling out with them ... They were anti-immigration and anti-multiculturalism, but they weren't overt, they didn't want to represent Canadians of European origins and they didn't wanna lose their jobs, which is understandable, because, you know, some of this stuff can really get you into hot water, right? You can get fired over it right? So they were afraid. (ED12)

In short, group membership is extremely fluid, and it is common for individuals to drift from one to the other for a variety of reasons.

> It's a process of discovery. So, you're, you know, in this skinhead group right around the streets, and you meet some guys: "hey why don't you come to this meeting about immigration?" And you thought: "Oh cool, people are meeting about immigration!" And they need security because the left-wing attacks them all the time. So we get to go and support the anti-immigration thing and crack a few skulls if we're lucky, right? But then, as you get in there, it's like you absorb all the information ... So I would

absorb everything that the group would have to offer and then I'd go: well you know what, they're not radical enough. I mean, if you look at any step, it's not moving like this. It's moving to a more ... radical position. (ED13)

For their part, most lone actors show a progressive passage from matrix entries (5) to (6), where they change their repertoire from sustained far-right exegesis online to crossing the line into deviant or criminal acts. Others jump almost immediately into violence. For instance, Corey Hurren, who attacked Rideau Hall in 2020, posted only a few anti–gun control and COVID-19 conspiracy theory messages before springing into action, all in a matter of a few weeks. Of course, at the time he was also under stress from personal bankruptcy, family problems, the difficulties of renewing his gun licence, and imminent loss of his vehicle (*National Post* 2021). The consulting psychiatrist diagnosed him with severe depression. This is not an isolated case; a sizable proportion of violent acts are committed by lone actors or by very small break-off groups with, at best, tenuous connections to wider networks of like-minded individuals.

Exits: Factors for desistance

Individual biographies tend to look like trajectories, with what we might understand as changes in speed and direction: one of our respondents left the neo-Nazi group he founded in between our interviews (ED1; the group itself still exists). Very few extremist biographies look like a before/after set of snapshots, implying a (sudden or gradual) pivotal shift between normality and extremism (e.g., a "radicalization"). Even group membership is not always a clear passage from one state to another, since individuals often change distance and engage in opportunistic forms of interaction dictated by the day's mood or events. For many, this evolution leads to a progressive distancing from extremist engagement or commitment.

As of late, criminology has taken interest in desistance from crime (McCuish, Lussier, and Chouinard Thivierge 2020; Villeneuve, Dufour, and Turcotte 2020). It is generally accepted that desistance can mean three different levels of disengagement from crime. Those are often portrayed as a sequence, from a more superficial to a deeper form, but as for the contexts of engagement and commitment described above, there is probably no mechanical process at work, no chronological succession of "stages."

In its most superficial meaning, desistance means that a significant reduction in the frequency and/or severity of criminal activity has occurred. This is referred to as primary desistance. This reduction may lead to a complete break, but that may be difficult to attain or may involve long-term efforts. Secondary desistance involves the adoption of prosocial replacement behaviours and a "reformed" personal identity. The deepest form of desistance occurs when the individual is fully reinstated in society and feels like he belongs with the generally law-abiding majority.

Obviously, this is heavily dependent on context factors: reformed as one may be, reinsertion is conditional on acceptance within society. It is equally obvious that this model is a poor fit with political forms of deviance and crime. First, the legal weight of the distinction between crime and no crime is far less clear since political opinion and speech are protected by the Charter. Second, the other key distinction, the duality between the individual and society, is also clearly invalid from a political or ideological point of view. Third, the pro- or anti-social duality is also irrelevant since most political criminals tend to justify their actions with altruistic motives.

Despite these objections, desistance theory may still be of help. Of particular interest is primary desistance, itself thought to have three facets, usually presented as "phases" (F.-Dufour and Brassard 2014). One is the separation phase, where changes occur in the places frequented by the individual and their social network. New peers enter the picture and delinquent ones tend to be less present. The critical phase involves introspection and a re-evaluation of behaviours, results, consequences, and life goals. Finally, the integration phase includes the adoption of a new social role and the reshaping of personal identity. F.-Dufour and Brassard identify three main sets of factors that transform individual trajectories. The "transformed" are those who feel marginalized and use crime to attain material gains that seem otherwise out of reach. Their desisting follows a problematization of their lifestyle as producing more negative than positive consequences. A few are faced with the despair that their actions have led to a biographical dead end, whether they see a way out or not:

> You do it for a cause, but when you're still young ... people who get into this, they don't see, twenty years later, that it led nowhere. But when you're young, you think you can change the world. And you're pumped up when two or three new guys come in, and you think it's going to get big. But it's a damn waste of time, in Quebec. There's nothing you can do about it, because everyone, everyone, everyone is against you. (ED37)

This respondent left his group because he was tired of the violence: "I said look, I've got five kids, I don't have the time for stupid fist fights." But he still thinks immigration is wrong, that governments tax too much, that he has a right to carry firearms, and he calls himself a "patriot." What is more, though he no longer partakes in violent activities and is not a member of any group, his "transformation" is only partial: he served two prison terms for illegal possession of multiple guns as late as 2018.

As is the case for some criminals in F.-Dufour and Brassard, one of our respondents reported having essentially let himself be arrested and convicted, which he later came to see as a threshold in his life:

> One of my guys and I, he was the guy I was kinda priming to take over my spot as a recruiter, a young guy ... and err, we got in trouble and got arrested one night. And he was full of tattoos, racist tattoos, and I'm like, "He's a young kid, he's gonna die if he goes to jail," so I took the charges and I went to jail for three years. (ED28)

The remorseful entered their criminal career from a mainstream, rather than marginalized, social position. They generally do not accept the criminal identity but feel guilt for at least some of the acts they committed.

> One time a little thing happened ... and my kid was there when they came to confront me or whatever, right, and I was thinking

> afterwards, like this is not gonna be the life I'm gonna teach my kid about. Like she'll have no memory of it, my daughter, she was like two at that time. So, I'm glad she'll have no memory. And that's what I'm trying to create now, she'll have the memory of me, you know, working to prevent this stuff, not being involved in it, being the president of this group. (ED34)

The rescued are steered from their career in criminality through interaction with individuals who help them "reform." Family members, institutions, peers, NGOs can directly affect an exit from the extremist path. None of our (admittedly, few) desisted respondents reported changing their life after this type of interaction. However, we did get information on this aspect from activists involved in that type of intervention. It is also a common story among some of the individuals who have become public about their past far-right activities, such as Elisa Hategan (Hategan 2014). Usually this is most likely to affect actual change when the circumstances are at their most dire for the subject.

By and large, desisting extremism consists in ending commitment to the ideology or to the group, and eventually disengaging altogether from the movement. This occurs when the benefits of continued participation (for the most part protection, friendship, excitement, a sense of meaning) no longer make up for the sacrifices involved (safety, peace, family, work). The way our desisting participants evaluate this is highly variable, but by far the most common reason invoked was the incompatibility of their lifestyle with their desire to raise a family. Not that this conflict is inevitable, however: "I couldn't teach my daughter to hate other people ... a lot of these guys they do that, like you'll go to parties and you'll see them teaching their child to *Seig heil* and teaching their kids the fourteen words like, for me, I can't" (ED34).

Note that there may be resistance from the group to terminating membership and group activities, especially if the desistance goes beyond mere distancing, towards a conflictual ideological position:

> Personally, early on I kept some friends from the group but at some point I became a kind of Judas because I began to fight

> against that, because I saw it was really bullshit. And then, that was it. I was beaten up, they stole my shirts. One, precisely because it was a [punk rock band] Bérurier Noir shirt, who are antifascists. And that, you don't show around because, to them, it's a direct attack. (ED8)

Of course, this form of violence is meant as a message not to the immediate target, who is not likely to rethink his departure, but to the remaining members who might reconsider their own membership or question some of the activities of the group. In other words, it is meant to prevent further desistance or dissent from the ranks and to redraw and strengthen the boundary between the in- and the outgroup.

Conclusion

The trajectories of our respondents, as those of defendants in the courts, are peppered with the peculiarities of human biographies. Yet there is a limited, identifiable set of factors that, in conjunction, are powerful attractors towards extremism. Individuals who are undereducated or have inadequate social interactions with family and nonextremist peers are likely to be impressed by groups that project power or are charismatic ideologues, especially if current events happen to highlight ideological cleavages (a legislator's motion condemning Islamophobia, for instance), local social polarization (an influx of refugees), or government power (like pandemic sanitary measures). Those who are educated and feel knowledgeable, while ideologically opposed to a seemingly unstoppable movement or trend, again given signal events in the news, may feel disempowered and decide to disseminate hate propaganda on the Internet. They may also pick up a firearm and massacre the faithful in a mosque.

Throughout this chapter we have shown how rational individuals, given a particular context, are pushed and/or pulled towards various groups. These factors range from the highly personal to the global, from the directly visible in everyday life to the highly abstract and ideological. Usually, only the extremely fragile engage with extreme movements when multiple such pressures come to bear at once, opening a window for engagement. For some, the window is an escape hatch that leads to a less stressful, less vulnerable, less lonely state and towards a new world of moral clarity, solidarity, and enlightenment. Of course, these factors operate in the world described in the previous chapters, where multiple groups and individuals are making intense use of mass communication to disseminate their perception of important issues, phenomena, or accidents, in large part by articulating them as workings of a vast conspiracy. But neither push nor pull factors act as strings that manipulate. Individuals have to learn to recognize them, to adopt them, and to "read" them properly in order to act accordingly – with the reading and the acting reinforcing each other, especially in group contexts. Choosing to act in defence of whiteness, for instance, both reinforces the white supremacist discourse and shows the way through example. It is important to remember that our respondents didn't wait for their convictions to be fully formed or fully compatible with the far right before they committed to their group's deviant and criminal acts. In fact, many never reached that level of ideological sophistication. In that, a group's ideology and repertoire of action are continual works in progress, constructed by individuals in a never-ending need to decide how to continue from moment to moment. It is an ongoing "ethnomethod," a toolbox used to make sense of the world and one's role within it.

The small minority of those who commit to a far-right movement or who develop beliefs associated with this ideology of the far right certainly represents a security threat. The matter is a little more complex with regards to the majority that contributes, by its ideological position and actions, to fuelling distrust towards political, social, and economic institutions. Yet in both cases simple police solutions have been popular and often called for by activists, politicians, and victims. In the next chapter we look at the different strategies of policing the far right, as they contribute to expanding or limiting political opportunity structures.

6 POLICING THE FAR RIGHT

Introduction

Sometime in 2017, Public Safety Canada (PSC) appears to have had an epiphany with regards to the threat of far-right violence. As with each of its previous yearly terrorist threat reports, in 2016 it was still claiming that

> the principal terrorist threat to Canada remains that posed by violent extremists who could be inspired to carry out an attack in Canada. Violent extremist ideologies espoused by terrorist groups like Daesh and al-Qaida continue to appeal to certain individuals in Canada. (PSC 2016, 3)

The next yearly report, though it still begins by underlining that "the main terrorist threat to Canada continues to stem from violent extremists inspired by terrorist groups, such as Daesh and al-Qaida" (PSC 2017, 3), adds the following:

> The extreme right-wing is not an ideologically coherent group and historically, extreme right-wing violence in Canada has been sporadic and opportunistic. Nonetheless, the shooting at the Islamic Cultural Centre of Quebec City in Ste-Foy, Quebec, on January 29, 2017, in which six people were killed and 19 others injured, is a reminder that attacks perpetrated by those who espouse extreme right-wing views can occur in Canada. As there

> has been a rise in hate-related incidents reported to police in Canada, there is always the potential for extreme right-wing motivated violence to occur in the future. (PSC 2017, 7)

The reason for the epiphany is obvious: one single attack at a mosque managed to kill and wound more Canadians than the sum of all "Islamist" terrorist attacks in Canadian history. This is the only mention of far-right violence, though seven pages are still dedicated to explaining the multiple (Islamist) threats to Canada. Yet it highlights an important shift in thinking. The following year, the threat report spends two pages (out of ten) on the far right (PSC 2018). In 2019 Blood and Honour and its violent offshoot Combat 18 were added to Canada's official list of terrorist entities. In 2021, just after demonstrators stormed the Capitol in Washington, DC, Atomwaffen Division, the Proud Boys, and the Base were also added to the list. Later in June it was the turn of the Three Percenters and Aryan Strikeforce.

That the list, until very recently, was composed almost exclusively of Islamist groups speaks volumes to the durable depth of the scars left by 9/11 on counterterrorism in Canada. It also shows that a slow but perceptible evolution is taking place. This chapter describes this evolution and accounts for its sluggishness.

National security policing

In Canada, political violence is usually considered to be a national security issue, especially if it can be legally defined as "terrorism." As such, it is part of the legally defined mandate of the federal Royal Canadian Mounted Police (RCMP) and even strictly local events are often elevated to policing structures where the RCMP must be present. From that point of view, the question then becomes whether the far right in Canada constitutes a threat to the security of the nation or if it constitutes terrorism. We believe that this approach is not likely to be fruitful, for two reasons. First, it bears repeating that the Canadian far right is not a uniform block with common objectives and methods, and therefore it escapes easy categorization. Second, where politically motivated violence indeed exists, it must be noted that the boundary between common crime and national security offences is, for the most part, the product of institutional responsibility, as designated by law. Identifying the distinction in the actual activities of criminals is a far thornier undertaking. Considering the distinction between teenage shoplifting and the 9/11 disaster, most politically motivated crimes are located far from both extremes.

Moreover, national security threats are identified before crimes are being conceived of and prepared, much less committed. This is the realm of what Brodeur (2007) referred to as "high policing," the surveillance and disruption of political activities deemed undesirable by the state. Of course, in a liberal democracy these are defined in the strictest terms and peaceful protest and dissidence in general are tolerated, if not encouraged. Within this framework, "political policing" consists in protecting democratic institutions and processes.

In practice, this means that policing institutions are given significant latitude in defining national security, national security threats, and adequate responses. In Canada, such matters are entrusted to the Canadian Security Intelligence Service (CSIS). The service's primary mission is to investigate and "advise" the prime minister of Canada in matters of national security and, when necessary, to notify federal police if criminal activities are detected or suspected.

The Canadian Security Intelligence Service (CSIS)

In its 2018 report, the Security Intelligence Review Committee (SIRC), whose mission was to monitor CSIS activities (it has since been replaced by the National Security and Intelligence Review Agency [NSIRA] and indirectly by the intelligence commissioner [IC], in charge of reviewing ministerial directives to CSIS), conducted a brief analysis of the service's work and noted that it had stopped specific surveillance of the far-right scene in March 2016, nine months before the mosque massacre in Quebec City (SIRC 2018, 19). The unfortunate sequence of events created a mini-scandal in the media. It also underlined once more the difficulty for intelligence agencies in monitoring and evaluating small-group or individual behaviour. One reason is that such behaviour is often (but certainly not always) unpredictable. Another is, we shall argue, that it is not deemed worthy of attention.

CSIS was created in 1984, in the wake of one of the worst political policing scandals in Canadian history, involving CSIS's predecessor, the RCMP's Security Service. Not that the scandal came as a surprise for those who were knowledgeable about the surveillance of political activity in Canada. In 1969, the Mackenzie Commission report had already underlined that the fight against communism was taking a toll on the RCMP's pristine image, as its constables were resorting to dirtier and dirtier tricks:

> Furthermore, there is a clear distinction between the operational work of a security service and that of a police force. A security service will inevitably be involved in actions that may contravene the spirit if not the letter of the law, and with clandestine and other activities which may sometimes seem to infringe on individuals' rights; these are not appropriate police functions. (Canada 1969, 21)

A few years later, a botched bombing committed by an RCMP corporal on behalf of the Italian mafia triggered a Royal Commission of Inquiry into new allegations against the RCMP's Security Service (McDonald Commission; Canada 1979). The corporal, who had injured his hand while setting the bomb, claimed in court he had done "much worse" for the RCMP. Indeed, investigations and testimony revealed that Security Service operatives had engaged in various illegal actions against official, legal political parties, institutions, and businesses under the pretext of fighting separatism in Quebec (including stealing databases, firebombing buildings, and conducting more than four hundred break-ins). Following the recommendations of the commission, the Security Service was abolished and replaced by a "civilian" service (i.e., one whose members would not be given the legal powers of sworn officers of the peace), CSIS.

Of course, at the beginning, the new CSIS agents were recruited from the group of the former Security Service investigators (and initially worked from the same offices). They carried with them the "case file" outlook that consists in building incriminating dossiers on, and eventually criminal cases against, subversive elements. More importantly, the Security Service culture also entailed that the only threats worthy of attention were those that could be linked to international foreign powers opposed to Canada or its allies. This included, primarily, the member countries of the Warsaw Pact (Whitaker et al. 2012, 368), as well as France in the case of Quebec separatists (especially after President De Gaulle's thunderous 1967 proclamation "vive le Québec libre" to an elated crowd in Montreal). The threats included spying, of course, but also the sponsoring of international terrorism by the Kremlin and the support of various "communist" political organizations intent on interfering with internal Canadian politics. For instance, the Front de libération du Québec had been very active in the 1960s, robbing banks, stealing from military depots, planting more than two hundred bombs in Montreal, kidnapping the British trade commissioner and the deputy premier of Quebec in 1970, eventually killing the latter. But in the mid-1960s the RCMP suspected that the FLQ also had links to Cuba and the Kremlin (Whitaker et al. 2012, 280). In the context of the 1960s anti-Soviet paranoia, this only added to the urgency felt by Canadian police agencies at the time, who felt justified in taking more extreme measures.

This legacy of a narrow focus on communists and separatists is one key reason why a few actual terrorist plots were overlooked by CSIS in its first years of existence, one resulting in the worst massacre in Canadian history: the infamous Air India bombing. In that case the threat was only taken seriously by CSIS in the few months prior to the massacre. The service had run electronic and physical surveillance of Sikh extremists who publicly, repeatedly swore to massacre Indians in revenge for the Indian Armed Forces destruction of the Golden Temple at Amritsar. This included two agents witnessing a bomb test in the woods (Leman-Langlois 2018; Canada 2010). Yet the entire affair was seen as an Indian problem or, at best, a local policing matter involving extremist Sikhs who mostly clashed with their co-religionists in and around Surrey, BC. Even when the problem was finally elevated to a top priority, the necessary resources were only allocated after the double bombing (Canada 2010, vol. 2, part 1, 345–53).

Over the following decades, the service evolved beyond recognition. In two decades, personnel would slowly change and more experts would be recruited, moving the culture slowly towards information analysis and evaluation instead of the criminal caseload model. The Air India Commission identifies the early 2000s as the threshold when old-style political policing finally took a backseat to modern intelligence analysis (Canada 2010; Gomez del Prado and Leman-Langlois 2020). One key factor, of course, is the intelligence electroshock of the 9/11 attacks in the USA. Only months before, CSIS still had difficulty in clearly identifying security threats, as illustrated by the infamous Ahmed Ressam case. Ressam, an Algerian refugee claimant, was recorded discussing attacks against targets in Canada and in the US, plotting his departure to Afghanistan to acquire fighting skills, and forging a false identity. His goodbyes to his roommates were also recorded. On his way to LAX, Ressam was stopped by a US Customs (now Border Protection) agent who discovered a homemade bomb in the trunk of his rental car (Leman-Langlois and Brodeur 2009; Leman-Langlois 2018b, 2019). Two years before 9/11, al Qaeda was still not on the service's radar and Ressam and his friends were just a frustrated "bunch of guys" whining and ranting against the West.

Another reason that made it difficult for CSIS to actively participate in the prevention of terror attacks was its relationship with police, and especially the RCMP. Until 2017, CSIS had no power to intervene directly and had to refer cases where crimes were suspected to the RCMP (it has since gained limited powers to disrupt suspicious or potentially threatening activities). At least in the years prior to 9/11, the precise form this reference could take was deemed highly problematic and the service couldn't reconcile its civilian advisory role, its spying techniques, and its obligation to report criminal conspiracies to the RCMP (Canada, 2010). On one hand, involving police – who would want to mount a case for public trial – meant exposing its assets, investigatory methods, sources, priorities, and tasking. From the police's point of view, using knowledge provided by CSIS risked tainting the evidentiary process, which would sink the eventual prosecution of those responsible (among other things, CSIS surveillance and search warrants were granted on the lower threshold of "investigative need" rather than the "reason to believe" imposed on police) (Gomez del Prado and Leman-Langlois 2020). Rules and policies were eventually put in place to both compel and strictly frame the exchange of information between CSIS and the RCMP. In particular, the One Vision framework for cooperation launched in 2012 set out the process by which the entities would exchange information and warnings. In 2015, One Vision 2.0 added deconfliction rules in order to avoid potential problems generated by CSIS's new field intervention powers introduced by changes in the CSIS Act (via Bill C-51). In short, the rules mean that barring emergencies, CSIS must quickly give notice to police when the potential for criminal acts appears significant but only by revealing the name and date of birth of a potential subject of interest. The RCMP's National Security Enforcement Sections (NSESs) are then activated but must start from the beginning, without the benefit – or liability – of CSIS investigative products. This minimal threshold for information sharing has been criticized as grossly insufficient for the security of Canadians, since it can delay a police response in cases of serious conspiracy (Forcese and Roach 2015).

Gauging the threat

Though CSIS repeatedly includes the mantra of "multifaceted complexity" in its yearly reports, from 2001 to 2018 the threats it identified were all essentially the same: Islamist organizations abroad who try to inspire or directly sponsor attacks in Canada. It must be underlined that in late 2001 CSIS was given an immediate, massive 30 per cent increase in its budget specifically to fight "Sunni Islamic Extremism" (SIRC 2002, 31). The high specificity of the budget meant that any additional staff or training were selected for their relevance to this new, relatively narrow set of threats. Note that CSIS's budget is (probably, details are confidential) mostly geared towards the conducting of thousands of individual security clearances for refugee claimants, federal staff, etc., every year, and consequently a 30 per cent global increase hides a far more significant increase in the more specific security intelligence functions.

During those nearly two decades, when "right-wing extremism" is mentioned at all in yearly reports, it is always to dismiss it: "Right-wing extremism has not been as significant a problem in Canada in recent years. Those who hold such extremist views have tended to be isolated and ineffective figures" (CSIS 2013). The 2016 report makes no mention of the far right at all. It contains a "terrorism timeline" covering the 2014–16 period, where all attacks are Islamist in nature and occur mostly abroad (resulting in undoubtedly tragic but entirely coincidental Canadian victims). The portrait is set against a vast background of multiple, but closely networked, terrorist organizations operating in remote, exotic regions of the world and inspiring violence in Canada or against Canadians abroad.

This core threat has been described in various ways over the years. This is partially due to CSIS's efforts to respond to accusations of insensitivity to the meaning of words such as "jihad" to ordinary Muslims, of conflating "Salafist" with "terrorist," or, for instance, of using language reinforcing the so-called Islamic State's contention to be truly and uniquely Islamic (Elghawaby 2016). Later reports attempt to entirely avoid the use of general language and instead replace it with phrases like "extremists who are inspired by terrorist groups such as Daesh and Al Qaeda" (CSIS 2018). Entire paragraphs are "agnostic" as to the actual source of the threat, built exclusively of intangible concepts:

> CSIS also remains concerned about the threat posed by those who harbor and support other forms of extremism. The globalization of terrorism, fueled by elaborate online propaganda by extremist groups, has expanded the breadth of radicalization and mobilization to violence. In some instances, individuals influenced by extremist ideology have travelled (or attempted to travel) abroad to participate in terrorist activity. Others have supported their extremist ideology through training, fundraising, recruitment and attack planning within Canada. (CSIS 2018, 19)

Yet the list of incidents and places in the world where CSIS claims such "extremism" takes root, in the end, shows that the only real threat is Islamic extremism.

The contours, function, and consequences of this threat are almost the same as that of communism in the 1920–80 era. Communism was such an overwhelmingly dominant threat that, as is evident in the documents of the time (see Kealy and Whitaker 1989, 1993), the RCMP was almost exclusively interested in members and "sympathizers" of communist organizations – even though their most subversive actions, as inventoried by RCMP, were anti-capitalist speeches. By contrast, Nazi and fascist organizations, even during the war, were only given cursory attention. Communism was perceived as a central motivating ideology connecting multiple conflicts worldwide and inspiring subversion in Canada (the RCMP's PROFUNC program, active until 1983, planned to imprison 16,000 identified Canadian communists and 50,000 sympathizers in the event of a war with the Soviet Union). Originally centred in the Kremlin, but with new cases breaking out all over the world, threats to Canada and its allies were multiplying. Needless to say, the fall of the iron curtain left a gaping hole in the national security apparatus's raison d'être.

Starting with 9/11, violent Islamism filled that gap very well, effectively erasing any genuine "multifaceted complexity" in foreign conflicts to present a centralized, structured threat. Just like communism, it has a perceived antagonistic agenda, dangerous to "Canadian values"; it has a few central command centres and multiple clients around the globe; it invests heavily in propaganda and convinces a marginal but notable number of Canadians and foreigners to join the global "jihad." Just like the communist threat, it is nearly immutable, vast, slow moving. It is the new cold war, everlasting, impossible to win, too important to lose. By comparison, the matter of the far right seemed truly inconsequential or at least not a proper "national security" issue.

We argue that this was due to a particular lens used on the objects rather than their respective properties. Further, the persistence of this lens today is due to organizational inertia: once personnel are recruited, trained, and experienced in tackling a particular issue, they become experts in that issue and cannot simply switch and become experts in an entirely different one. The training investment is also a heavy loss, for instance, if hundreds of hours spent on Arabic and Qur'anic studies are no longer needed. In 2010 then CSIS director Richard Fadden explained, "So in some cases, for our purposes, somebody has to study for two or three years. It is excruciatingly expensive, just in plain cash bucks. And it's expensive in that it takes an experienced officer off-line for two or three years" (CTV News 2010). Such experts also tend to evaluate new potential threats with the yardsticks elaborated for the old ones: for instance, sponsorship of a foreign enemy power. Finally, the organizational structure also contributes to the inertia because it has been dedicating teams, budgets, recruitment strategies, training, and career incentives to a now obsolete hierarchy of issues.

As we have seen, catastrophic events can help put an end to organizational inertia. The mosque massacre was instrumental in a significant shift in focus at Public Safety Canada, which (appears to have) quite suddenly realized there was a potential for violence from the far right. But even the relatively euphemistic language used in the PSC report quoted above was rejected by CSIS proofreaders as exaggerated. When PSC was preparing its report, it submitted the draft text to CSIS for suggestions and comments. Documents obtained by journalist Stewart Bell (2018) under the Access to Information Act reveal that CSIS took issue with PSC's decision to identify the far right as a problem in Canada (the documents were shared with us for the purposes of this chapter, while PSC refused to respond to our repeated access to information requests). The unnamed CSIS reviewers disagree with almost every part of the draft text that has to do with the intensity or size of the threat. In one instance CSIS commentators suggested that a paragraph about the far right start by stating that "Within the broader context of extremism in Canada, the number of right-wing extremists who promote or are willing to engage in politically-motivated violence is extremely small" (email from CSIS to PSC, correspondent names redacted). At the time, the service's view was that the far right as a whole fell within the act's exceptions to the threats listed above: "lawful advocacy, protest or dissent, unless carried on in conjunction with any of the activities referred to in paragraphs (a) to (d)" (CSIS Act, Interpretation).

Yet one year later, the 2018 CSIS report suddenly claims that "*Since 2014* [emphasis added], all Five Eye partners have experienced violent attacks or plots perpetrated by individuals influenced, in whole or in part, by their far-right-wing views" (CSIS 2018, 23). There is no explanation as to why the 2014, 2015, 2016, or 2017 reports made no mention of these attacks and plots (including in the 2016 "terrorism timeline"). Note that the report, like the following one in 2019, still marks Islamist terrorists as the main threat to the national security of Canada, even though there are no attacks or plots attributed to them. Since 2020 CSIS has adopted an entirely new vocabulary, complete with complex acronyms, but with no reference to terrorism, to describe types of extremism. Racist, misogynistic, and other types of threats typical of the far right are now accounted for, but the language used to refer to actual events and risks is more opaque than ever.

Intelligence is the cogent organization of complex, sometimes massive, often contradictory information. We know for a fact that CSIS intelligence analysis personnel, individually and as specialized groups, have a far more nuanced and detailed perception of the proverbial threat environment than that portrayed in the various public reports from CSIS or PSC, both meant for public consumption and political communication. As such, however, the reports do set a framework and expectations for the attribution of resources, be they human, financial, or legal (as evident with the inscription of new terrorist entities on the official list). In other words, whether they reflect the state of knowledge and analysis within the organizations, we believe they are indicative of their overall agenda. Consequently, it is no surprise to read, in the 2023 Report of the Public Inquiry into the 2022 Public Order Emergency (Canada 2023), that CSIS still had almost no information on the multiple far-right entities embedded in the Freedom Convoy.

The way forward

The main questions for the way forward are a) to what extent is the far right, as groups or as individuals, likely to commit crimes, other illegal acts, or other behaviours that might be made unlawful in the future; and b) whether any of these actions amount to threats to national security. If they do not, they are a police matter and the national security apparatus, including CSIS, should simply remain unconcerned.

The first aspect is easy to elucidate. As chapter 2 above has shown, the far-right nebula encompasses multiple ideologies and types (including absence) of organization, from Sovereign Citizens to clandestine militias, with Incels and anti-government avengers in between. Each of these subcategories has prompted hundreds of criminal infractions (property crimes, hate crimes, threats, violence) and other violations (tax code, municipal bylaws, etc.). That they are likely to continue seems like a glaring understatement. Of course, these infractions were not committed by "the far right" as a group, such as 9/11 was committed by al Qaeda.

The second interrogation is whether this inventory of infractions constitutes, in whole or in part, a threat to national security. That is a more complex matter, and it revolves around two principal issues. The first one is the practical definition of "national security" under use. One common definition is the "grand" view of the threats to and vulnerabilities of the sovereign state, including of course invasions, ballistic bombing attacks, embargoes, commercial and economic sanctions, blockades, and the like. Under this definition, the very existence of the nation must be threatened. Despite the hyperbolized statements of the immediate post-9/11 era, terrorism is not, and has never been, such an existential threat. Like most asymmetric conflicts, it is defined by a corresponding asymmetry of the risks, one that dramatically favours the nation state. In the past decades we have repeatedly seen very limited individual threats being treated as terrorism and national security issues, which shows that the grand view of national security, though popular among politicians and columnists, is clearly not the operational one.

On a less grandiose level, national security may refer to the security of the key elements that allow the nation to function as a system. These can be evoked by a series of concepts such as human, economic, political, or ecological security. More tangibly, one might consider the vulnerability of critical infrastructures, among which can be found governmental administrations at multiple levels, key industries (chemicals, energy), water and electrical distribution networks, financial institutions, transportation (rail, air, bridges), health, and communications. Typically, these infrastructures are on the list of targets of most terror groups. In Canada most were attacked at some point in recent history, with highly variable results (Leman-Langlois and Brodeur 2009). The financial sector was targeted by the FLQ in the 1960s. Air transport was attacked by the Air India conspirators. Montreal's central rail station was bombed in 1984, as were railway tracks in British Columbia in the 1970s, dozens of times, by the Sons of Freedom. The electrical distribution network was targeted by a fringe group in Quebec in 2004 and by Direct Action in BC in 1982. Politicians, diplomats, representatives, and sites of government administration were attacked multiple times by various groups and individuals. It has become difficult to keep track of threats against government officials coming from anti-government conspiracy theory aficionados on the far right. For instance, on 2 July 2020 a reservist from Manitoba drove to Ottawa to kill the prime minister of Canada. After nearly two hours of police negotiation, he was arrested on the grounds of the PM's residence at Rideau Hall with two shotguns, one handgun, and a rifle equipped with a high-capacity magazine. The list goes on but, notably, has had no effect on Canada's status as one of the countries on the planet *least* affected by terrorism (Leman-Langlois and Brodeur 2009).

Canada has no legal definition of national security, but the CSIS Act describes four categories of activities that constitute threats:

> (a) espionage or sabotage that is against Canada or is detrimental to the interests of Canada or activities directed toward or in support of such espionage or sabotage,
> (b) foreign influenced activities within or relating to Canada that are detrimental to the interests of Canada and are clandestine or deceptive or involve a threat to any person,
> (c) activities within or relating to Canada directed toward or in support of the threat or use of acts of serious violence against persons or property for the purpose of achieving a political, religious or ideological objective within Canada or a foreign state, and
> (d) activities directed toward undermining by covert unlawful acts, or directed toward or intended ultimately to lead to the destruction or overthrow by violence of, the constitutionally established system of government in Canada. (CSIS Act, 1985 [2024], 3)

Most of the illegal activities committed by groups and individuals on the far right would probably fall under (c) or (d) above, with (b) clearly obvious in many cases, such as Russian disinformation meant to disrupt democratic processes by exaggerating political polarization. Because of the historical reasons mentioned above, data collection and analysis, and thus reporting, by the service are explicitly restricted to these categories. There is a further, crucial exclusion of "lawful advocacy, protest or dissent." Yet, as we have seen in the previous chapters, activities on the far right are spread over the entire spectrum between protest and violent massacre. This represents a difficult challenge for political policing.

Each category can be subjected to a different interpretation, which may make that category more or less restrictive. For instance, violence has multiple definitions and may or may not include intimidation, threats, destruction of property, harassment, etc. It is clear from the above discussion that where far-right entities have been concerned, so far, the restrictive interpretation dominates.

One aspect of our collective, national vulnerability has been neglected. In everyday practice the normal functioning and efficiency of the government and its agencies is predicated not simply on the well-being of elected officials and civil servants but also on basic consent by the majority of citizens. When this minimal cohesion breaks down, or appears to, even the full deployment of policing is quickly overrun and military action may be required, usually with results ranging from less than optimal to catastrophic. Therefore, we suggest that violent attacks deliberately designed to, or that can reasonably be expected to, generate conflict and insecurity, usually by pitting populations against one another, can be thought of as national security threats against critical political infrastructure: for example, "the constitutionally established system of government in Canada." On 6 June 2021 a vehicle-ramming attack on a Muslim family in London, Ontario, showed how an individual, small-scale attack can inflame society at the local and national levels and fuel social polarization. It also showed the power of the radical Islamophobic discourse in recruiting and mobilizing receptive individuals.

National security surveillance should be more closely aligned with the actual potential of the various forms of threats rather than the now outdated vision that gives top priority to local manifestations of international (jihad) networks. In fact, this vision no longer fits even the current jihadi extremism itself. Neither of the two 2014 pro-ISIS attackers had tangible ideological, financial, or tactical contacts outside of Canada (or inside, for that matter). That is also true of the BC legislature attack plotters or the Via Rail plotters. If any kind of democratic political policing is going to take place in Canada, it will have to invest far less in the tracking of violent international far-right groups and far more in monitoring national propaganda and ideology networks that are the incubators of violent attacks and hate speech. This will not, or rarely will, identify individual threats but will go a long way in shaping policy and steering preventative efforts – assuming a governmental desire to follow up and address the issue. The identify-and-list process that has so far dominated the new interest in far-right extremists will not work, for multiple reasons: a) the list is obsolete within minutes of its update, if not before, so it will be no help in preventing financing, training, etc.; b) most groups do not have clearcut membership rules; c) most groups encourage individual rather than group action; d) this approach causes groups to disband immediately, negating surveillance efforts; and e) it entirely ignores the vastness and inscrutability of the far right.

The detection and identification of individual or small group threats is mostly a true mission impossible. Even if Canada had an intelligence institution dedicated to open-source collection, and for that it would first need to build a democratically acceptable legal framework for navigating social media (and other sources), it would be hopeless to attempt to identify actual violent attackers in the sea of hate, propaganda, and endless conspiracy scenarios on the web. The 2022 Ottawa Freedom Convoy siege illustrates this well: the group was essentially a flash mob of citizens tired of COVID-19 restrictions, of anti-vaccine crusaders, Trudeau haters, and conspiracy theorists. It also contained a substantial number of far-right anti-government and neo-Nazi extremists, some already under the scrutiny of CSIS and the RCMP. It is unclear at this point whether attention was paid to the networking, recruiting, and mainstreaming efforts that prompted the participation of these extremists. They are building the next wave of far-right-inspired violence but, as usual, sorting out the violent from the merely oppositional remains a challenge. Plotters do not have detectable behaviour or speech patterns and often move quite suddenly from the standard bellyaching and propagandizing to climbing into a car with an entire arsenal (the Rideau Hall attacker ran a conspiracy website for twenty years before driving to Ottawa) or to using their vehicle as a deadly weapon (e.g., the London attacker in June 2021 and the Toronto attacker in 2018). As has been the case for years, the individual identification of dangerous elements will continue to come from walk-ins, anonymous calls, informers, disgruntled co-conspirators, and worried family members.

Policing and criminal law

First and foremost, outright political violence is a police matter. Beyond media sensationalism and the industrial use of fear stoking about existential threats, beyond the politicians' righteous wrath and the fury of pundits, all of which are most effective at glorifying terrorists and increasing the power of their propaganda, the simple reality is far less grandiose. In fact, for the most part, the actors of hate and terrorism are otherwise ordinary humans dealing with local problems in the definitional and practical frameworks suggested by disjointed, chaotic, conflictual snippets of hateful ideologies and the hortatory power of social movements.

Terror

The dominant counterterrorist strategy today consists of using the Criminal Code not only as a repressive but as a preventative tool. Though the trend started sometime before the 9/11 attacks, that event has been a major driver in what Asp (2013) refers to as the criminalization of nonconsummate offences. That was the main objective of the Canadian Anti-Terrorist Act of 2001 (ATA):

> The ATA was founded primarily on the principle of the prevention of terrorist acts. Offences such as knowingly instructing the carrying out of any activity for a terrorist group or knowingly facilitating a terrorist group are specifically defined to be offences, regardless of whether the ultimate terrorist activity is carried out and regardless of whether the accused knows the specific nature of the terrorist activity being contemplated. By creating such offences, the law takes into account both the manner in which terrorist groups actually operate and the fundamental need for prevention. (Justice Canada, https://www.justice.gc.ca/eng/cj-jp/ns-sn/act-loi.html)

The killings, mutilations, kidnappings, and hijackings that are the basic tactics of terrorists were criminalized before the ATA. But ordinary penal laws can only be said to be "preventative" in their political communication aspects, where they clearly identify the acts that will not be tolerated by the state and attempt to deter their perpetration by the threat of punishment. But the actual mobilization of the state always *follows* the crime. The advent of 9/11 caused a catastrophic conceptual crisis, making it glaringly obvious that terrorists were entirely immune to the deterrent power of penal sanctions. No matter how harsh, punishment cannot deter from suicide, a conclusion made inescapable by the indelible images of airplanes deliberately crashed into buildings at high speed (Leman-Langlois 2003).

Consequently, most of the anti-terrorism laws adopted by many states in the aftermath of the 9/11 attacks involved the use of laws to punish pre-terrorist activities. Unfortunately, they also all rest on the (false) assumption that terrorist acts always require an important preparatory phase, consisting of multiple separate actions that could be criminalized and therefore used to identify and to stop them. The ATA followed this trend by introducing entirely new offences to the Criminal Code, including the financing of terrorist entities, training for terrorist purposes, supporting, and counselling (financing was part of UN Security Council resolution 1373). They can now be found in Part II.1 of the code. In the years following, more were added, including travelling abroad and disseminating propaganda for the purposes of terrorism. Now two decades later, we must conclude that the 9/11 attack, with its worldwide plotting and financing, its long-term preparation, and its vast network of accomplices, was not a harbinger of a new era of mass terrorism but a statistical oddity. The result is that our anti-terrorism laws are inadequate to tackle contemporary terrorism.

Though one can see the link between learning to make bombs, buying the necessary materials, or encouraging others to do so and the goal of violent destruction, in many other instances the link between the new pre-terrorist crimes and an eventual violent act is less obvious (travelling, propaganda, counselling, etc.). Regardless, this multiplication of pre-terror offences has generated almost all terrorism cases in Canada, even though, *stricto sensu*, no actual terrorism was expected or, therefore, prevented (Nesbitt and Hagg 2020). Note that the pre-terrorist offences were also punished in proportion not to the actual elements of the act but to those of the possible, imaginable but still unplanned attacks (Nesbitt, Oxoby and Potier 2019). One of us was once asked by a senator in committee why sending the value of a hamburger to a terrorist group abroad should not be punished as a fully formed terrorist act.

Meanwhile, though the 2017 Quebec City mosque attack was an act of terrorism under almost all known definitions (a few exceptions, for instance, require group organization), like most other acts of far-right violence it could not be prosecuted as such. One key difficulty in prosecuting terrorist acts is, quite simply, that as a political crime the political motivation of the accused must be demonstrated in court. Unless the attacker left a letter, a manifesto, or a video explaining his or her actions and linking them directly to an ideology, the demonstration will be easily countered by the defence. The mosque attacker did have far-right propaganda on his computer, was a regular follower of xenophobic programming on the Internet, and had viewed the Columbine videos hundreds of times. Yet this was deemed insufficient to establish a clear link between ideology, methodology, and the actual attack. Even his post-arrest confession to a social worker, to the effect that Muslims were dangerous and had to be dealt with, was not regarded as sufficient evidence of motive at the time of the attack. Bissonnette, the mosque attacker, was declared guilty of six counts of murder and forty-one of attempted murder. One recent exception to this norm is the case of the alleged perpetrator of the London ram-attack against a Muslim family, in June 2021, who did face terrorism charges. His original four counts of first-degree murder and one of attempted murder were eventually upgraded to terrorism under 83.01(1)(b) of the Criminal Code. At the end of the trial held in early 2024, the judge clearly established that the accused had engaged in terrorist activities. She even considered it to be a textbook case (Dubinski 2024).

One other way to fulfill the motive requirement is to link the suspect to an officially listed terrorist group, as members are understood to share the motives of the group. As already mentioned, the list is published and maintained by the government on the recommendation of the minister for Public Safety Canada and its agencies, especially CSIS (see Public Safety Canada 2021). Until recently, this official list was composed almost exclusively of Muslim extremist groups, with few exceptions (such as the now inactive Tamil Tigers, Aum Shinrikyo, and ETA). During the two decades of its existence, the list has certainly had the effect of exaggerating the apparent prevalence of international Muslim extremist terror networks in political violence.

Furthermore, the high level of attention given to "jihad" organizations generated a problematic set of expectations regarding violent networks on the far right: that they would be equally connected, that they would have the same flair for branding and comparably cogent grievances, objectives, and repertoires of action. Yet the far right, as it exists today, has fewer international players and more conflicting ideologies, and, as we have seen, is mostly a collection of subjects confronting immediate, local problems. Given that, it seems inevitable that violence from the far right is not likely to be labelled as "terrorist" in courtrooms, not seen as part of a network, and, by way of consequence, not identified as a threat to national security. It also explains why the far right is often considered to be non-violent, especially by local police: outbursts of violence are systematically attributed to "crackpots" and lone actors, while the larger groups remain on social media or run well-disciplined demonstrations and are generally respectful of authority (for instance, ED17 explains that his group coordinates their activities with the police).

In addition to the populations they identify as dangerous, far-right groups also often target governments and their representatives, much like terrorists in general. During the 2022 Freedom Convoy crisis, Diagolon sympathizers sought to attack frontline officers at the Coutts, Alberta, border crossing, which was blockaded by anti-sanitary-measures protesters at the time. The group was already under police surveillance, and with the help of agents who had infiltrated it, as well as wiretaps, RCMP officers were able to arrest thirteen individuals and seized a cache of weapons and armour near the protest site.

What the Rouleau Commission showed, however, is that when the entities are less well defined, with an implicit, sporadic, or absent membership structure, identifying policing strategies becomes much more difficult, which can lead to paralysis. The RCMP and Ontario Provincial Police did gather intelligence on the protest at large and CSIS did the same on undisclosed individuals linked to extremism, but by and large that intelligence never translated into action. Local Ottawa police largely disregarded it before and during the crisis. The Privy Council Office had difficulty gathering the various reports and digesting them in actionable form. In the end, for a complex series of interconnected reasons, the disruption of a critical infrastructure (the federal government) was allowed to continue for three weeks. One of those reasons was the incapacity of all policing organizations involved to understand and properly evaluate the degree of extremism of the anti-government core of protesters. Another was the hesitation in taking any form of preventive action towards extremists who had not committed or clearly planned to commit obvious, immediately identifiable criminal offences.

Hate

One other tool in the legal toolbox is the "hate crime" designation. Statistics Canada keeps records of hate crimes in Canada, which is interesting but not very compelling because the number of instances is far higher than that reported by police. Statistics Canada's data on victimization from hate crime leads us to conclude that the vast majority are not reported but also that a sizable proportion are in fact reported but simply not recorded as such by police (for a study in the USA, see Pezzella 2019).

Legally, in Canada hate crimes can take two distinct forms. The first is hate speech: the dissemination of hate at various levels of formalization, rationalization, or emotional content. In some cases, hate speech is heavily "researched" and minutely documented, resulting in a heady mix of true, fictional, and/or misleading historical, statistical, and scientific "facts." At other times it is pure hate poetry and consists of hortatory proclamations that mostly aim at stirring emotions. Either way it is notoriously difficult to prevent, stop, or prosecute because of freedom of speech protections. At the same time social media corporations, whose products are the main channels of diffusion for this material, have been reluctant to censor it. There are four main reasons for this. First, there remain political and legal uncertainties associated with censorship, politics, and government power, only exaggerated by the multiple jurisdictions in which these corporations operate;

second, they are wary of accepting general responsibility for the content uploaded by their users, which would lead to a manifold increase in their commitment to police that content; third, of course, because controversial discourse generates traffic, engagement, and revenue; fourth, there is no clear distinction in content or intensity threshold that separates hate speech from accepted political discourse.

The second type of hate crime results when the motivation for what is otherwise an ordinary crime is hate for a recognizable population group (identifiable by a common characteristic such as religion, gender, ethnicity, colour, etc.). In that case, much like the terrorism qualification, the identification of the crime as a hate crime allows the Crown to request a more severe sentence. The logic of increasing the sentence in those cases is that the crime has repercussions for an entire population rather than simply its primary and secondary victims. Ethically speaking, the main problem is that it creates a sentencing premium for an element of the crime that consists of thought. Discussion of these and other legal and political aspects would take us outside the limits of this book, but in practice the main hurdle with using this provision is that, as mentioned with terrorism, motive must be proven.

The genealogy of hate crimes differs from that of terrorism in one key aspect. Hate crime laws tend to be enacted after civil society groups, usually marginal ones or those that are culturally disempowered despite their large numbers (i.e., women), fight for and obtain the needed additional legal protections of their rights. One negative consequence of this process is that laws offer a piecemeal, per-group protection and exclude other groups until they also succeed in being heard (Martin 2020). On the contrary, anti-terrorism laws are enacted when majority groups feel threatened by smaller ones, especially if they appear to be sponsored by or, at least, influenced by foreign entities (either state or non-state actors). The negative consequence comparable to that of hate crime laws is that anti-terrorist laws are often conceived with specific groups in mind and can easily appear xenophobic or at least unfair, as obvious in the entities list described above. This different genealogy has also led to one other key distinction between the two: each is the primary responsibility of different sets of institutions, with high-policing, national security, high-budget organizations directed towards terrorism and low-policing, street-crime agencies concentrating on hate crime.

Both the historical and institutional distinctions are external to the actual nature of the two types of action. Criminologically speaking, most acts motivated by hate are nearly indistinguishable from most acts of terrorism. They share foundational characteristics, among which are the rejection of identified outgroups as dangerous, illegitimate, or parasitic, as well as the conviction that direct intervention is required, either in discourse or in physical form. As the analysis above demonstrates, it would be a mistake to assume that hate crimes are a lesser form of violence than is terrorism. They in fact may generate far more damage, especially when compared to "pre-terrorist" crimes. Both types of crime converge heavily in their conceptualization, legal definitions, and tangible consequences at the psychological and sociological levels. A popular way to set them apart has been to consider hate crimes as crimes motivated by hate against a particular social group, while crimes motivated by a political objective would be considered acts of "terrorism." Yet our data shows that most members of the far right tend to give political legitimacy (on a highly varying scale of complexity) to their racism and misogyny. Conversely, many types of politically motivated objections are nothing more than unconvincing rationalizations of fear and hatred.

Outside of criminalized terror and hate, there exist many behaviours not yet prohibited or which are illegal but rarely investigated or prosecuted. They must be considered when attempting to draw a picture of the overall threat posed by the far right. For example, screamingly alarmist xenophobic or anti-government fake news may not be clearly illegal but has motivated multiple potentially dangerous actions, such as the aforementioned storming of the grounds of Rideau Hall or the attempts to exercise "citizen's arrests" on politicians (including a case where CBC journalist Daniel Thibeault was mistaken for Bloc Quebecois MP Mario Beaulieu or another in August 2022 in which members of a fringe group attempted to arrest the entire Peterborough police service, which illustrate well the potential for chaos). The Criminal Code had a provision against "false news" until the early

1990s when, in the case of notorious Nazi propagandist Ernst Zündel (who also claimed there was a secret Nazi flying saucer air base in Antarctica), the Supreme Court struck it down as an unjustifiable restriction on freedom of expression. The use of fake news by the far right is not a new thing; only the means of distribution have changed. Finally, as of late, many large protest groups who originally had no link to the far right have been thoroughly colonized by it (sometimes via all-encompassing conspiracy theories like QAnon), most notably the COVID-19 anti-mask and anti-sanitary-measure movement, the anti-vaxx movement, the "yellow vests" protests of 2018–19, as well as large portions of the anti-globalization movement.

One more example of behaviour that is strictly legal is intimidation, humiliation, and other forms of "soft violence" as described in Meyers (2019). Though never clearly morphing into explicit threats or physical assault, such attacks, especially because of their constant, repeated nature, can exert a heavy toll on their targets. Consequences include social stigma and exclusion, group polarization, and various forms of individual psychological affliction for direct and indirect victims (family, friends).

One last flaw in the criminal justice approach resides within its political communication aspect. From the authorities' point of view, it may not be efficient to call on the artillery of "terrorism" and "hate crime." Netting a terrorist group on the verge of committing an attack produces much-needed political capital for the police and other collaborating organizations but hate crimes may simply generate more paperwork and statistics that look bad. Prosecuting for hate crimes or terrorism without an invulnerable evidentiary path to political or "hate" motives is a risky investment of effort. Not to mention that the more serious the crime, the less impact the qualifications have: murderers are already automatically condemned to the maximum sentence included in the Criminal Code. However, the proverbial messages being sent, in all these cases, are that 1) only Muslims can commit terrorist acts (one journalist called the mosque massacre "reverse terrorism"); 2) the state does not recognize group vulnerability when it is directed at minority groups, and when it does, with unrestrained embellishment, it is to bemoan even failed attacks as existential threats when Muslim extremists are involved; and 3) the far right is essentially not a producer of violence.

Policing the community

Much has been written on community policing, but suffice to say that its basic strategy is to form stronger ties with the community in order to boost primary social control mechanisms and to increase police knowledge and understanding of local social dynamics (Gomez del Prado and Leman-Langlois 2020). Its value in counterterrorism (CT) divides experts. Some argue that the necessities of traditional policing tactics – clandestine operations, recruitment of informants, massive surveillance – tend to undermine the goals of the more preventive actions. Others maintain that, on the contrary, closer ties with people make CT tactics redundant since everyone in the community despises terrorists and is eager to report them to a consent-based, trustworthy police force (Murray 2007). In other words, CT and community-oriented policing (COP) tactics are either conflicting or redundant.

As it happens, both sides of this debate have premised their argument on the idea that terrorism is the product of a certain sub-population within the community, usually Arabic-descent Muslims, or the so-called Muslim community. Some (like de Guzman 2002) starkly dismiss community policing as a counterterrorist tool, since the terrorists and terrorist sympathizers who form the community cannot be reasoned with or trusted. Responding to that grossly xenophobic point of view, Murray argues on the contrary that it is by getting close to the ordinary members of the community who are not sympathetic to terrorists that community police officers will be able to get information and tips about suspicious behaviours. Either way, terrorism emerges as a (by-)product of a community, a postulate that has no substance at all and only reflexively refers to the observer's peculiar way of segmenting and labelling communities and their members. And it is not helpful when the terrorists come from the majority population.

Much thinking about community policing as a means to counter terrorism revolves around abstract ideals or premises that are highly disputable or simply false (Gomez del Prado and Leman-Langlois 2020):

- The word "community" in the COP literature refers to a geographically defined population, in utter disregard for its diversity in terms of class, age, ethnic background, religious affiliation, actual presence in the area (those who spend their working day outside the area vs those who stay, for instance), experience in collective and personal victimization or in fact, despite its geographic foundations, key geographic/urban/architectural differences between neighbourhoods. Given this, the idea that community-oriented police can gain the trust of "the community" appears simplistic at best and far removed from an actual preventive tactic.
- When "community" is, at the same time, also used to identify subsets of the overall "community," as in "the Muslim community," it also erases profound variations and tends to assume a high level of communication, strong interpersonal relationships or networks, commonalities in worldviews, alignment of personal objectives and values, etc. This is a highly dangerous misconception and in fact tends to lead to profiling and over-policing, which in turn generates multiple flashpoints of conflict between police and residents, who feel they are not being treated fairly.
- It is hoped that both police organizations and individual officers can eschew, at least temporarily, the criminal justice investigation outlook and favour local problem-solving aimed at reinforcing informal social controls and collective efficacy. It seems likely that this "problem-oriented policing" (POP) could be a powerful strategy in tackling neighbourhood-wide problems of ethnic or political polarization, including those involving racism, xenophobia, and the like. In this case, the problem is organizational: for various reasons, in practice POP has generally been limited to a niche occupation for limited numbers of staff. It is not valued, does not lead to recognition and promotion within the organization, and adds nothing to

the organization's political capital because it is not as media-genic as arrests and criminal trials.

- It was once thought that police officers might be trained to become emergency social problem solvers with a mix of psychology, sociology, and social work skills added to classic police training. This has hit two massive stumbling blocks: officers do not have the time nor the inclination for the (unrewarded) extra training; classic police training, to a large extent, conflicts with social work, especially around the manner in which legal authority can be deployed. Yet what is needed in broken and dysfunctional neighbourhoods is rarely an extra dose of classic patrol surveillance, ticketing, and arrests, which are the basic tools of street policing.
- It is still widely assumed that political violence is the work of clandestine groups that take the time to recruit, organize, and plot attacks during an extended period of time during which potential community intelligence gathering and sharing might lead to preventive arrests or disruptive action. We have seen that this is often not the case.

At the same time, some of the arguments in favour of policing terrorism at the ground level instead of mobilizing national security or deploying mass, hi-tech surveillance are entirely sound:

- The COP approach may sound particularly inappropriate to those who think of political violence as the product of vast, international networks. As we have seen, however, the clear majority of political violence, terrorism, and hate crime occur locally; those responsible may be inspired by distant internet propaganda or world events but they are mostly triggered by local problems and act locally, at the neighbourhood level. They are often accompanied by local political polarization.
- Few victims of hate crimes report them to the police, and the most common reason given for that is the lack of trust in police. In 2019, more than 60 per cent of those who did not report a crime did so because they thought they would not

be taken seriously by police (Statistics Canada 2019). Others think the police is itself a xenophobic organization, and for some it is the conviction that criminal arrests are not the solution. Each of these rationales points to COP and POP as proper approaches for both the prevention and repression of hate crimes.

- Neighbourhood safety greatly outreaches police legal competence, expertise, or power. It must be understood as a co-production of multiple recognized, respected entities and not as a set of exclusive tasks for the police. There is no demand for, and in fact no offer of, police social workers. Employing police officers to respond to emergency social problems generates high risks and has in fact led to calls to "defund" the police and to reallocate funds to social services. At the first line of contact, police may be uniquely positioned to identify potential problems, which they should then funnel towards the proper services rather than watch, investigate, infiltrate, and arrest. This requires that police organizations and individual officers gain and maintain public trust and that they be prepared to relinquish some responsibilities to other agencies – exactly what the original COP strategies provided for.

To the extent that community policing involves building public trust and favouring non-criminal solutions to individual local problems, it does seem particularly well designed to address the interrelated problems of community polarization, radicalization, extremism, and the hate and terror crimes they produce – in large part because instead of taking charge of them it relies on proper, adapted responses from relevant organizations. Non-police advising committees can be useful in facing neighbourhood polarization and radicalization (one of us is a member of such a group, which includes school officials, social workers, psychologists, etc.). The goal of such a committee is to make sure that only the most extreme and urgent cases are dealt with through criminal justice intervention, while the rest are channelled to the appropriate social service.

The reality is that many cases that do not belong in the justice system are still brought to court and sanctioned; the individuals found guilty are sent to prison while the correctional system has no deradicalization program in place. The criminal justice outcome is preferred by a good portion of the public at large but also by many advocates of minority rights who want infringers to be punished. Yet the reality is that the millions of dollars spent on such high-profile investigations and trials, including the massive staging of "sting" operations, informers, undercover operatives, etc., would almost certainly be better spent on prevention and non-police intervention.

Police organizations do not benefit politically from the diversion of potentially high-profile cases to prevention mechanisms. Conversely, spectacular arrests and "foiled plots" are uniquely well positioned to counter the scandals that plague contemporary policing, in particular when attacks still take place after police are notified, as in the Couture-Rouleau case. Couture-Rouleau had repeatedly been in contact with police for months prior to his final meltdown in 2014, first with local police, whom his father, with no other resource available, called on in desperation. Provincial police had better expertise and were also consulted, with the RCMP finally being brought on board and interviewing the subject at least twice and having his passport cancelled when he tried to leave for Turkey. Yet a few weeks later Couture-Rouleau rammed his car into two military personnel, launching a wave of public insecurity and a deluge of new anti-terror criminal measures – measures which, incidentally, would have made no difference in the Couture-Rouleau case. Alex Stavropoulos, an Incel who attempted to kill a mother and her child, had a history of clashes with police, during one of which he was struck by a conductive energy weapon (commonly referred to as a Taser) while screaming "white power."

Such stories illustrate one of the challenges of policing where a mix of politics, religion, and mental health elements combine in a potentially explosive manner. At what point can we intervene and with what authority? When is the individual going to be dangerous? What if we lose track of them, only to see them re-emerge later with a bomb, like Ahmed Ressam? The wait for a crime to be committed can be hazardous, and the temptation to accelerate the process difficult to resist.

The Couture-Rouleau debacle also illustrates the difficulty of resource allocation. Following his attack, the RCMP moved some 200 investigators away from their organized crime tasks to work on the terrorism problem. In essence, the reassignment was a communications move designed to protect or recapture political capital. Within a few months investigators were re-assigned to their old postings, as no new case had appeared on the radar. All along, what Couture-Rouleau needed was simply mental health resources, which he never got.

The way forward

Traditional policing tactics all converge on a single practical goal, which is used to measure their success: the charging of individuals under the Criminal Code. Of course, there are many cases where this is the appropriate response and repressive policing is what is needed, including tactical response teams if necessary. We do not propose to end criminal investigations into terrorism or hate crimes, nor do we claim that psycho-social intervention or deradicalization programs are surefire, infallible solutions. We simply want to challenge the supremacy of the criminal justice approach.

First, as we have seen, it is difficult to successfully prosecute individuals under the terrorism or hate crime provisions as laid out in the Criminal Code. The articles in the code are essentially archaic or based on an "idealized" version of terrorism that is extremely rare. Further, it is sometimes counterproductive to criminalize many of the damageable activities in which the far right engages. Ernst Zündel's fight against the old "false news" section 181 of the Criminal Code quickly turned into a heroic fight for "free speech" and gave standard Nazism the varnish of a noble pursuit of liberty for all Canadians; what is more, Zündel won and the section was struck down. It seems obvious that state intervention should at least avoid giving hate a new pulpit from which it can disseminate propaganda.

Second, the criminal approach has led to paradoxes in which clearly terrorist acts were never labelled as such, while extremely low-level offences of "pre-terrorism" have been elevated to national security issues. This is in part because of the discrepancy in difficulty when qualifying Muslim extremists and far-right extremists as terrorists; so far, the likelihood of Muslims being labelled terrorists has been infinitely higher than that of white, non-Muslim Canadians.

Third, the insistence on using a criminal investigation process has produced another unwanted consequence: persons clearly burdened by mental health issues have been caught in penal nets, sometimes in large-scale undercover operations where police agents led them on towards the commission of an offence. To date the most notorious cases were that of Amanda Korody and John Nuttal, in which the presiding judge declared, "the world has enough terrorists; we do not need the police to create more," and that of the "VIA Rail plot" in which two separate psychiatrists found the main culprit was in poor mental health.

Fourth, the constant insistence on spectacular, highly organized, networked, international terrorism has led to a severe underestimation of the actual threats. For instance, neo-Nazi groups have started intimidating journalists but when one case finally appeared in front of a judge, she stopped the prosecution from detailing the politics of the group, accepting the defence's argument that the incident was a "joke." Seven members of the group had stormed Vice Media's Montreal office and offered a "prize" to a journalist covering the far right in Canada. The judge even rebuked the prosecutor for his exaggeration and his attempts at entering "corrosive and inappropriate" evidence such as the SS logo of the group. The Appeals Court has since partially reversed this judgment and the accused has been convicted of breaking and entering but, tellingly, not of the criminal harassment and intimidation charges.

Finally, massive police operations and spectacular trials lead to the glorification of terrorism, hate, and terrorists or to their positioning as powerful opposition to the state or to its institutions. The constant repetition of how dangerous they are, how well organized, determined, and motivated by rational political ends, produces the opposite effect to what is needed.

Nonstate social controls

On 12 May 2018 residents of Rosemont, in Montreal, marched to voice their objection to the presence of an active neo-Nazi propagandist in their neighbourhood. During the previous week a story in the *Montreal Gazette* had revealed that "Zeiger," one of the main editors of the online hate magazine *Daily Stormer* (deliberately reminiscent of Julius Streicher's *Der Sturmer*), was in fact one Gabriel Sohier-Chaput, a self-employed communications consultant. The story had been brought to the *Gazette* by two Concordia University journalism students who had been given a trove of contents taken from a Discord chat room dedicated to neo-Nazism named Montreal Storm. Sohier-Chaput was actively recruiting on that platform, creating what he called a book club where members would meet in person – it is in organizing one such meeting that Sohier-Chaput's home address was revealed (*Gazette* 2018, 2018a). Discord has since closed the group and others like it. The self-proclaimed antifascists who had raided the chat room went further than the media and put up posters denouncing Sohier-Chaput and giving his home address. The 12 May march ended at that location, where the crowd was met by both police in riot gear and a contingent of Soldiers of Odin who were there to counterprotest.

Months later, on 30 October, the Montreal police service obtained an arrest warrant for Sohier-Chaput, who no longer lived at his previous address and was in fact in hiding. The warrant followed a complaint by B'nai Brith Canada, filed in May. At his trial in March 2022 Sohier-Chaput claimed, in classic alt-right form, that his writing was meant to be sarcastic. He was later found guilty of promoting hatred.

Sohier-Chaput's short-lived time in the far-right infosphere reached thousands and managed to recruit some fifty to one hundred active, real-world extremists through his "book club." For our purposes, his story also illustrates how a network of state and non-state actors can interact and produce massive social control. At the time of writing, the case is under appeal, but, regardless of the outcome, it will in all probability be dwarfed by the informal reaction to which he has already been subjected. In this section we focus on non-state entities, which we categorize into four groups: antifascist vigilantes, the media, industrial stakeholders, and the public at large.

As seen in chapter 4, "digital vigilantism" refers to a process whereby individuals and groups choose to organize and coordinate various retaliatory efforts against selected targets on digital platforms. The main weapon is to cause intense and enduring shame via unwanted forms of visibility. This is an important aspect since maximized and at the same time calculated and selective visibility is an important propaganda tool for adherents of the far-right infosphere. The strategy of digital vigilantes is to circumvent, defeat, or subvert the structured, fine-tuned images projected by the targeted entities.

This is what happened to Zeiger: a deliberate strategy to "name and shame" was adopted, starting with the publication of his personal information ("doxxing"). Militants then followed with the organization of a march and various attempts at direct and indirect (via his neighbours) intimidation. The overall climate of harassment and humiliation may be viewed as potentially or directly threatening the target's physical safety. In other words, the identification and dissemination of information is not simply meant to be preventive, through a form of neutralization: it also affords the power to directly sanction those being targeted. At other times, public charges on the Internet may also be intended to prompt police or judicial authorities to recognize an offence, a crime, or an injustice or to cause public opinion to evolve over a particular issue (Loveluck 2016). Ultimately, digital vigilantism is an attempt to counter behaviours considered deviant but that are not taken seriously by institutionalized authorities.

Other than the trawling of Discord forums, digital vigilantes have been active in the past few years, with spectacular coups such as the theft of the entire Ironmarch.org database, which was subsequently posted to the Internet, forcing the closing of the group. But, as we have seen with Zeiger, antifascist vigilantes do not confine themselves to the Internet and other forms of technological action; they are also active in person, organizing marches and (counter-)protests, sometimes getting far-right events cancelled. In March 2015 a Pegida event in Montreal was called off when one hundred of its members were besieged by nine hundred counterprotesters (Lindeman 2015). In Winnipeg a fight broke out between the far-right Canadian Coalition of Concerned Citizens (CCCC), Soldiers of Odin, and counterdemonstrators from "Fascist Free Treaty 1" when the federal government was debating a motion against Islamophobia (CTV News 2017).

In many ways, journalism may be involved in doxxing. Uncovering clandestine groups of extremists, naming them, describing their actions, and exploring their personal biographies is part of good reporting (while obviously stopping at revealing personal information such as addresses, phone numbers, and the like). The work of Ryan Thorpe (2019), of the *Winnipeg Free Press*, illustrates this. Thorpe, intrigued by recruitment posters in his area of town, followed their lead to an extremist group which he pretended to join. The group was the Base, an accelerationist neo-Nazi outfit known to train with live weapons in the United States that has members in Canada. Thorpe outed the group and its members in his paper. One, an active recruiter for the Base, was a reservist with the Canadian Armed Forces. Another was the founder of the neo-Nazi forum Fascist Forge (where the Base was heavily promoted). All are now incarcerated.

The media often collaborates with digital antifascists, as was the case in the story above; once incriminating information was collected from Discord discussions, it was shared first with journalism students who picked up the investigation and ultimately with the *Montreal Gazette* and other traditional media. In this case, however, the story does not seem to have gained much traction in the news cycle, despite repeated court appearances. At the end of this road, we also find academics, who often rely in whole or in part on media reports to complete their research about the far right.

The third group of entities involved in controlling the far-right discourse are the industrial stakeholders. The *Daily Stormer*, Sohier-Chaput's main communication channel, has an interesting history. Founded by Andrew Anglin, who attempted to excuse Heather Heyer's death during the Unite the Right rally by piling scorn on the victim, the website was banned first by domain registrar and hosting service GoDaddy, then Google, Cloudflare, and others (Lavin 2018). It is now registered through a chain of nebulous shells and resides on unidentifiable servers. Though ultimately failed, the efforts of the service providers caused the site to bounce around and made it temporarily difficult to find. But the actual impact on readership is unknown.

Though smaller or hidden entities continue to enable the creation and dissemination of extreme content, in general the larger actors have been very active in closing accounts and servers. Under fire from civil society, Facebook, Twitter (now X), and the like now regularly and proudly report closing multiple hate channels, sometimes thousands at a time.

Finally, it often comes down to public involvement. It should be noted that members of the public can participate in vigilante shaming without entirely realizing they are part of an information distribution strategy. It is easy enough to like, republish, or comment on posts that aim at outing extremists and calling public attention to their actions. In fact, much doxxing and media reporting would have limited effect on those targeted if no public reaction was present or at least possible. By and large, mass reactions tend to respond to initial calls or revelations by active political organizations or individuals – and, conversely, are counted upon by them. For example, Milbrandt (2020) describes how the public at large was recruited by activists to identify participants in the Unite the Right rally in Charlottesville. Through the @YesYoureRacist Twitter/X accounts, members of the public were invited to "make them famous." Even though only a small minority of the public is mobilized by such calls to virtual or physical action, it has often proven to be more than enough to intimidate the intended targets, who usually choose to disappear at least temporarily.

Conclusion

In the end, once again as illustrated by the Zeiger story, mobilization across civil society, whether it starts with the ordinary public, organizations dedicated to outing neo-Nazis, or the media, may force key individuals to act and take more official, direct measures against extremists who cross the line. Both industrial service providers and police finally acted to put an end to Sohier-Chaput's fifteen minutes of fame, banning him from his platforms and taking him to court. Of course, any of the actors in that network may commit various errors, with potentially disastrous consequences for those on the receiving end of the intervention. Police, media, and civil society organizations may identify and pursue innocent persons and destroy their reputation in the process. Members of the public, free of any form of requirement for corroboration, confidentiality, or post-facto accountability, are only more likely to make such crucial mistakes, especially those who are more concerned with the fame that doxxing others can bring them than with the accuracy of the information.

After this succinct overview of institutional and non-institutional forms of controls, the overall conclusion is simply that the outlook is bleak. While organizations in charge of national security and policing are struggling to adapt to the issue, when not to simply identify it, the Canadian government's solution has been to introduce new legislation to counter "online harms," further dissolving the problem in a vague, overly broad, confusing, and potentially divisive strategy based on censorship. In other words, solutions seem out of reach for the authorities, who are caught in a practical conflict between inaction and misguided overreaction, both dangerous for Canadian citizens.

Of course, most of this problem disappears when individuals elect to commit clear-cut criminal offences or to engage in obvious criminal plotting or egregiously explicit hate speech. If the Freedom Convoy crisis has shown anything, it is that this all-or-nothing criminal justice strategy is not serving national security well. It has also shown that critical infrastructures can be threatened by persons who do not plan on committing the types of crimes traditionally associated with terrorism. At the same time, we must avoid, at all costs, the aggressive tactics that some policing organizations have adopted over the years, sometimes with the objective of protecting the government from mere embarrassment (*National Post* 2012). Clearly, a national discussion about what constitutes national security, and how to best protect it, is long overdue.

CONCLUSION

During the fall of 2022, the Public Order Emergency Commission heard multiple witnesses, including police and intelligence service personnel, Freedom Convoy organizers, Ottawa residents, and city officials. The narrative unfolding before Justice Paul Rouleau betrayed a gross lack of preparation by the Ottawa Police Service (OPS). It also revealed the ineffectiveness of communication channels between intelligence brokers at CSIS, the RCMP, the Privy Council Office, the Ontario Provincial Police (OPP), and the Ottawa Police Service (OPS). To put it simply, the threat represented by the protest had been severely underestimated.

Such hearings are required whenever the government activates the temporary additional powers afforded by the Emergencies Act. They are meant to ascertain the legitimacy of the government's decision, as well as the way it was implemented by various agencies. It is telling that the act, like the 1914 War Measures Act which it replaced in 1988, has been invoked only once in peacetime. The original act was used to respond to the Front de libération du Québec (FLQ) crisis in October 1970 and caused a historically momentous scandal. Its replacement has been invoked only once and that was in February 2022, during the Freedom Convoy occupation, combined with border crossing blockades in Coutts (Alberta) and Windsor.

The FLQ crisis and the Freedom Convoy occupation have almost nothing in common other than the government's call for emergency powers. Yet we believe that a few important teachings can be derived from a comparison between the two events. The two crises were significant, both in terms of objective public safety and for the maintenance of Canadians' confidence in their state institutions. The FLQ had kidnapped a British diplomat and the deputy premier of Quebec, eventually killing the latter. The Freedom Convoy arrived not only with trucks but with an army of sympathizers, colonized by cliques of various far-right anti-government extremist groups, with money and with plans to stay until their demands were met, and with no alternative path to resolution. Constant minor clashes and harassment caused the exasperation of residents and created a highly volatile context with a high potential for violence.

Though of a different nature, implications, and legal definitions, both situations were quite serious. Yet, it could easily be argued that the response was disproportionate, born out of surprise, misreading the situation, and an utter lack of preparedness. Neither crisis threatened public order, welfare, or the safety of the state. Better planning and basic prevention (e.g., diverting trucks away from the Ottawa city core in 2022; giving the deputy premier a bodyguard after multiple explicit threats had been made against politicians in 1970) would have averted the administrative panic response.

After the dust settled, it became obvious that, in both cases, declaring a state of emergency was of little help in solving the immediate problem, and it seems unlikely to have prevented repetition: quite the opposite, in fact, since the forceful removal of trucks and protesters allowed them to save face and to reinforce their "state oppression" discourse. There is particular context for this. As we've explained in earlier chapters, such massive events are supercharging the far right. They are ideal sites for mainstreaming extreme ideas; for fostering distrust and hatred against governmental institutions, the media, and politicians; for recruiting new followers; for financing; for networking in person or through technological mobilization.

In 1970, the government seemed to have a poor grasp of the general state of affairs leading to the crisis. Whether it was deliberate is still a matter of debate: it is now obvious that throughout the 1960s the RCMP and Montreal police seemed to have had a reasonably good understanding of the FLQ's strengths, weaknesses, and modes of operation, but the political discourse was almost entirely out of step with that knowledge (Whitaker et al. 2012). In 2022, the intelligence on the coming convoy seemed to have been spotty at best, with Ottawa Police essentially taken by surprise by what they thought would be a weekend drive to the nation's capital. Two weeks before the event, the Ontario Provincial Police warned that many convoy participants were prepared to stay much longer (*National Post* 2022). There is no sign that the OPP, the RCMP, or CSIS monitored the convoy during the early organizational stages (which were partly conducted on open forums) or once on the highways. CSIS's Integrated Terrorism Assessment Centre (ITAC) had recognized a few far-right extremists in the convoy's organization in the weeks prior to the event (*Guardian* 2022), but it is not clear what conclusions or potential outcome analyses were produced. It is also not clear whether this fact was considered sufficient to monitor social media use by these targets (CSIS's evidence, at their request, was presented in camera to Justice Rouleau). Finally, the actual problems in transmitting, receiving, or understanding this information may never be known, but neither the Ottawa police chief nor his intelligence officer seems to have assimilated the available information.

Besides the sketchy intelligence, another explanation for the lack of preparation is that the contemporary far right is typically on very good terms with police services and policing in general. Their discourse is usually infused with law-and-order tropes and professed respect for military and military-like authority structures. What is more, former military and police officers can be found in many far-right organizations. This may explain in part why marching La Meute members usually had little trouble with police, who were busy arresting counterprotesters (Montpetit 2017). The Rouleau inquiry also heard testimony to the effect that convoy organizers received support, training, and intelligence from both active and retired police officers (McLeod, Dickson, and Walsh 2002). In the United States many Washington police officers assisted the rioters during the 6 January storming of the Capitol building (Mogelson 2022).

One last teaching is that authorities consistently demonstrate an inability to differentiate subgroups involved in a crisis. In 1970, RCMP and Montreal police proceeded indiscriminately to arrest Quebec nationalists, intellectuals, and artists, broadly confusing terrorism, dissent, protest, and free speech – which eventually proved disastrous for the RCMP, who eventually lost their national security intelligence mandate (in 1984). In 2022, the wild variety of those taking part in the convoy seems to have had the opposite effect: none were given proper attention. Not that taking seriously the self-appointed "Queen of Canada" or 5G conspiracy buffs is particularly easy. Yet what has become evident in the last decade is that even the most eccentric have a potential for creating situations that can easily degenerate out of control. In a bizarre incident sometime later, supporters of the Queen of Canada attempted to arrest the entire Peterborough police force.

Though it was not its central objective, we hope that this book will contribute to alleviating the difficulties in sorting out and prioritizing sites, groups, trends, and events for enhanced attention. Equally important is the form this attention might take: as we have seen in the pages above, one stubborn paradox is that the obvious solutions to most aspects of the problem are almost always the wrong ones. Declaring a state of emergency is no exception and is more likely to galvanize groups than to normalize the situation.

Our general portrait of the far right in Canada, fragmentary as it is, and partially already out of date as it comes off the press, certainly helped meet other objectives. An overarching one was to move away from the spectacular yet rare uses of violence and other anxiety-inducing activities of extremists, to a perhaps less clear, but certainly more realistic, portrayal of life on the far right.

We started on this path by first adopting a wider, more encompassing definition, in order to better situate the topic and avoid focusing on the utterly marginal, as if it had evolved in a cultural test tube, entirely outside of mainstream culture, politics, economics, and history. We began by observing groups and individuals who dealt in the usual themes of xenophobia, nationalism, anti-feminism, anti-government paranoia, and antisemitism. These are still at the core of the far right as a whole, but from there, the worldviews branch out wildly, sometimes borrowing issues and motifs from the left, creating hybrids such as antisemitic and Islamophobic feminism. Various groups will stress some aspects over others, approach those in their idiosyncratic way, develop their own repertoire of action, and usually disagree on some aspect of the wider ideological family. In that context it is very difficult to find a unifying ideological marker for the far right, even if, for the outside observer, some of the nuances that cause arguments and rifts within the movement can seem insignificant. From the inside, one overarching common aspect is not ideological: it is that groups and individuals converge on one version or another of opposition, and this opposition shapes both their discourse and their repertoire of action.

To draw the contours of our object we had to resort to an analytical definition that uses three vast categories of ideologies as varying ingredients of the far right. Our 3D definitional matrix and its six resulting types manage to instill a modicum of order within the vast, fluctuating ideologies of the far right. The cohesion, durability, mode of action, and influence of groups is significantly shaped by the group's relationship to the three dimensions we identified: to authorities, to violence, and to identified others. The relationship to authority captures anti-state, anti-institution, anti-science, anti-media, and anti-(university-)education variations on the far right. As oppositional movements, far-right groups find institutions easy targets, since they function by establishing and imposing regulatory, ethical, or policy frameworks. In this case, the dominant discourse is positioned to mobilize "freedom," a universal good (although only in its doubly narrowed concept of freedom from [non-group] rules, but that nuance is generally lost).

The second dimension involves the positioning of the group with relation to violence. We noted that violence has many iterations, roughly divided between physical and psychological (including threats), and that, most importantly, only a limited number of those iterations are illegal. Some that are illegal, such as hate speech, are limited to specific target groups and difficult to prosecute. Quite a few more are legally allowed but can elicit negative public responses, which most groups tend to avoid, preferring to show a more sanitized face. It is never entirely banned, however; as we have shown in chapter 5, real and symbolic violence is a powerful draw for many individuals on the far right.

Finally, perhaps the most central aspect of our matrix is the construction of others or outgroups. In its most radical form, the rejection of entire population groups implies or explicitly involves the rejection of basic democratic building blocks such as the concept of citizenship, equal rights, and the rule of law. On that level it connects to and overlaps with the rejection of institutions of the first dimension. From masculinists to white supremacists the division of society into essentialized groups usually implies the presence of natural or inevitable social conflicts. It also implies a value ranking of groups or at least a radical preference for one's identified group. The ways in which the groups are carved out, singled out, and evaluated is particular to most individual groups. Of course, the concept of "race" survives and continues to be particularly cogent to a majority of those on the far right. For others, it has morphed (in public speech or in actual worldview) into a more legalistic, less culturally archaic concern for immigration or cultural incompatibility. As well, there are political others: elites, the media, politicians, those on the left, or active antifascists – or all of the above.

Chapter 2 has demonstrated how the definitions matrix can identify ideological families on the far right, through their style of membership, their activities, their core beliefs, and other facets. Contrary to the usual approach, we deliberately avoided drawing a complete list of far-right entities for multiple reasons: it would quickly become out of date; individuals move from group to group or are members of multiple groups at a time, hopelessly distancing the nomenclature from the reality; multiple groups and lone actors don't have an "official" name. We believe that particular names and banners do not matter that much, and that more importance should be given to particular worldviews and repertoires of action. That is why the definitional matrix is far more useful in mapping the field than a group inventory would be.

In chapter 3, we then reviewed the multiple processes by which far-right groups, with the exception of the most violent, attempt to build broad legitimacy among the public and relevance in relation to both day-to-day events and a rapidly changing global culture. This is achieved or not, of course, with highly variable levels of success. The method is the usual one-two punch: first, recast key elements of the context as urgent identity and survival problems; second, project particular expertise (e.g., common sense, popular, non-elite, non-corrupt) and suggest practical solutions.

As moral entrepreneurs, when far-right actors attempt to conquer the public or at least to occupy a portion of public space, they best identify a key issue already in the public eye. A global pandemic is such an opportunity, though rare and short-lived. Economic crises can also serve, as long as the impact is directly felt by those being courted. Far removed, theoretical, philosophical, or merely potential calamities are far less powerful and tend to appeal only to the converted. Global migrations are less immediately dramatic but likely to remain topical for the foreseeable future, particularly if the media continues to show images of people emerging from the woods to enter Canada at unofficial border crossings. It does help that mainstream identitarian politics have been active in keeping the immigration and integration issues on the agenda; far-right groups can pick up the baton from there.

Our study of La Meute, arguably at the mildest end of the far right, showed how closely it polices interactions on its Facebook pages and how hostile language is (mostly) kept within socially acceptable boundaries. That is because the goal is to appeal to the largest portion of society. At the height of its popularity, the leadership was constantly reminding anyone listening (on social media and in the traditional media) that its group was one of the largest ever, sometimes claiming up to 60,000 members. That number was grossly inflated and intended to convey the message that not all those members could be racist fascists; their concerns must be widespread and rational, and by extension both their idiosyncratic definition of the problem and its proposed solution must be equally legitimate. Which also makes the existence of the group fundamentally important, since it represents the voice of the people.

Like any moral entrepreneurship project, La Meute was originally organized around a pressing issue that became a concern for large portions of the population, especially after 9/11: Islamization and the danger of (extremist) Muslims abroad and at home. Once the al Qaeda/ISIS wave of terrorism passed and the issue left the headlines, La Meute quickly moved on to the (illegal) migration of Haitians across the border with the USA. Its reappropriation of popular security and identity/integration themes is far from unique to La Meute. We chose it as a case study precisely because of the powerful way it illustrates the main strategy for mainstreaming far-right ideas.

It is important that this largely discursive strategy takes root in what we have referred to as the far-right "infosphere," a vast, organically growing, largely contingent network of content producers, co-producers, and "prosumers" actively constructing multiple (and oftentimes contradictory) far-right versions of reality. Much has already been written about the infamous "echo chamber" created by the automated curation of content by social media bots, which tends to systematically produce an increasingly reflexive and narrow world for users, especially if they are expressing niche, marginal interests to begin with. In chapter 4, we explained why this portrayal is incomplete, as it essentially relegates the user to being a puppet at the hands of all-powerful reality-bending databots or information masters. What we have seen, instead, is that users take pride and find empowerment, encouragement, validation, and support in actively participating in this construction. Others think it is exciting, funny, or entertaining. Many simply enjoy the omnipresent underlying violence, the vindictiveness, and the hate they find there. The echo chamber also fails to account for the porousness of the far-right infosphere and the ways it connects to gradually less extremist discourse and eventually to mainstream politics. That last aspect we have only briefly touched on in this book, but it is certainly worth attention.

As others have already noted, the (re)casting of events and information in far-right language is not limited by any sort of distinction between truth and falsehood, the real and the imagined. Conspiracy theories abound, to a point where they have become part and parcel of the far right, and it is now difficult to imagine what either the nebula of entities or its infosphere might look like without them. We have argued that contrary to a popular point of view, these theories are not simplifications that serve to account for overly complex realities. Some in fact consist of added layers of complexity to what are, by all other accounts, relatively straightforward events. Rather, they serve to systematically interpret current events in ways that assign responsibility for ills and gratitude for virtue to entities previously identified as evil or good.

Our approach to the infosphere as a "bio-technical" network underlined the co-creation of the language, concerns, goals, and strategies of the far right, where various human agents and various machines interact and generate the containers (aesthetics, style, codes, grammar) and the contents (videos, streams, memes, posts). It is crucially important to note, like McLuhan, that both carry various explicit and implicit messages, and then, with Latour, that these messages are partly determined by technologies and partly by their users. We don't mean this in the usual sense where platform bots curate and structure communications and information (though they certainly do that) but in the ways they help shape all messages. Influencers, prosumers, and mere "likers" format their message according to what they understand to be the most powerful uses of the technology. In turn, the various technologies, complete with their capabilities, shortcomings, rules, and policies, are manipulated, subverted, and hacked by their users. Entire movements, like the alt-right, were born out of that system.

Moving from group strategy and macro context effects, chapter 5 delves into the microscopic mechanics of group recruitment, membership, activities, and eventual retreat. It first accounts for our decision to entirely eschew the popular concept of "radicalization": though perhaps useful to therapists and other intervention professionals, it in almost no way describes what individuals on the far right experience, inflict, inspire, or aspire to. It poorly accounts for the multiple variables at work in encountering, approaching, engaging with, or participating in far-right group activities, especially those that have to do with the social, political, cultural, demographic, technological, or economic context in which they exist. The human experience of extremism is vastly complex, and though we identified several similarities in pathways, personal biographies, or immediate social context, they stubbornly resist being boiled down to a single "radicalization" process.

Our account of personal commitment to the far right does not evoke the concept of factors, reasons, or causes in the usual way, which may be disconcerting. Throughout the book, we have adopted an ethnomethodological outlook, where such concepts are meant to convey that various objects, some experienced, some felt, some imagined, become part of how individuals make sense of their context, usually in social groups. Our causes and factors are not deterministic. Our overarching account of engagement and commitment is that, for the most part, individuals are looking for ways to cope with everyday life. In the broader array of human possibilities, our respondents adopted strategies offered by an entity in the vast nebula of the far right. In that, neither the individuals, the groups, nor their wider network are extraordinary.

Individuals join the far-right movement family, in words and in deeds, in groups or alone, for a multiplicity of reasons. We have shown that these reasons interact, with a powerful multiplier effect. None of our respondents could pinpoint the moment when they first set foot on the path to engagement and participation in a far-right group, and the explanation is simple: it was the result of an interaction of factors, some obvious and recognized by the individuals themselves (current events, accidents, or outright, explicit recruitment), others far less so (psychosocial vulnerabilities, unemployment, personal network effects). All occur on independent timelines, with highly variable levels of subjectively experienced intensity and different applied meanings.

Those are the explanatory causes. But what about the political causes? We do not think that people join the far right by accident and might otherwise have joined an environmentalist group, a religious cult, or a mainstream political party. Though we have underlined the weight of contingent life incidents, such as current events or family networks, for instance, the reality is that various ideologies on the far right do appeal rationally to those at the meeting point of particular push and pull factors. The extreme values, decisiveness, approaches, discourse, and actions of the far right can be seductive to those who come to feel that social, cultural, and political ills need radical remedies.

Finally, in the last chapter we saw that one key part of this sociopolitical context is the various types of responses offered to (real and imagined) trends and events in the far right, as seen from the outside. We have looked at actions taken by civil society and by private industry and governments. As oppositional movements, far-right groups tend to be particularly preoccupied by the shape and function of various authorities, and especially by their regulatory outputs. But they are also concerned by other forms of less official social control. The back-and-forth between far-right and antifascist groups is a staple of an ideological underworld of sorts, and only appears on media radars when it degenerates to the point of causing deaths – which is to say, rarely. But we have seen how some members of skinhead groups, for instance, define themselves almost entirely through such encounters, not often directly experienced but constantly recalled and retold. In fact, the threat of Antifa now also commonly appears in non-extremist conservative discourse and serves the same function, to bring groups together by pointing to a common enemy (regardless of whether it exists or not).

Other typical enemies of the far right are the media as a whole and any journalist individually. Being an active member of a news agency is now far more dangerous than it was just a few years ago. Journalists are being bullied online and off and are targeted for "citizen's arrests," and their reputation is under constant, intense attack. As the media grapples with two other crises – dwindling revenue and the incapacity to compete with the explosion of non-professional, unskilled sources for audiences – there is a high potential for catastrophic collapse of the current industrial media structure, severely hampering the already fragilized democratic edifice. This cascade effect would of course produce the ideal conditions for a forceful rise of the far right, the proportions of which were last seen a century ago.

Paradoxically for some, official policing authorities are at the same time respected because of their dedication (or at least mandate) to enforce laws and maintain order and despised as antagonists because of their status as agents of the state. Many police organizations also seem confused by this contradiction. In the last forty years the far right has been seen as a collection of ideologues, with a few individual outliers occasionally committing street crimes better left to local police patrols and statistically insignificant. For historical reasons, national security efforts have traditionally been directed elsewhere. A few propagandists have been prosecuted, with mixed results; some have been sued by other citizens, with equally variable outcomes. A few alarm bells have started to sound, including the 2017 mosque massacre, the 6 January uprising in the USA, and the Freedom Convoy in February 2022. But chapter 6 has shown that policing organizations have yet to find their bearings in this new world of disorganized, police-friendly, eccentric, high-tech, local extremism that routinely recruits police officers. Politicians are quick to jump on surveillance and enforcement solutions: censorship, user identification, data collection and retention, warrantless search of devices, of privately owned data sources, and the like. In 2021 the Liberal government promised an "online harms" bill, but expert consultations did not go as planned, when most suggested practical measures met with fundamental objections related to citizen autonomy, privacy, and freedom of speech. None of these repressive solutions is likely to have a significant reduction, interdiction, deterrent, or preventive effect on so-called "online harms"; rather, they will introduce further fluidity and unpredictability in the movement, making it harder, rather than easier, to police.

The aim of this book was never to offer a range of potential solutions to aspects of the far right one might deem dangerous, irritating, illegal, illegitimate, or otherwise undesirable. In fact, we have given little thought to populating these categories or even to how this might be done in a reasonably objective, unbiased manner. Given the key characteristics of the far-right nebula, as well as those of the entities that might be mobilized in implementing such solutions, the first, most pressing warning that we can offer is that a general approach is utterly impossible. Furthermore, in the event that we simply lack imagination and one such strategy can indeed be devised, it would almost certainly be undesirable: the nets would be too broad, catching armchair revolutionaries and radical terrorists alike; experience shows it would disproportionately, if not exclusively, catch the proverbial "low hanging fruit," those who do not excel at organizing, hiding, and manipulating; it would immediately be embroiled in political and legal contests. We can only hope this book has made this obvious.

Practical solutions do not abound, to say the least. And most are likely to target individuals, one at a time, locally. When the criminal justice system is mobilized, the key principle is understatement. This holds true for state responses to any social movement. Any language that aggrandizes the threat, the numbers, the skills, the organization, or the ideology (in that case, by voicing abhorrence for instance) has a galvanizing effect on the opposition. The equivalent is also true during trials or incarceration, where any ostentatious precaution should be avoided ("supermax" designations for holding cells, snipers on roofs, paramilitary or tactical group escorts, grandiose rhetoric from the prosecution or from the bench, and the like). We are fully aware how unlikely these warnings are to be followed.

But the justice system is not the best tool we have. In fact, there have been many instances, lately, where it was wrongly employed, processing individuals with indisputable mental health (from clear, acute pathologies to temporary but intense stress), drug, and other significant individual (family, work, school) problems. Most times, however, such cases fall entirely through the cracks of the system, escaping the attention of police and social services. The overwhelming majority should be dealt with using social work approaches: at the level of communities, where early signs of polarization must be countered; at the level of families, where the problems that give rise to political or ideological violence are also the root of multiple other personal issues; and obviously for individuals whose psychosocial problems may morph into hate and violence. Multiple research and intervention programs already exist, in most Canadian municipalities, to tackle these problems (one of us is active in one such program). But funding, staffing, and training are notoriously lacking at all of these levels, even though benefits would spread far, far beyond the simple prevention of extremism, polarization, and hate.

The one overall, nation-wide strategy that will bear fruit is the fight against disinformation, including conspiracy theories. Though it is probably pointless to attempt to detoxify those who are already deeply involved in searching for, creating, or disseminating disinformation that they believe in, aiming at prevention is promising. In our opinion, countering disinformation is more likely to succeed than attempting to censor every new theory appearing online daily, if not hourly. This will require a strong and diverse media, government and police transparency that foster public trust, and media literacy starting in school.

That, of course, is just the tip of the far-right iceberg. Most of its individual and group components manage to avoid the main hazards listed above: they do not commit crimes, explicitly spread hate, or encourage, support, or join with those who do. Their existence may annoy liberal sensibilities, but it is not only legal and legitimate, it is in fact required in any polity that calls itself democratic. Though they often act as a transmission belt between the depths of the extreme and the mainstream, they also serve to insulate and to occupy political space on the right.

In short, though some instances of violent, highly disruptive, threatening behaviour seem to call for stern measures and though we have repeatedly stated the high potential for disaster, the current context is highly volatile, and imprudent interventions can easily generate unwanted consequences. We are at a crossroads of multiple vulnerabilities, where loss of public confidence in institutions, growing spheres of disinformation, economic and environmental insecurities, technological unpredictability, news media fragility, and identity politics, all of which are launching pads for the far right, could radically alter our political landscape in the next few years.

ACKNOWLEDGMENTS

This book is the final product of research we started in 2013 thanks to a SSHRC grant [435-2013-0872]. It would not have been possible without the contributions of the people we met and who accompanied us throughout this long and tortuous adventure. Our gratitude goes first and foremost to the students who served as our research assistants. Involved at many stages of the research, we have seen them evolve, grow, and acquire new knowledge and skills. In addition to their professionalism and commitment, we were able to count on their sense of humour and resilience. The fieldwork was not a smooth ride, and on several occasions, we had to adjust our strategies. Several of our students accompanied us in the field, taking part in the interviews we conducted with active and veteran activists from far-right groups. We thank them all for their invaluable support and creativity! Over the years, this great team has included at Université Laval: Bénédicte Collignon, Marie-Soleil Normandin, Alex Wood, Johanna Massé, Émilie Fort, Maryse Catellier-Boulianne, Mélanie Rembert; at Université de Montreal: Rosalie Chevrette, Valentine Crosset, Maxime Bérubé, and Laurie-Anne Beaulieu. To all of you, whether you've been with us for one session or several years, we owe you a huge debt of gratitude!

The list of colleagues who have commented on and evaluated the preliminary outputs of this research is too long to be mentioned here. Two special mentions are in order, however. First, we are extremely grateful to the reviewers who evaluated the first version of this manuscript. Through their constructive remarks, they have greatly contributed to improving the document and pushing us to position ourselves even more clearly within a rapidly expanding field of study. Second, colleagues at our respective universities and the research teams with which we are affiliated have offered us over the years, in addition to their listening skills, a necessary and demanding critical eye, which has enabled us to move forward. Special thanks go to our colleagues at the Centre international de criminologie comparée and the now-defunct Canadian Network for Research on Terrorism, Security and Society.

Finally, this research would not have been possible without the participation of members of far-right groups. Thank you to all those who agreed to meet us and grant us an interview. Thank you for sharing with us your experiences, perceptions, and perspectives on a number of social issues. It hasn't always been easy ... In fact, it was very complicated. But we couldn't imagine doing research on such a hot topic without hearing from the people who make these movements, even if it was a demanding exercise.

REFERENCES

Adams, Josh, and Vincent J. Roscigno. 2005. "White Supremacists, Oppositional Culture and the World Wide Web." *Social Forces* 84 (2): 759–78.

Akkerman, Tjitske. 2012. "Comparing Radical Right Parties in Government: Immigration and Integration Policies in Nine Countries (1996–2010)." *West European Politics* 35 (3): 511–29.

– 2015. "Immigration Policy and Electoral Competition in Western Europe: A Fine-Grained Analysis of Party Positions over the Past Two Decades." *Party Politics* 21 (1): 54–67.

Akkerman, Tjitske, Sarah L. de Lange, and Matthijs Rooduijn, eds. 2016. *Radical Right-Wing Populist Western Parties: Into the Mainstream?* (New York: Routledge).

Alonso, Sonia, and Sara Claro di Fonseca. 2012. "Immigration, Left and Right." *Party Politics* 18 (6): 865–84.

Archambault, Emil, and Yannick Veilleux-Lepage. 2019. "The Soldiers of Odin in Canada: The Failure of a Transnational Ideology." In *Vigilantism against Migrants and Minorities*, edited by T. Bjørgo and M. Mareš, 272–85. London: Routledge.

Art, David. 2020. "The Myth of Global Populism." *Perspectives on Terrorism* 20 (3): 999–1011. doi:10.1017/S1537592720003552.

Arzheimer, Kai. 2009. "Contextual Factors and the Extreme Right Vote in Western Europe, 1980–2002." *American Journal of Political Science* 53 (2): 259–75.

Asp, Petter. 2013. "Preventionism and Criminalisation of Nonconsummate Offenses." In *Prevention and the Limits of the Criminal Law*, edited by Andrew Ashworth, Lucia Zedner, and Patrick Tomlin, 22–46. Oxford: Oxford University Press.

Atton, Chris. 2006. "Far-Right Media on the Internet: Culture, Discourse and Power." *New Media & Society* 8 (4): 573–87.

Avalos, Alberto. 2017. "50K 'Gen Z' High School Students Identify as Republican." *Hispanic Heritage Foundation*, 27 October 2017. https://hispanicheritage.org/50000-generation-z-high-school-students-identify-republican/.

Back, Les. 2002. "Aryans Reading Adorno: Cyber-Culture and Twenty-First Century Racism." *Ethnic and Racial Studies* 2 (4): 628–51.

Badawy, Adam, Emilio Ferrara, and Kristina Lerman. 2018. "Analyzing the Digital Traces of Political Manipulation: The 2016 Russian Interference Twitter Campaign." In *Proceedings of The Web Conference*, WWW'18, 259–65. New York: ACM. doi: 10.1109/ASONAM.2018.8508646.

Bail, Christopher. 2014. *Terrified: How Anti-Muslim Fringe Organizations Became Mainstream*. Princeton: Princeton University Press.

Bail, Christopher A., Brian Guay, Emily Maloney, Aidan Combs, D. Sunshine Hillygus, Friedolin Merhout, Deen Freelon, and Alexander Volfovsky. 2020. "Assessing the Russian Internet Research Agency's impact on the Political Attitudes and Behaviors of American Twitter Users in Late 2017." *Proceedings of the National Academy of Sciences of the United States of America* 117 (1): 243–50.

Bale, Tim. 2008. "Politics Matters: A Conclusion." *Journal of European Public Policy* 15 (3): 453–64.

Bale, Tim, Christoffer Green-Pedersen, André Krouwel, Kurt Richard Luther, and Nick Sitter. 2010. "If You Can't Beat Them, Join Them? Explaining Social Democratic Responses to the Challenge from the Populist Radical Right in Western Europe." *Political Studies* 58 (3): 410–26.

Barkun, Michael. 2017. "President Trump and the 'Fringe.'" *Terrorism and Political Violence* 29 (3): 437–43.

Barnes, Samuel H., and Max Kaase, eds. 1979. *Political Action: Mass Participation in Five Western Democracies*. Beverley Hills and London: Sage Publications.

Bar-On, Tamir. 2018. "The Radical Right and Nationalism." In *The Oxford Handbook of the Radical Right*, edited by Jens Rydgren, 17–41. Oxford: Oxford University Press.

Baron, Stephen W. 1997. "Canadian Male Street Skinheads: Street Gang or Street Terrorists?" *Canadian Review of Sociology and Anthropology* 34 (2): 125–54.

Barrett, Stanley. 2015 (1987). *Is God a Racist? The Right-Wing in Canada*. Toronto: Toronto University Press.

Bartley, Allan. 2020. *The Ku Klux Klan in Canada: A Century of Promoting Racism and Hate in the Peaceable Kingdom*. Halifax: Formac Publishing Company Limited.

Bauman, Zigmunt. 2000. *Liquid Modernity*. London: Polity Press.

Belew, Kathleen. 2018. *Bring the War Home: The White Power Movement and Paramilitary America*. Cambridge and London: Harvard University Press.

Bell, Stewart. 2018. "Documents Reveal Internal Debate over Threat of Canadian Right Wing." Global News. https://globalnews.ca/news/4188139/far-right-extremely-small-csis/.

Benford, Robert D. 2016. "Social Movements and the Dramatic Framing of Social Reality." In *The Drama of Social Life*, edited by Charles Edgley, 139–55. New York: Taylor and Francis.

Benford, Robert. D., and David A. Snow. 2000. "Framing Processes and Social Movements: An Overview and Assessment." *Annual Review of Sociology* 26 (1): 611–39.

Bergeron, Patrice. 2017. "Attentat dans une mosquée de Québec: un acte terroriste difficile à prévenir, selon Couillard." *HuffPost*, 30 January 2017.

Bergmann, Eirikur. 2020. *Neo-Nationalism: The Rise of Nativist Populism*. London: Palgrave Macmillan.

Bernauer, Julian. 2017. "A Fourth Wave of Populism? Trajectories of Populist Radical Right Parties in Europe, 2000–2017." *11th ECPR General Conference*. https://ecpr.eu/Filestore/PaperProposal/afb62469-c7aa-4d52-9328-2a037ac7844b.pdf, last time consulted 19 June 2019.

Berntzen, Lars Erik. 2018. "The Anti-Islamic Movement: Far Right and Liberal?" PhD thesis, European University Institute. https://www.researchgate.net/publication/324128275_The_AntiIslamic_Movement_Far_Right_and_Liberal_Introduction.

Bertram, Luke. 2016. "Terrorism, the Internet and the Social Media Advantage: Exploring How Terrorist Organizations Exploit Aspects of the Internet, Social Media and How These Same Platforms Could Be Used to Counter Violent Extremism." *Journal for Deradicalization* (7): 225–52.

Betz, Hans-George. 2017. "Nativism across Time and Space." *Swiss Political Science Review* 23 (4): 335–53.

– 2018. "The Radical Right and Populism." In *The Oxford Handbook of the Radical Right*, edited by Jens Rydgren, 86–104. New York: Oxford University Press.

Blee, Kathleen M. 2002. *Inside Organized Racism: Women in the Hate Movement*. California: University of California Press.

Blee, Kathleen M., and Kimberly A. Creasap. 2010. "Conservative and Right-Wing Movements." *Annual Review of Sociology* 36 (1): 269–86.

Blee, Kathleen M., and Amy McDowell. 2012. "Social Movement Audiences." *Sociological Forum* 27 (1): 1–20.

Bornjo, Tore, and Jacob Aasland Ravndal. 2019. "Extreme-Right Violence and Terrorism: Concepts, Patterns, and Responses." *ICCT Brief, International Centre for Counter-Terrorism*, 1–22. https://www.jstor.org/stable/pdf/resrep19624.pdf.

Boumaza, Magali, and Aurélie Campana. 2007. "Enquêter en terrain difficile." *Revue française de science politique* 57 (1): 5–25.

Bourdieu, Pierre. 1999. *Language and Symbolic Power*. Cambridge, MA: Harvard University Press.

Bourne, Mike. 2012. "Guns Don't Kill People, Cyborgs Do: A Latourian Provocation for Transformatory Arms Control and Disarmament." *Global Change, Peace and Security* 24 (1): 141–63.

Bowden, Tom. 1978. *Beyond the Limits of the Law.* Harmondsworth: Penguin.

Boyd, Danah. 2019. "The Fragmentation of Truth." Paper presented at the Knight Media Forum, Knight Foundation, 27 February 2019.

Brennan, Mary C. 1995. *Turning Right in the Sixties: The Conservative Capture of the GOP.* Chapel Hill and London: University of North Carolina Press.

Brodeur, Jean-Paul. 2007. "High and Low Policing in Post-9/11 Times." *Policing* 1 (1): 25–37.

– 2009. "Comment définir le terrorisme?" In *Terrorisme et antiterrorisme au Canada,* edited by Stéphane Leman-Langlois and Jean-Paul Brodeur, 17–37. Montreal: Presses de l'Université de Montréal.

Bruns, Alex, Stephen Harrington, and Edward Hurcombe. 2021. "Coronavirus Conspiracy Theories: Tracing Misinformation Trajectories from the Fringes to the Mainstream." In *Communicating COVID-19,* edited by Monique Lewis, Eliza Govender, and Kate Holland, 229–49. Switzerland: Palgrave Macmillan, Cham. https://doi.org/10.1007/978-3-030-79735-5_12.

Burgess, Jean, and Joshua Green. 2009. *YouTube: Online Video and Participatory Culture,* with contributions by Henry Jenkins and John Hartley. 1st ed. Cambridge, UK: Polity.

– 2018. *YouTube: Online Video and Participatory Culture,* with contributions by Henry Jenkins and John Hartley. 2nd ed. Cambridge, UK: Polity.

Busher, Joel, and John Morrison. 2018. "Micro Moral Worlds of Contentious Politics: A Reconceptualization of Radical Groups and Their Intersections with One Another and the Mainstream." *Mobilization: An International Quarterly* 23 (2): 219–36.

Caiani, Manuela, and Andřej Císař. 2019a. "Radical Right Movement Parties in Europe: An Introduction." In *Radical Right Movement Parties in Europe,* edited by Manuela Caiani and Andřej Císař, 2–10. London and New York: Routledge.

– 2019b. "Movements, Parties and Movement Parties of the Radical Right: Towards a Unified Approach." In *Radical Right Movement Parties in Europe,* edited by Manuela Caiani and Andřej Císař, 10–26. London and New York: Routledge.

– 2019c. "Conclusion: Movements vs. Parties, Movements and Parties, Movements or Parties? Types of Interactions within the Radical Right." In *Radical Right Movement Parties in Europe,* edited by Manuela Caiani and Andřej Císař, 230–43. London and New York: Routledge.

Caiani, Manuela, and Patricia Kröll. 2015. "The Transnationalization of the Extreme Right and the Use of the Internet." *International Journal of Comparative and Applied Criminal Justice* 39 (4): 331–51.

– 2017. "Nationalism and Populism in Radical Right Discourses in Italy and Germany." *Javnost/The Public* 24 (2): 1–19.

Caiani, Manuela, and Linda Parenti. 2016. *European and American Extreme Right Groups and the Internet*. London and New York: Routledge.

Caiani, Manuela, and Donatella della Porta. 2011. "The Elitist Populism of the Extreme Right: A Frame Analysis of Extreme Right-Wing Discourses in Italy and Germany." *Acta Politica* 46 (2): 180–202.

Caiani, Manuela, Donatella della Porta, and Claudius Wagemann. 2012. *Mobilizing on the Extreme Right: Germany, Italy, and the United States*. Oxford: Oxford University Press.

Cameron, Dell, and Tom Gizmodo. 2022. "New Leak Suggests Most Users Funding Canada's 'Freedom Convoy' Reside in U.S." *Gizmodo*, 14 February 2022. https://gizmodo.com/givesendgo-leak-freedom-convoy-canada-trucker-protest-d-1848534782.

Campana, Aurélie, and Samuel Tanner. 2019. *Meanwhile in Canada: Anti-Muslim Ordinary Racism and the Banalization of Far Right Ideology*. TSAS Research Paper. https://www.tsas.ca/publications/anti-muslim-ordinary racism-and-the-banalization-of-far-right-ideology/.

Campbell, Andy. 2022. *We Are Proud Boys: How a Right-Wing Street Gang Ushered in a New Era of American Extremism*. New York: Hachette Book.

Canada, Government of. 1979. *Commission of Inquiry Concerning Certain Activities of the Royal Canadian Mounted Police*. Hull: Government of Canada Publishing Centre.

– 2010. *Air India Flight 182: A Canadian Tragedy*. Report of the Commission of Inquiry into the Investigation of the Bombing of Air India Flight 182. Ottawa: Government of Canada.

– 2023. *Report of the Public Inquiry into the 2022 Public Order Emergency*. Ottawa: Government of Canada.

Canadian Armed Forces. 2018. *White Supremacy, Hate Groups, and Racism in the Canadian Armed Forces*. 2000-1040 MPCIS. Military Police Criminal Intelligence Section, Criminal Intelligence Report. Released under the Access to Information Act of Canada.

Canadian Security Intelligence Service. 1985. *Canadian Security Intelligence Service Act* C-3. Last amended on 13 July 2019, http://laws-lois.justice.gc.ca/eng/acts/c-23/

– 2013. *CSIS Public Report 2011–2013*. Ottawa: Government of Canada.

– 2015. *CSIS Public Report 2013–2014*. Ottawa: Government of Canada.

– 2018. *CSIS Public Report 2018*. Ottawa: Government of Canada.

– 2019. *CSIS Public Report 2019* Ottawa: Government of Canada.

Cardon, Dominique. 2008. "Le Design de la Visibilité. Un Essai de Cartographie du Web 2.0." *Réseaux* 6 (152): 93–137.

Carranco, Shannon, Jon Milton, and Christopher Curtis. 2018. "Alt-right in Montreal: Anti-fascists Ramp Up Fight against Neo-Nazis." *The Montreal Gazette*, 16 May 2018. https://montrealgazette.com/news/local-news/alt-right-in-montreal-anti-fascists-ramp-up-fight-against-neo-nazis.

Carter, Elisabeth. 2005. *The Extreme Right in Western Europe: Success or Failure?* Manchester: Manchester University Press.

– 2018. "Right-Wing Extremism/Radicalism: Reconstructing the Concept." *Journal of Political Ideologies* 23 (2): 157–82.

Chavez, Leo R. 2013. *The Latino Threat: Constructing Immigrants, Citizens, and the Nation*. Redwood City: Stanford University Press.

Claxton, Matthew. 2017. "Former Langley Libertarian Candidate Detained in Italy." *The Abbotsford News*, 17 May 2017. https://www.abbynews.com/news/former-langley-libertarian-candidate-detained-in-italy/.

Covington, Paul, Jay Adams, and Emre Sargin. 2016. "Deep Neural Networks for YouTube." RecSys '16, Proceedings of the 10th ACM Conference on Recommender Systems. https://doi.org/10.1145/2959100.2959190.

Crosset, Valentine, and Benoit Dupont. 2022. "Cognitive Assemblages: The Entangled Nature of Algorithmic Content Moderation." *Big Data & Society* 9 (2): 1–13.

Crosset, Valentine, Samuel Tanner, and Aurélie Campana. 2019. "Researching Far Right Groups on Twitter: Methodological Challenges 2.0." *New Media & Society* 21 (4): 939–61.

CTV News. 2010. "Canadian Spies Heading Overseas to Learn Arabic." CTV News, 14 July 2010. https://www.ctvnews.ca/canadian-spies-heading-overseas-to-learn-arabic-1.532373.

– 2011. "Neo-Nazis, Anti-racists Hold Rallies in Calgary." CTV News, 19 March 2011. http://www.ctvnews.ca/neo-nazis-anti-racists-hold-rallies-in-calgary-1.620930.

Daniels, Jessie. 2009. *Cyber Racism: White Supremacy Online and the New Attack on Civil Rights*. Lanham, MD: Rowman & Littlefield Publishers.

– 2018. "The Algorithmic Rise of the Alt-Right." *Context* 17 (1): 60–5.

della Porta, Donatella. 2008. "Research on Social Movements and Political Violence." *Qualitative Sociology* 31 (3): 221–30.

– 2013. *Clandestine Political Violence*. Cambridge: Cambridge University Press.

della Porta, Donatella, and Diani Mario. 2009. *Social Movements: An Introduction*. Hoboken: John Wiley & Sons.

della Porta, Donatella, and Dieter Rucht. 1995. "Left-Libertarian Movements in Context: A Comparison of Italy and West Germany, 1965–1990." In *The Politics of Social Protest: Comparative Perspectives on States and Social Movements*, edited by Craig J. Jenkins and Bert Klandermans, 229–72. Minneapolis: University of Minnesota Press.

Delpéteau, François. 2018. "Relational Thinking in Sociology: Relevance, Concurrence and Dissonance." In *The Palgrave Handbook of Relational Sociology*, edited by François Delpéteau, 3–33. London: Palgrave Macmillan.

Devoir, Le. 2020. "Manifeste Contre le Dogmatisme Universitaire." *Le Devoir*, 30 January 2020. https://www.ledevoir.com/opinion/idees/571818/manifeste-contre-le-dogmatisme-universitaire.

Diani, Mario, ed. 1992. "The Concept of Social Movement." *The Sociological Review* (40): 1–25.

– 2013. "Networks and Social Movements." In *The Wiley Blackwell Encyclopedia of Social and Political Movements*, edited by David A. Snow, Donatella della Porta, Bert Klandermans, and Doug McAdam. Hoboken: Wiley-Blackwell. Available online.

Donovan, Jason, and Danah Boyd. 2019 "Stop the Presses? Moving from Strategic Silence to Strategic Amplification in a Networked Media Ecosystem." *American Behavioral Scientist* 65 (2): 333–50.

Downs, William M. 2002. "How Effective Is the Cordon Sanitaire? Lessons from Efforts to Contain the Far Right in Belgium, France, Denmark and Norway." *Journal für Konflikt und Gewaltforschung* 4 (1): 32–51.

Dubenko, Anna. 2017. "Right and Left on the Violence in Charlottesville." *New York Times*, 14 August 2017. https://www.nytimes.com/2017/08/14/us/politics/trump-charlottesville-left-right-react.html.

Dubinski, Kate. 2024. "Judge Rules Killer of London, Ont., Muslim Family Committed Terrorism, Calling It a 'Textbook Example.'" CBC News, 22 February 2024. https://www.cbc.ca/news/canada/london/veltman-muslim-family-conviction-killing-1.7121217.

Durham, Martin. 2007. *White Rage. The Extreme Right and American Politics.* London and New York: Routledge.

Edgley, Charles. 2016. *The Drama of Social Life: A Dramaturgical Handbook.* London and New York: Routledge.

Elghawaby, Amira. 2016. "Want to Hurt the Islamic State? Call It Something Else. How Politicians and Media Refer to the Terrorist Group May Actually Help in Countering Its Destructive Narratives." *National Council of Canadian Muslims*, 23 February 2016. https://www.nccm.ca/want-to-hurt-the-islamic-state-call-it-something-else/.

Ellinas, Antonis A. 2010. *The Media and the Far Right in Western Europe: Playing the Nationalist Card.* Cambridge: Cambridge University Press 2010.

F.-Dufour, Isabelle, and Renée Brassard. 2014. "The Convert, the Remorseful and the Rescued: Three Different Processes of Desistance from Crime." *Australian & New Zealand Journal of Criminology* 47 (3): 313–35.

Feenberg, Andrew. 1999. *Questioning Technology.* London and New York: Routledge.

Feith, Jesse. 2018. "'We Can't Tolerate It': Anti-racists Protest against Neo-Nazi in Rosemont." *The Montreal Gazette*, 15 May 2018. https://montrealgazette.com/news/local-news/anti-racists-to-march-in-rosemont-la-petite-patrie-against-neo-nazi-on-saturday.

Fielitz, Maik, and Nick Thurston, eds. 2016. *Post-Digital Cultures of the Far Right: Online Actions and Offline Consequences in Europe and the US*. New York: Columbia University Press.

Forcese, Craig, and Kent Roach. 2015. *False Security: The Radicalization of Canadian Anti-Terrorism*. Toronto: Irwin Law.

Fraser, David. 2022. "Almost $6M in Freedom Convoy Money Captured as Months-Long Injunction Ends." CBC News, 2 February 2022. https://www.cbc.ca/news/canada/ottawa/freedom-convoy-injunction-ends-money-captured-1.6438103.

Fredette, Chantal, and Jean-Pierre Guay. 2014. "Définir et mesurer l'adhésion à la culture des gangs de rue." *Criminologie* 47 (2): 295–315.

Freilich, Joshua D., Nelson A. Pichardo Almanzar, and Craig J. Rivera. 1999. "How Social Movement Organizations Explicitly and Implicitly Promote Deviant Behavior: The Case of the Militia Movement." *Justice Quarterly* 16 (3): 655–83.

Frigoli, Gilles, and Gilles Ivaldi. 2017. "L'extrême droite et l'Islam: Fractures idéologiques et stratégies électorales." *Hommes & Migrations* 1316: 27–34.

Futrell, Robert, Pete Simi, and Anna E. Tan. 2019. "Political Extremism and Social Movements." In *The Wiley Blackwell Companion to Social Movements*, 2nd ed., edited by David A. Snow, Sarah A. Soule, Hanspeter Kriesi, and Holly J. McCammon, 17–42. Hoboken: Wiley-Blackwell.

Galbraith, James K. 2017. "Grexit, Brexit, Fixit ... The Dynamics of Division in the Age of Trump." *Political Insights* 8 (3): 381–8.

Ganesh, Bharath. 2018. "The Ungovernability of Digital Hate Culture." *Journal of International Affairs* 71 (2): 30–49.

Gattinara, Pietro. 2019. "Neo-Facist Movement Parties in Italy: The Extreme Right Between Electoral and Protest Politics." In *Radical Right Movement Parties in Europe*, edited by Manuela Caiani and Andřej Císař, 80–95. London and New York: Routledge.

Gerbaudo, Paolo. 2012. *Tweets and the Streets: Social Media and Contemporary Activism*. London: Pluto Press.

– 2019. *The Digital Party: Political Organisation and Online Democracy*. London: Pluto Press.

Gest, Justin, Tyler Reny, and Jeremy Mayer. 2018. "Roots of the Radical Right: Nostalgic Deprivation in the United States and Britain." *Comparative Political Studies* 51 (13): 1694–719.

Giugni, Marco, Paul Koopmans, Florence Passy, and Paul Statham. 2005. "Institutional and Discursive Opportunities for Extreme-Right Mobilization in Five Countries." *Mobilization: An International Quarterly* 10 (1): 145–62.

Goffman, Erving. 1974. *Frame Analysis: An Essay on the Organization of Experience.* Cambridge, MA: Harvard University Press.

Goldstone, Jack A. 2003. "Bringing Institutionalized and Noninstitutionalized Politics." In *State, Party and Movements*, edited by Jack A. Goldstone, 1–25. Cambridge: Cambridge University Press.

Gomez del Prado, Grégory, and Stéphane Leman-Langlois. 2020. *Le policing au Canada et au Québec.* Montreal: Éditions Yvon Blais.

Gottschalk, Michel, and Simon Gottschalk. 2004. "Authoritarianism and Pathological Hatred: A Social Psychological Profile of the Middle Eastern Terrorist." *The American Sociologist* 35 (2): 38–59.

Gottschalk, Peter, and Gabriel Greenberg. 2007. *Islamophobia: Making Muslims the Enemy.* New York: Rowman & Littlefield Publishers.

Grant, Meghan. 2022. "Coutts Arrests: New Details on the Men and Women Charged in Border Blockade." CBC News, 17 February 2022. https://www.cbc.ca/news/canada/calgary/coutts-arrests-charges-border-protest-1.6354587.

Guardian. 2022. "Canada Was Warned before Protests That Violent Extremists Infiltrated Convoy." *Guardian*, 17 February 2022. https://www.theguardian.com/world/2022/feb/17/ottawa-protests-anti-terror-agency-warned-violent-extremists.

Gurr, Ted. 1986. "The Political Origins of State Violence and Terror." In *Government Violence and Repression: An Agenda for Research*, edited by Michael Stohl and George A. Lopez, 45–71. Westport: Greenwood Press.

Gusfield, Joseph R. 2000. *Performing Action: Artistry in Human Behavior and Social Research.* London and New York: Routledge.

Hafez, Farid. 2014. "Shifting Borders: Islamophobia as Common Ground for Building Pan-European Right-Wing Unity." *Patterns of Prejudice* 48 (5): 479–99.

Hamm, Mark. 2009. "From the Klans to Skinheads: A Critical History of American Hate Groups." In *Hate Crimes.* Volume 1: *Understanding and Defining Hate Crimes*, edited by Barbara Perry and Brian Levin, 95–107. Westport and London: Praeger.

Han, Kyung Joon. 2015. "The Impact of Radical Right-Wing Parties on the Positions of Mainstream Parties Regarding Multiculturalism." *West European Politics* 38 (3): 557–76.

Hankes, Keagan. 2016. *SPLC Analysis: Small Community of Extremists on Twitter Responsible for Majority Messages.* Montgomery: Southern Poverty Law Center.

Hanna, Jeanne, and Joel Busher. 2019. "UKIP and the UK's Radical Right: A Tale of Movement Party Success?" In *Radical Right Movement Parties in Europe*, edited by Manuela Caiani and Andřej Císař, 46–62. London and New York: Routledge.

Hannah, Matthew N. 2021. "A Conspiracy of Data: QAnon, Social Media, and Information Visualization." *Social Media & Society* 7 (13): 1–15.

Harrington, Brooke, and Gary A. Fine. 2000. "Opening the 'Black Box': Small Groups and Twenty-First-Century Sociology." *Social Psychology Quarterly* 63 (4): 312–23.

Hart, Jacob Davey, Eisha Maharasingam-Shah, Ciaran O'Connor, and Aoife Gallagher. 2021. *An Online Environmental Scan of Right-wing Extremism in Canada.* Beirut, Berlin, London, Paris, and Washington: Institute for Strategic Dialogue.

Hategan, Elisa. 2014. *Race Traitor: A Memoir. The True Story of Canadian Intelligence Service's Greatest Cover-Up.* Toronto: Incognito Press.

Hawley, George. 2017. *Making Sense of the Alt Right.* New York: Columbia University Press.

– 2019. *The Alt Right: What Everyone Needs to Know.* New York: Oxford University Press.

Hayes, Molly, and Colin Freeze. 2020. "Police Lay First Terrorism Charge for Toronto Case Involving Misogyny." *The Globe and Mail*, 19 May 2020. https://www.theglobeandmail.com/canada/article-police-lay-first-terrorism-charge-for-toronto-case-involving-misogyny/.

Hedlund, Anna, and Steven Sampson. 2023. "Involved and Detached. Emotional Management in Fieldwork." In *The Entanglements of Ethnographic Fieldwork in a Violent World*, edited by Nerina Weiss, Erella Grassiani, and Linda Green, 93–113. Milton Park, Abingdon, Oxon: Routledge.

Hegghammer, Thomas. 2013. "The Recruiter's Dilemma: Signalling and Rebel Recruitment Tactics." *Journal of Peace Research* 50 (1): 3–16.

Heinze, Anna-Sophie. 2018. "Strategies of Mainstream Parties Towards their Right-wing Populist Challengers: Denmark, Norway, Sweden and Finland in comparison." *West European Politics* 41 (2): 287–309.

Helly, Denise. 2012. "Islamophobia in Canada? Women's Rights, Modernity, Secularism." *RECODE Online Working Papers Series* 11: 1–24.

Hirsch-Hoeffler, Sivan, and Cas Mudde. 2013. "Right-Wing Movements." In *The Wiley Blackwell Encyclopedia of Social and Political Movements*, edited by David Snow, Donatella della Porta, Bert Klandermans, and Doug McAdam. Hoboken: Wiley-Blackwell. https://doi.org/10.1002/9780470674871.wbespm381.

Horgan, John. 2008. "From Profiles to Pathways and Roots to Routes: Perspectives from Psychology on Radicalization into Terrorism." *The Annals of the American Academy* 618: 80–94.

– 2014. *The Psychology of Terrorism*. 2nd ed. London and New York: Routledge.

Horsti, Karina. 2015. "Techno-cultural Opportunities: The Anti-immigration Movement in the Finnish Mediascape." *Patterns of Prejudice* 49 (4): 343–66.

Howard, Philip, N. 2020. *Lie Machines: How to Save Democracy from Troll Armies, Deceitful Robots, Junk News Operations, and Political Operatives*. New Haven and London: Yale University Press.

Humphreys, Adrian. 2021. "Corey Hurren on Rideau Hall Attack: 'I Figured as Soon as I Got on the Property, I Would Get Shot Down.'" *National Post*, 3 March 2021. https://nationalpost.com/news/canada/corey-hurren-on-rideau-hall-attack-i-figured-as-soon-as-i-got-on-the-property-i-would-get-shot-down.

Hutter, Swen, Hanspeter Kriesi, and Jasmine Lorenzini. 2019. "Social Movements in Interaction with Political Parties." In *The Wiley Blackwell Companion to Social Movements*, 2nd ed., edited by David A. Snow, Sarah A. Soule, Hanspeter Kriesi, and Holly J. McCammon. Hoboken: Wiley-Blackwell. https://doi.org/10.1002/9781119168577.ch18.

Ignazi, Piero. 1992. "The Silent Counter-revolution: Hypotheses on the Emergence of Extreme Right-Wing Parties in Europe." *European Journal of Political Research* 22 (1–2): 3–34.

Jamin, Jérôme. 2009. *L'imaginaire du complot. Discours d'extrême droite en France et aux États-Unis*. IMISCOE Dissertations. Amsterdam: Amsterdam University Press.

Jaskulowski, Krzysztof. 2010. "Western (Civic) versus Eastern (Ethnic) Nationalism: The Origins and Critique of the Dichotomy." *Polish Sociological Review* 171 (3): 289–304.

Jenkins, H. 2006. *Fans, Bloggers, and Gamers: Exploring Participatory Culture*. New York: New York University Press.

Johansson, Thomas, and Marcus Herz. 2019. *Youth Studies in Transition: Culture, Generation and New Learning Processes, Young People and Learning Processes in School and Everyday Life 1*. New York: Springer International Publishing.

Johnson-Cartee, K.S. 2004. *News Narratives and News Framing: Constructing Political Reality*. Lanham: Rowman & Littlefield Publishers.

Johnston, Hank. 1996. "A Methodology from Frame Analysis: From Discourse to Cognitive Schemata." In *Social Movements and Culture*, edited by Hank Johnston and Bert Klandesmans, 217–46. Minneapolis: University of Minnesota Press.

Jost, John. 2017. "Ideological Asymmetries and the Essence of Political Psychology." *Political Psychology* 38 (2): 167–208.

Kealy, Gregory, and Reg Whitaker. 1989. *RCMP Security Bulletins: The War Series, 1939–1941*. St John's: Canadian Committee on Labour History.

– 1993. *RCMP Security Bulletins: The War Series, Part II, 1942–1945*. St John's: Canadian Committee on Labour History.

Kelly, Annie. 2017. "The Alt-right: Reactionary Rehabilitation for White Masculinity." *Soundings* 66: 68–78.

Kimmel, Michael. 2013. *Angry White Men: American Masculinity at the End of an Era.* New York: Nation Books.

– 2018. *Healing from Hate: How Young Men Get Into – and Out of – Violent Extremism.* Oakland: University of California Press.

Kincaid, John D. 2017. "Theorizing the Radical Right: Directions for Social Movements Research on the Right-wing Social Movements." *Sociology Compass* 11 (5): 1–10.

Kinsella, Warren. 2001. *Web of Hate: Inside Canada's Far Right Network.* Toronto: Harper Collins.

Klandermans, Bert, and Suzanne Staggenborg, eds. 2002. *Methods of Social Movement Research*, vol. 16. Minneapolis: University of Minnesota Press.

Knupfer, Helena, Ariadne Neureiter, and Jörg Matthes. 2023. "From Social Media Diet to Public Riot? Engagement with 'Greenfluencers' and Young Social Media Users' Environmental Activism." *Computers in Human Behavior*, 139.

Koehler, Daniel. 2014. "The Radical Online: Individual Radicalization Processes and the Role of the Internet." *Journal for Deradicalization* (1): 116–34.

– 2015. "Contrast Societies: Radical Social Movements and Their Relationships with Their Target Societies a Theoretical Model." *Behavioral Sciences of Terrorism and Political Aggression* 7 (1): 18–34.

Kohn, Hans. 1944. *The Idea of Nationalism: A Study of Its Origins and Background.* New York: The Macmillan Company.

Koopmans, Ruud, Paul Statham, Marco Giugni, and Florence Passy. 2005. *Contested Citizenship: Immigration and Cultural Diversity in Europe.* Minneapolis: University of Minnesota Press.

Koulouris, Theodore. 2018. "Online Misogyny and the Alternative Right: Debating the Undebatable." *Feminist Media Studies* 18 (4): 750–61.

Krebs, Valdis E. 2002. "Uncloaking Terrorist Networks." *First Monday* 7 (1).

Kriesi, Hanspeter. 2012. *Political Conflict in Western Europe.* Cambridge and New York: Cambridge University Press.

Krishnan, Manishna. 2015. "A Group of White Supremacists Is Promoting Itself on Canadian University Campuses." *Vice News*, 14 September 2015. https://www.vice.com/en_ca/article/dp5x7j/a-group-of-white-supremacists-is-promoting-itself-on-canadian-university-campuses.

Kruglanski, Arie, Michele Gelfand, Jocelyn Bélanger, Anna Sheveland, Malkanthi Hetiarachchi, and Rohan Gunaratna. 2014. "The Psychology of Radicalization and Deradicalization: How Significance Quest Impacts Violent Extremism." *Advances in Political Psychology* 35: 69–93.

Latour, Bruno. 2005. *Reassembling the Social: An introduction to Actor-Network Theory.* Oxford: Oxford University Press.

– 2007. *L'espoir de Pandore. Pour une vision réaliste de l'activité scientifique.* Paris: La Découverte.

Laub, John, and Robert Sampson. 2003. *Shared Beginnings, Divergent Lives: Delinquent Boys to Age 70.* Cambridge, MA: Harvard University Press.

Lavin, Talia. 2018. "The Neo-Nazis of the Daily Stormer Wander the Digital Wilderness." *The New Yorker,* 7 January 2018. https://www.newyorker.com/tech/annals-of-technology/the-neo-nazis-of-the-daily-stormer-wander-the-digital-wilderness.

Lean, Nathan. 2012. *The Islamophobia Industry: How the Right Manufactures Fear of Muslims.* London: Pluto Press.

Lefranc, Sandrine, and Isabelle Sommier. 2009. "Les Émotions et la Sociologie des Mouvements Sociaux." In *Emotions ... Mobilisation! Mobilisation!,* edited by Christophe Traini, 273–93. Paris: Presses de Science Po.

Leman-Langlois, Stéphane. 2003. "Rationalité pénale moderne et terrorisme, peut-on contrôler le 'méga-crime' à l'aide du système pénal?" In *Comprendre l'acte terroriste,* edited by Dianne Casoni and Louis Brunet, 113–19. Presses de l'Université du Québec.

– 2018a. "Terrorism and Counterterrorism in Canada." In *The Routledge Handbook of Terrorism and Counter-Terrorism,* edited by Andrew Silke, 504–16. London and New York: Routledge.

– 2018b. "Terrorisme au Canada." *Cahiers de la sécurité et de la justice* 43: 118–25.

– 2019a. "Technologies of Surveillance." In *The Handbook on Social Control,* edited by Mathieu Deflem, 347–60. Hoboken: Wiley-Blackwell.

– 2019b. "Prévention et répression du terrorisme au Canada." In *Nouveau traité de sécurité. Sécurité intérieure et sécurité urbaine,* edited by Maurice Cusson, Olivier Ribaux, Étienne Blais, and Michel Max Raynaud, 179–90. Montreal: Éditions Hurtubise and Quebec: Septentrion.

Leman-Langlois, Stéphane, and Jean-Paul Brodeur, eds. 2009. *Terrorisme et antiterrorisme au Canada.* Montreal: Presses de l'Université de Montréal.

Leonardi, Paul M. 2010. "Digital Materiality? How Artifacts without Matter, Matter." *First Monday* 15 (6). https://doi.org/10.5210/fm.v15i6.3036.

Lewis, Rebecca. 2018. "Alternative Influence, Broadcasting the Reactionary Right on YouTube." *Data & Society,* 1–61. https://datasociety.net/wp-content/uploads/2018/09/DS_Alternative_Influence.pdf.

Lindeman, Tracy. 2015. "PEGIDA Québec Cancels March after Anti-Racist Groups Convene." CBC News, 28 March 2015. cbc.ca/news/canada/montreal/pegida-québec-cancels-march-after-anti-racist-groups-convene-1.3013592.

Lombroso, Daniel. 2020. "Why the Alt-Right's Most Famous Woman Disappeared." *The Atlantic*, 16 October 2020. https://www.theatlantic.com/politics/archive/2020/10/alt-right-star-racist-propagandist-has-no-regrets/616725/.

Loveluck, Benjamin. 2016. "Le vigilantisme numérique, entre dénonciation et sanction." *Politix* 3 (115): 127–53.

– 2020. "The Many Shades of Digital Vigilantism: A Typology of Online Self-Justice." *Global Crime* 21 (3–4): 213–41.

Lubbers, Marcel. 2019. "What Kind of Nationalism Sets the Radical Right and Its Electorate Apart from the Rest? Pride in the Nation's History as Part of Nationalist Nostalgia." *Nations and Nationalism* 25 (2): 449–66.

Macdonell, Beth. 2017. "Tense Times as Opposing Rallies Clash at Winnipeg City Hall." CTV News, 19 March 2017. https://winnipeg.ctvnews.ca/tense-times-as-opposing-rallies-clash-at-winnipeg-city-hall-1.3331418.

Mammone, Andrea, Emmanuel Godin, and Brian Jenkins. 2013. *Varieties of Right-Wing Extremism in Europe.* London and New York: Routledge.

Marantz, Andrew. 2019. *Antisocial: Online Extremists, Techno Utopians and the Hijacking of the American Conversation.* London: Penguin Books.

Marcil, Yannick, and Mathieu Rousseau. 2018. "Péter la Balloune de La Meute." *On Jase.org* (no longer online), https://onjase.org/post/2018/01/08/52-peter-balloune-la-meute.

Marighella, Carlos. 1969. *Mini-Manual of the Urban Guerilla.* Utrecht: Foreign Languages Press. https://foreignlanguages.press/wp-content/uploads/2020/11/S03-Marighella-Minimanual-2nd-Printing.pdf.

Marsh, Alan. 1977. *Protest and Political Consciousness.* Beverly Hills and London: Sage Publications.

Martin, Jenni. 2020. "Eliminate Hate: Hate Crimes and Hate Speech in Canada." *The Journal of Intelligence, Conflict, and Warfare* 3 (1): 33–46.

Marwick, Alice, and Rebecca Lewis. 2017. "Media Manipulation and Disinformation Online." *Data & Society*, 15 May 2017. https://datasociety.net/pubs/oh/DataAndSociety_Media ManipulationAndDisinformationOnline.pdf.

Massinon, Stephan. 2013. "As Calgary's White Supremacist Groups Fade, Expectations for Peaceful Anti-racism Rally Rise." *Calgary Herald*, 22 March 2013. http://www.calgaryherald.com/life/Calgary+white+supremacist+groups+fade+expectations+peaceful+anti+racism+rally+rise/8140273/story.html.

Maxwell, Angie, and Stephanie Schulte. 2018. "Racial Resentment Attitudes among White Millennial Youth: The Influence of Parents and Media." *Social Science Quarterly* 99 (3): 1183–99.

McCuish, Evan, Patrick Lussier, and Stéphanie Chouinard Thivierge. 2020. "Retour sur le concept de maturité dans le contexte du désistement de la délinquance durant la transition adolescence-vie adulte." *Criminologie* 51 (1): 199–224.

McLeod, Marsha, Janice Dickson, and Merieke Walsh. 2022. "Creator of Far-Right, Anti-Government Group Testifies That He Received Police Information during Convoy Protests." *The Globe and Mail*, 4 November 2022. https://www.theglobeandmail.com/politics/article-creator-of-far-right-anti-government-group-testifies-that-he-received/.

McVeigh, Rory, Daniel J. Myers, and David Sikkink. 2004. "Corn, Klansmen, and Coolidge: Structure and Framing in Social Movements." *Social Forces* 83 (2): 653–90.

Melucci, Alberto. 1995. "The Process of Collective Identity." In *Social Movements and Culture*, edited by Hank Johnston and Bert Klandermans, 41–63. Minneapolis: University of Minnesota Press.

Meyers, Sarah. 2019. "Is There a Gap in Canada's Hate Crime Laws? The Identification of Soft Violence as a Tool for Current Right-wing Extremist Social Movements." *The Journal of Intelligence, Conflict, and Warfare* 2 (2): 1–14.

Meyers, Sarah, and Sieglinde Rosenberger. 2015. "Just a Shadow? The Role of Radical Right Parties in the Politicization of Immigration, 1995–2009." *Politics and Governance* 3 (2): 1–17.

Milbrandt, Tara. 2020. "Digital Vigilantism and Virtuous Denunciation after Charlottesville." In *Introducing Vigilant Audiences*, edited by Daniel Trottier, Rashid Gabdulhakov, and Quian Huang, 215–58. Cambridge, UK: Open Book Publishers.

Mogelson, Luke. 2022. *The Storm Is Here: An American Crucible*. New York: Penguin Press.

Momani, Bessma, and Ryan Deschamps. 2021. "Canada's Right-Wing Extremists: Mapping Their Ties, Location, and Ideas." *Journal of Hate Studies* 17 (2): 36–46.

Mondon, Aurélien, and Aaron Winter. 2017. "Articulations of Islamophobia: From the Extreme to the Mainstream?" *Ethnic and Racial Studies* 40 (13): 2151–79.

Montpetit, Jonathan. 2017. "Far-Right Group Claims PR Victory after Duelling Protests in Quebec City." CBC News, 20 August 2017. https://www.cbc.ca/news/canada/montreal/quebec-far-right-la-meute-1.4254792.

Mudde, Cas. 1995. "Right-Wing Extremism Analyzed: A Comparative Analysis of the Ideologies of Three Alleged Right-Wing Extremist Parties (NPD, NDP, CP '86)." *European Journal of Political Research* 27 (2): 203–24.

– 2002. *The Ideology of the Extreme Right*. New York: Manchester University Press.

– 2007. *Populist Radical Right Parties in Europe*. Cambridge, UK: Cambridge University Press.

– 2009. *Populist Radical Right Parties in Europe*. Online edition. Cambridge, UK: Cambridge University Press.
– 2010. "The Populist Radical Right: A Pathological Normalcy." *West European Politics* 33 (6): 1167–86.
– 2013. "The 2012 Stein Rokkan Lecture: Three Decades of Populist Radical Right Parties in Western Europe: So What?" *European Journal of Political Research* 52 (1): 1–19.
– 2016. "The Study of Populist Radical Right Parties: Towards a Fourth Wave." C-REX Working Series Papers, Center for Research on Extremism, 1: 1–25.
– 2017a. *The Far Right in America*. London and New York: Routledge.
– 2017b. *The Populist Radical Right: A Reader*. London and New York: Taylor & Francis.

Munger, Kevin, and Joseph Phillips. 2022. "Right-Wing YouTube: A Supply and Demand Perspective." *The International Journal of Press/Politics*, 27 (1): 186–219.

Murray, John. 2005. "Policing Terrorism: A Threat to Community Policing or Just a Shift in Priorities?" *Police Practice and Research: An International Journal* 6 (4): 347–61.

Murthy, Dhiraj, and Sangay Sharma. 2019. "Visualizing YouTube's Comment Space: Online Hostility as a Networked Phenomena." *News, Media and Society* 21 (1): 191–213.

Nadeau, Frédérick. 2020. "Parcours d'engagement dans l'extrême-droite Québécoise: une ethnographie (2014–2017)." Thesis, Université du Québec – Institut national de la recherche scientifique, Thèse en études urbaines. https://espace.inrs.ca/id/eprint/10392/.

Nadeau, Frédérick, Martin Geoffroy, and Hiba Qchiqach. 2021. "L'extrême-droite au Québec. Une chronologie des évènements et de la violence (2010–2020)." Centre d'expertise et de formation sur les intégrismes religieux, les idéologies politiques et la radicalisation (CEFIR), Cégep Edouard-Montpetit. 1–42. https://cefir.cegepmontpetit.ca/wp-content/uploads/2021/05/CEFIR-Rapport-de-recherche-Chronologie-v3.pdf.

Nadeau, Frédérick, and Denis Helly. 2016. "Une extrême-droite en émergence? Les pages Facebook pour la Chartes des Valeurs Québécoises." *Les Terrains de la Laïcité au Québec* 57 (2–3): 505–21.

Nagle, Angela. 2017. *Kill All Normies: Online Culture Wars from 4Chan and Tumblr to Trump and the Alt Right*. Winchester, UK and Washington: Zero Books.

Nardi, Christopher, and Catherine Lévesque. 2022. "Ottawa Police Plagued by Infighting and an Insurrection against Chief during Protests, Inquiry Hears." *National Post*, 19 October 2022. https://nationalpost.com/news/politics/ottawa-police-inquiry.

National Post. 2012. "'Embarrassment to the Canadian Government' Considered Security Threat at Toronto G20 Summit: Documents." *National Post*, 10 June 2012. https://nationalpost.com/news/canada/embarrassment-to-the-canadian-government-considered-security-threat-at-toronto-g20-summit-documents.

Nesbitt, Michael, and Dana Hagg. 2020. "An Empirical Study of Terrorism Prosecutions in Canada: Elucidating the Elements of the Offences." *Alberta Law Review* 57 (3): 595–648.

Nesbitt, Michael, Robert Oxoby, and Meagan Potier. 2019. "Terrorism Sentencing Decisions in Canada since 2001: Shifting Away from the Fundamental Principle and towards Cognitive Biases." *UBC Law Review* 52 (2): 553–629.

Netolitzky, Donald. 2016. "The History of the Organized Pseudolegal Commercial Argument Phenomenon in Canada." *Alberta Law Review* 53 (3): 609–42.

Neveu, Érik. 2002. *Sociologie des Mouvement Sociaux*. Paris: Découverte.

– 2015. *Sociologie Politique des Problèmes Publics*. Paris: Armand Colin.

Newman, Benjamin, Jennifer L. Merolla, Sono Shah, Danielle Cesarez Lemi, Loren Collingwood, and Karthick S. Ramakrishnan. 2021. "The Trump Effect: An Experimental Investigation of the Emboldening Effect of Racially Inflammatory Elite Communication." *British Journal of Political Science* 51 (3): 1138–59.

Norocel, Ov Cristian. 2022. "Gendering Web2.0 Sociotechnical Affordances of Far-Right Metapolitics." *Social Media & Society* 8 (3): 1–11.

O'Gorman, Rick, and Andrew Silke. 2015. "Terrorism as Altruism: An Evolutionary Model for Understanding Terrorist Psychology." In *Evolutionary Psychology and Terrorism*, edited by Max Taylor, Jason Roach, and Ken Pease, 149–63. London and New York: Routledge.

Olsen, Nathan. 2018. "For Our Many, Not Our Few: Austehen and the Anti-immigration Left." *Politik: Perspektives* IV (3): 11–2.

Ouellet-Vézina, Henri. 2017. "Des affiches d'Atalante Québec à l'Université Laval." *Impact Campus*. 6 September 2017. http://impactcampus.ca/actualites/des-affiches-datalante-quebec-a-luniversite-laval/.

Özkirimli, Umut. 2010. *Theories of Nationalism: A Critical Introduction*. New York: Palgrave Macmillan.

Pape, Robert. 2005. *Dying to Win: The Strategic Logic of Suicide Terrorism*. New York: Random House.

Parent, Richard, and James Ellis. 2014. "Right-Wing Extremism in Canada." *TSAS Working Paper* 14 (3): 1–40.

– 2016. "The Future of Right-Wing Terrorism in Canada." *TSAS Working Paper* 16 (12): 1–44.

Payerhin, Marek, and Cirus Ernesto Zirakzadeh. 2006. "On Movement Frames and Negotiated Identities: The Case of Poland's First Solidarity Congress." *Social Movement Studies* 5 (2): 91–115.

Pedahzur, Ami, and Leonard Weinberg. 2001. "Modern European Democracy and Its Enemies: The Threat of the Extreme Right." *Totalitarian Movements and Political Religions* 2 (1): 52–72.

Pélouas, Anne. 2017. "Au Québec, l'Extrême Droite Cherche à Surfer sur Charlottesville." *Le Monde*, 21 August 2017. http://www.lemonde.fr/ameriques/article/2017/08/21/au-quebec-l-extreme-droite-cherche-a-surfer-sur-charlottesville_5174625_3222.html#a5JdhoVDu4Yc7BkL.99.

Perrin, Andrew, and Monica Anderson. 2019. "Share of US Adults Using Social Media, Including Facebook, Is Mostly Unchanged since 2018." *Pew Research Institute.* https://www.pewresearch.org/short-reads/2019/04/10/share-of-u-s-adults-using-social-media-including-facebook-is-mostly-unchanged-since-2018/.

Perry, Barbara. 2014. "Gendered Islamophobia: Hate Crime against Muslim Women." *Social Identities* 20 (4): 74–89.

Perry, Barbara, and Ryan Scrivens. 2015. *Right Wing Extremism in Canada: An Environmental Scan.* Ottawa: Public Safety Canada.

– 2017. "Uneasy Alliances: A Look at the Right-Wing Extremist Movement in Canada." *Studies in Conflict & Terrorism* 39 (9): 819–41.

– 2019. *Right-Wing Extremism in Canada.* Cham: Palgrave MacMillan.

Perry, Barbara, Jeff Gruenewald, and Ryan Scrivens. 2021. *Right-Wing Extremism in Canada and the United States.* Switzerland: Palgrave McMillan.

– 2022. *Right-Wing Extremism in Canada and in the United States.* Cham: Palgrave MacMillan.

Pezzella, Frank, Matthew D. Fetzer, and Tyler Keller. 2019. "The Dark Figure of Hate Crime Underreporting." *American Behavioral Scientist.* https://doi.org/10.1177/0002764218823844.

Phillips, Whitney. 2015. *This Is Why We Can't Have Nice Things. Mapping the Relationship between Online Trolling and Mainstream Culture.* Cambridge, MA, and London: MIT Press.

– 2018. "The Oxygen of Amplification: Better Practices for Reporting on Extremists, Antagonists and Manipulators." *Data & Society.* https://datasociety.net/output/oxygen-of-amplification/.

Pirro, Andrea. 2019. "Lo and Behold: Jobbik and the Crafting of a New Hungarian Far Right." In *Radical Right Movement Parties in Europe,* edited by Manuela Caiani and Andřej Císař, 151–67. London and New York: Routledge.

Pitsula, James M. 2013. *Keeping Canada British: The Ku Klux Klan in 1920s Saskatchewan.* Vancouver: University of British Columbia Press.

Pollard, John. 2016. "Skinhead Culture: The Ideologies, Mythologies, Religions and Conspiracy Theories of Racist Skinheads." *Patterns of Prejudice* 50 (4–5): 398–419.

Potter, Jonathan, and Margaret Wetherell. 1998. "Social Representations, Discourse Analysis and Racism." In *The Psychology of the Social*, edited by Uwe Flick, 138–55. Cambridge, UK: Cambridge University Press.

Poyting, Scott, and Barbara Perry. 2007. "Climates of Hate: Media and State Inspired Victimisation of Muslims in Canada and Australia since 9/11." *Current Issues in Criminal Justice* 19 (2): 151–71.

Presse Canadienne, La. 2017. "Des banderoles anti-immigration déployées à Montréal." *La Presse Canadienne*, 22 August 2017. http://ici.radio-canada.ca/nouvelle/1051619/banderoles-anti-immigration-montreal-stade-olympique-atalante.

Public Safety Canada. *2016 Public Report on the Terrorist Threat to Canada*. Ottawa: Government of Canada.

– *2017 Public Report on the Terrorist Threat to Canada*. Ottawa: Government of Canada .

– *2018 Public Report on the Terrorist Threat to Canada*. Ottawa: Government of Canada.

– 2021. "Currently Listed Entities." Last modified 25 June 2021. https://www.publicsafety.gc.ca/cnt/ntnl-scrt/cntr-trrrsm/lstd-ntts/crrnt-lstd-ntts-en.aspx.

Rémillard, David. 2015. "La Meute, un groupe contre 'l'invasion de l'islam.'" *Le Soleil*, accessed 6 December 2018. https://www.lapresse.ca/le-soleil/actualites/societe/ 201512/28/01-4935114-la-meute-un-groupe-contre-linvasion-de-lislam.php.

Rocha, Roberto. 2018. "Data Sheds Light on How Russian Twitter Trolls Targeted Canadians." CBC News, 3 August 2018. https://www.cbc.ca/news/canada/russian-twitter-trolls-canada-targeted-1.4772397.

Rooduijn, Matthijs, Sarah L. de Lange, and Wouter van der Brug. 2014. "A Populist Zeitgeist? Programmatic Contagion by Populist Parties in Western Europe." *Party Politics* 20 (4): 563–75.

Rosenbaum, Jon H., and Peter C. Sederberg. 1976. "Vigilantism: An Analysis of Establishment Violence." In *Vigilante Politics*, edited by Jon H. Rosenbaum, and Peter C. Sederberg, 3–29. Philadelphia: University of Pennsylvania Press.

Ross, Jeffrey Ian. 1992. "Contemporary Radical Right-Wing Violence in Canada: A Quantitative Analysis." *Terrorism and Political Violence* 4 (3): 72–101.

– 1995. "The Structure of Canadian Terrorism." *Peace Review* 3 (4): 355–61.

Rousseau, Cécile, Christian Savard, Anna Bonnel, Richard Horne, Anousheh Machouf, and Marie-Hélène Rivest. 2023. "Clinical Intervention to Address

Violent Radicalisation: the Québec Model." *International Journal of Forensic Mental Health* 22 (3): 222–32.

Rydgren, Jens. 2007. "The Sociology of the Radical Right." *Annual Review of Sociology* 33: 241–62.

– 2018. *The Oxford Handbook of the Radical Right*. Oxford: Oxford University Press.

Sageman, Marc. 2004. *Understanding Terror Networks*. Philadelphia: University of Pennsylvania Press.

Satzewich, Victor. 2011. *Racism in Canada*. Oxford: Oxford University Press.

Schmid, Alex. 2014. "Violent and Non-Violent Extremism: Two Sides of the Same Coin?" *The International Centre for Counter-Terrorism – The Hague* 5, no. 5. https://www.icct.nl/publication/violent-and-non-violent-extremism-two-sides-same-coin.

Schmuck, Désirée, and Jörg Matthes. 2019. "Voting 'against Islamization'? How Anti-Islamic Right-Wing, Populist Political Campaign Ads Influence Explicit and Implicit Attitudes toward Muslims as Well as Voting Preferences." *Political Psychology* 40 (4): 739–57.

Schulze, Heidi Julian Hohner, Simon Greipl, Maximilian Girgnhuber, Isabell Desta, and Diana Rieger. 2022. "Far-Right Conspiracy Groups on Fringe Platforms: A Longitudinal Analysis of Radicalization Dynamics on Telegram." *Convergence* 28 (4): 1103–26.

Scrivens, Ryan. 2015. "Understanding the Collective Identity of the Radical Right Online: A Mixed-Methods Approach." PhD diss., Simon Fraser University. https://summit.sfu.ca/item/17632.

Scrivens, Ryan, Amanda Isabel Osuna, Steven M. Chermak, Michael M. Whitney, and Richard Frank. 2022. "Examining Online Indicators of Extremism in Violent Right-Wing Extremist Forums." *Studies in Conflict and Terrorism* 26 (11): 1–25.

Scrivens, Ryan, and Barbara Perry. 2016. "Resisting the Right: Countering Right-Wing Extremism in Canada." *Canadian Journal of Criminology and Criminal Justice* 59 (4): 534–58.

Scrivens, Ryan, Thomas W. Wojciechowski, and Richard Frank. 2020. "Examining the Developmental Pathways of Online Posting Behavior in Violent Right-Wing Extremist Forums." *Terrorism and Political Violence* 34 (8): 1721–38.

Security Intelligence Review Committee. 2018. *Building for Tomorrow: The Future of Security Intelligence Accountability in Canada*. Ottawa: Public Services and Procurement Canada.

– 2002. *SIRC Report 2001–2002: An Operational Audit of the Canadian Security Intelligence Service*. Ottawa: Public Works and Government Services Canada.

Sedgwick, Mark. 2010. "The Concept of Radicalization as a Source of Confusion." *Terrorism and Political Violence* 22 (4): 479–94.

Smith, Haedyn. 2021. "Rememoration, 'Sticky Associations,' and Social Media Performativity in the Pegida Movement." Diss., DePaul University. https://via.library.depaul.edu/etd/313.

Snow, David A. 2004. "Framing Processes, Ideology, and Discursive Fields." In *The Blackwell Companion to Social Movements*, edited by David A. Snow, Sarah A. Soule, and Hanspeter Kriesi, 380–412. Malden, MA: Blackwell Pub.

Snow, David A., and Robert D. Benford. 1988. "Ideology, Frame Resonance, and Participant Mobilization." *International Social Movement Research* 1 (1): 197–217.

Snow, David A., Burke E. Rochford Jr, Steven K. Worden, and Robert D. Benford. 1986. "Frame Alignment Processes, Micromobilization, and Movement Participation." *American Sociological Review* 51 (4): 464–81.

Snow, David A., and Sarah A. Soule. 2010. *A Primer on Social Movements*. New York: W.W. Norton & Company.

Southern Poverty Law Center. 2016. "Alternative Right." *Southern Poverty Law Center*. https://www.splcenter.org/fighting-hate/extremist-files/ideology/alternative-right.

Sprinzak, Ehud. 1995. "Right-Wing Terrorism in a Comparative Perspective: The Case of Split Delegitimization." *Terrorism and Political Violence* 7 (1): 17–43.

Statistics Canada. *Police-Reported Hate Crime in Canada, 2017*. Ottawa: Statistics Canada.

Steinberg, Marc W. 1999. *Fighting Words: Working-Class Formation, Collective Action, and Discourse in Early Nineteenth Century-England*. Ithaca: Cornell University Press.

Stodulka, Thomas, Samia Dinkelaker, and Ferdiansyah Thajib, eds. 2019. *Affective Dimensions of Fieldwork and Ethnography*. Cham: Springer.

Tanner, Samuel, and Aurélie Campana. 2014. "The Process of Radicalization: Right-Wing Skinheads in Quebec." TSAS *Working Paper* (14) 7: 1–50.

– 2020. "'Watchful Citizens' and Digital Vigilantism: A Case Study of Far Right in Quebec." *Global Crime* 21 (3–4): 262–82.

Tanner, Samuel, Valentine Crosset, and Aurélie Campana. 2020. "Far-Right Digital Activism as Technical Mediation: Anti-Immigration Activism on YouTube." In *Introducing Vigilant Audiences*, edited by Daniel Trottier, Rashid Gabdulhakov, and Qian Huang, 129–60. Cambridge, UK: Open Book Publisher.

Taylor, Verta, and Nella Van Dyke. 2004. "'Get Up, Stand Up': Tactical Repertoires of Social Movements." In *The Blackwell Companion to Social Movements*, edited by David A. Snow, Sarah A. Houle, and Hanspeter Kriesi, 262–93. London: Blackwell Publishing Ltd.

Thorpe, Ryan. 2019. "Homegrown Hate." *The Winnipeg Free Press*, 12 June 2019. https://www.winnipegfreepress.com/local/homegrown-hate-547510902.html.

Tilly, Charles. 1984. "Les origines du répertoire de l'action collective contemporaine en France et en Grande-Bretagne." *Vingtième siècle. Revue d'histoire* (4): 89–108.

– 2003. *The Politics of Collective Violence.* Cambridge, UK: Cambridge University Press.

– 2005. *Trust and Rule.* Cambridge, UK: Cambridge University Press.

– 2007. "Trust Networks in Transnational Migration." *Sociological Forum* 22 (1): 3–24.

Tomsen, Stephen, and James W. Messerschmidt. 2020. "Masculinities and Interpersonal Violence." In *The Emerald Handbook of Feminism, Criminology and Social Change,* edited by Sandra Walklate, Kate Fitz-Gibbon, JaneMaree Maher, and Jude McCulloch, 185–202. Bingley, UK: Emerald Publishing Limited.

Traverso, Enzo. 2016. *The End of Jewish Modernity.* London: Pluto Press.

Trottier, Daniel. 2017. "Digital Vigilantism as Weaponisation of Visibility." *Philosophy & Technology* 30 (1): 55–72.

Tufekci, Zynep. 2017. *Twitter and Tear Gas. The Power and Fragility of Networked Protest.* New Haven and London: Yale University Press.

Van Dijk, Teun A. 2006. "Ideology and Discourse Analysis." *Journal of Political Ideologies* 11 (2): 115–40.

Van Dyke, Nella, and David S. Meyer. 2016. *Understanding the Tea Party Movement.* New York and London: Routledge.

Vergani, Matteo, Muhammad Iqbal, Ekin Ilbahar, and Greg Barton. 2018. "The Three Ps of Radicalization: Push, Pull and Personal. A Systematic Scoping Review of the Scientific Evidence about Radicalization into Violent Extremism." *Studies in Conflict and Terrorism* 43 (10): 854–86.

Vertigans, Stephen. 2007. "Beyond the Fringe? Radicalisation within the American Far-Right." *Totalitarian Movements and Political Religions* 8 (3): 641–59.

Villeneuve, Marie-Pierre, Isabelle F.-Dufour, and Daniel Turcotte. 2020. "Désistement assisté. Vecteur d'intégration sociocommunautaire pour des adolescents engagés dans une délinquance grave ou persistante." *Criminologie* 53 (1): 225–52.

Weeks, Brian E., Alberto Ardèvol-Abreu, and Homero Gil de Zúñiga. 2017. "Online Influence? Social Media Use, Opinion Leadership, and Political Persuasion." *International Journal of Public Opinion Research* 29 (2): 214–39.

Weiss, Nerina, Erella Grassiani, and Linda Green, eds. 2023. *The Entanglements of Ethnographic Fieldwork in a Violent World.* Milton Park, Abingdon, Oxfordshire: Routledge.

Wendling, Mike. 2018. *Alt Right: From 4chan to the White House.* Halifax and Winnipeg: Fernwood Publishing.

Whitaker, Reginald, Gregory Kealy, and Andrew Parnaby. 2012. *Secret Service: Political Policing in Canada from the Fenians to Fortress America.* Toronto: University of Toronto Press.

Wintrobe, Ronald. 2006. *Rational Extremism: The Political Economy of Radicalism.* New York: Cambridge University Press.

Wodak, Ruth. 2018. "The Radical Right and Antisemitism." In *The Oxford Handbook of the Radical Right,* edited by Jens Rydgren, 61–84. Oxford: Oxford University Press.

Wooley, Samuel C., and Philip N. Howard. 2019. "Introduction: Computational Propaganda Worldwide." In *Computational Propaganda: Political Parties, Politicians, and Political Manipulation on Social Media,* edited by Samuel C. Wooley and Philip N. Howard, 3–20. New York: Oxford University Press.

Young, Kevin, and Laura Craig. 1997. "Beyond White Pride: Identity, Meaning and Contradiction in the Canadian Skinhead Subculture." *The Canadian Review of Sociology and Anthropology* 34: 175–206.

INDEX

Page numbers with (t) refer to tables.